BEFORE THE VOLCANO

REVERBERATIONS
OF IDENTITY
ON MONTSERRAT

JONATHAN SKINNER

ARAWAK PUBLICATIONS

Å R A W A K PUBLICATIONƧ
17 Kensington Crescent
Kingston 5
Arawak@OfficeEmail.net

08 07 06 05 04   5 4 3 2 1

University of the West Indies Library Cataloguing in Publication Data

Skinner, Jonathan.

Before the volcano : reverberations of identity
on Montserrat / Jonathan Skinner.
p. cm.

Includes bibliographical references.
ISBN: 976-8189-21-5

1. Montserrat — Civilization.
2. Montserrat — Social life and customs.
3. Ethnology — Montserrat.   I. Title.

F2082.S54 2004   972.975

Credits:

(Associated Press) *The Guardian*: "Eruption Reaches Montserrat Capital"
    (5 August 1997: 9)
The Independent: "Emerald Isle Taken by Storm", by Lucretia Stewart (2
    April 1996)
(DCT Syndication) *The Courier and Advertiser*: "Volcano Island Call" (26
    August 1995: 13); and "Student Recalls Volcano Island Ordeal" (6
    September 1995: 4)

Cover and book design by Karen L. Collins
Cover artwork by Gary Manly

BEFORE THE VOLCANO

The dust of exploded beliefs may make a fine sunset.
— Madan

What is then this ethnographer's magic, by which he is able to evoke the real spirit of the natives, the true picture of tribal life?
— Malinowski

CONTENTS

ACKNOWLEDGEMENTS

This book has benefited from many individuals and organisations to whom I would like to extend my gratitude. Rhetorically, I divide the following thanks into three stages. Before working on Montserrat, I would like to thank Tristan Platt, the late Ladislav Holy, David Riches and Nigel Rapport for inspiring and encouraging my drift into social anthropology as an undergraduate and post-graduate student at St Andrews University, Scotland. In addition, before departing for Montserrat, I received gracious amounts of financial assistance from my parents – John and Beti Skinner, the Department of Social Anthropology at St Andrews University, the University of St Andrews itself, the Russell Trust and the Carnegie Trust.

Whilst on Montserrat I was fortunate to receive the hospitality and assistance of the following – to name but a few (unless public figures, names have been changed for reasons of privacy): the late Pippa Irish and Sally Oswald; Josh Irish and Abdul Weekes; Doc and "The Fire-Fighter Posse"; Chedmond Browne; the staff at the Montserrat National Trust, ZJB Radio, the Montserrat Public Library, and the University of West Indies Extra-Mural Department; the members of the Maroons Creative Writers' Group led by Sir Howard Fergus; the Government of Montserrat, and His Excellency the former Governor of Montserrat (Frank Savage).

Since my return from Montserrat I have been greatly assisted by Nigel Rapport – friend, colleague and opponent as a true academic sportsman. During the writing of this work, my employers – Stephen Magee of the Teaching English as a Foreign Language Department at the University of St Andrews, and Cathy Di Domenico at the University of Abertay-Dundee – entertained my musings and gave me some much needed space so that I could write, and some much needed money so that I could live. A Sutasoma Award made by the Royal Anthropological Institute precipitated a turning point in my writing, followed much later by *The Sociological Review* Fellowship at the University of Keele. It was in the heart of the Keele community in the Midlands that I was able to reflect upon my manuscript, to tinker with it, displace and anonymise it where I thought it appropriate, and retain and sustain it where I thought it necessary. And it was as Visiting Fellow at the Refugee Studies Centre, and member of Linacre College, at the University of Oxford that I was able to finally complete this manuscript for publication.

Passages of this book have been tried and tested on academic university audiences at St. Andrews, Atlanta, Tubingen, Belfast, Manchester Metropolitan, North London, Goldsmiths College, Kent and Keele; and upon individuals such as Barnaly Pandé, Ali Malcolm-Smith, Salma Siddique, Sue Lewis, Robert Paine, J. Hillis Miller, David Riches again, and Jim Fernandez: I can therefore have no excuses and accept all blame and responsibility for its shortcomings. I am grateful to James Carrier and Sarah Sneddon for proof-reading the manuscript, to Pansy Benn who has been a pleasure to work with in taking this text to press, and to the two anonymous referees for their constructive comments. Finally, I would like to pay especial thanks to Mils Hills and Barnaly Pandé – and Nigel, for a third and last time – for joining me on the many stages of this prosaic-passionate enterprise.

I dedicate this book to those affected by the Chances Peak volcano, both those alive and dead. May this be of some assistance.

JPS
Linacre College, Oxford
2002

[I]n the course of our presentation, Gluckman said, "You're absolutely wrong about this – it's not that way at all," and then he explained how it was. On he went, and in the course of the explanation, the decisive crucial factor was that the Zulu said this – he gave it as a quotation from an important Zulu chief.

Well, that was fine. They were very polite and hospitable, and I think Max then took us all out and bought us beer. Yonina and I ended up at Max's house and stayed for dinner, and someplace along that time – I don't know whether it was Yonina or I – but we suddenly realised: Max Gluckman had worked in Zululand, and it was a well known, well established, well authenticated fact that all of his field notes had been burned up in an unfortunate fire. He had them all in a little out-house behind – and while he was away doing something, his field notes burned up.

So the next day we said to Max, "Are you sure that the decisive piece of evidence" – we repeated the statement of the Zulu informant.

"Oh," he said. "Absolutely!"

So we said, "Max, if your field notes all burned up, and you don't have any, you have a good memory – to remember verbatim what was said."

"Oh," he said, "that was not memory, verbatim. That was structurally correct."

So we began to explore what was structurally correct, and he said, "That's what a Zulu informant would have said had I asked him the right question."

So we went back to London feeling that, somehow – very interesting, anthropology, isn't it? That's the way it's done.

– Schneider

An Academic Preface – "Take only impressions, leave only monographs": Reading and Writing Anthropology and Ethnography

> *[M]ost ethnographic monographs are fiction even if the author intended otherwise.*
>
> *– Edmund Leach*

Tourists who travel to the islands of the Caribbean, to Papua New Guinea or Morocco are encouraged to be environmentally friendly, to preserve and conserve the tourist destination for the others who undoubtedly follow behind them. In their contact with other places and other peoples, tourists are encouraged to "Take only photographs, leave only footprints". The ideal tourist is one who, thus, leaves undisturbed the corals off Thailand's Ko Samui island, fails to score his name in the side of the Sphinx in Egypt, and refrains from hiring a member of Jamaica's "foreign service" – a "Rent-A-Rasta" – to fulfil his or her sexual fantasies. Responsible, ethical and politically correct, the ideal tourist comes and goes: their footprints on exotic shores are washed away; their baggage is returned intact laden with souvenirs; their values and lifestyles are reaffirmed; and their "sacred journey" – their pleasure pilgrimage – is consigned to the cognitive hold of their memory as they continue with their everyday profane professions. Tourists, however, rarely live up to such an ideal. Many tourists are racked with the desire to travel and encounter difference, and with that, the desire to collect or leave a sign, immortalising signatures and souvenirs – appropriate and appropriated lodestones of their transitory presence and experience. Such touristic desires correspond, strikingly, with anthropology: According to van den Berghe (1996: 552), "Tourism can even be seen as a mirror of anthropology itself: both constitute a quest for the other. In a sense, ethnic tourism is amateur anthropology, or anthropology is professional tourism." Whether or not there is a correspondence or a confusion between tourism and anthropology, van den Berghe writes (1996: 552), "[p]erhaps, in the end, we all yearn to achieve better self-understanding by looking at others".

This book is an anthropologist's "tour" of life and living on a British colony in the Caribbean, a place where identity is claimed and contested by anthropologists, poets, calypsonians, development workers, and Black radicals. This research tour – with its colonial and tourist resonances – took place on Montserrat at a time when questions and expressions of identity, nationhood and independence were reverberating about the island, a time just before the dramatic volcanic eruption of Mount Chance in 1995. That time is entered in the ethnography which starts in Chapter 1. That time is prefaced by an academic discussion of the nature of anthropology and ethnography. This is an important theoretical and disciplinary section – an "academic preface" – which sets out the ideas behind how this book was researched, how it was written, and how it can be read. For those more concerned with Montserrat than a questioning and an examination of the nature of anthropology and ethnography – with the underpinnings and mechanics of this book – I recommend that you only lightly dip into this academic preface, and that you perhaps return to it for a more thorough reading after reading the book from the beginnings of Chapter 1, "Montserrat place and Mons'rat neaga".

This "academic" preface is not specifically about these particular tourism/anthropology claims or about the tourist visits to the islands of the Caribbean, to Papua New Guinea or Morocco. It is about the visits of anthropologists in general – anthropologists who, I argue, instead of taking photographs and leaving footprints, take impressions of their visits and leave for posterity monographs about their visits. Whether it be Thomas Eriksen (1992) in Trinidad, Marilyn Strathern (1991) in Papua New Guinea, or Clifford Geertz (1968) in Morocco, I argue here that all anthropologists gain are but impressions – his or her own, and those of others. These impressions I refer to as "anthropological impressions": subjective world-views – multiple realities as I, using the work of cultural psychologist Richard Shweder, would like to explain them. They grow out of individual and group experiences, converging as inter-subjective constellations, diverging as incommensurable positions.

They are multiple. And they are partial – partial in the sense that there is a diversity of impressions, but not one complete and whole impression.

As an academic preface to this book, it is here that I set out my conceptual tool kit: it is here that I construct my impressionistic anthropology out of pre-existing definitions of anthropology, social theories and artistic experiments. First, I establish and explain my postmodern and anthropological convictions. Secondly, I propose an impressionistic principle of human understanding. Thirdly, I look at its implications for reading and writing anthropology. And, finally, I give some direction as to the reading and writing of the rest of this book which embodies these arguments. Taken together, the sections in this academic preface set up a conceptual base underpinning the rest of the book which is, essentially, an experimental ethnographic exemplification of this impressionistic anthropology.

ANTHROPOLOGY: AN UNCOMFORTABLE AND UNCERTAIN (ANTI−)DISCIPLINE

Let me begin this academic preface with an examination of the nature of my anthropology, which I consider to be uncomfortable and uncertain by necessity. Anthropology is a subject that has been described variously by its professional practitioners as "an inquisitive, challenging, uncomfortable discipline" (Firth 1981: 200); as a "virtual anti-discipline" (Hart 1990: 10); as a social science "born omniform" (Geertz 1993b: 21). As an (anti-)discipline, anthropology draws forth many such ambiguous, effusive and ineluctable comments. Firth (1981: 200) goes on to add that this "uncomfortable discipline" works by "questioning established positions and proclaimed values, [and] peering into underlying positions". These indeterminate remarks precipitate my discussion of the nature of anthropology, of what James Fernandez (1986: ix) considers to be a very pragmatic but uncertain enterprise.

More specifically, Fernandez (1986: ix) identifies anthropology's main concern as "how humans in real situations get things done". This is done by "doing ethnography", the activity of both conducting first-hand ethnographic research (fieldwork) and ethnographic writing (the monograph, such as this). Through this ethnographic "method and genre" (Atkinson 1990: 1), the anthropologist gains material about humans in different places and situations which, according to Daniel Miller (1994: 1), can then be generalised with other ethnographic observations to either confirm or refute models of "modern" life. Ethnographic practice and praxis would appear to be anthropology's building blocks. This observation, generalisation and comparison of human life strikes a chord with Kirsten Hastrup (1995: x) who believes that there is "a distinct anthropological project, the object of which is to provide ground for comparison and generalisation of social experience on the basis of concrete ethnography". And certainly, despite the epistemological problem of how anthropologists recognise units of comparison before making generalisations (Holy 1987: 13), the work of our anthropologists in Trinidad, Papua New Guinea and Morocco are testimony to this goal: Eriksen (1992) compares his visits to Trinidad with a visit to Mauritius to generalise some comments about ethnicity and nationalism; Strathern (1991) generalises her knowledge of Papua New Guinea with the wider Melanesian ethnographic region to enter into a discussion about cross-cultural comparisons; and Geertz (1968) contrasts observations on Islam in Morocco with Islam in Bali as a way of developing theoretical observations about the social role of religion in general.

My own comparative, partial and impressionistic anthropology is a "pick-n-mix" anthropology taken from modern British "social" anthropology and contemporary American "cultural" anthropology. As a British social anthropologist, I have been influenced by the work of "functionalist" fieldworkers Bronislaw Malinowski (1978[1922]) and Alfred Radcliffe-Brown (1922). It was Malinowski (1978: 24, 25) who advocated a period of fieldwork for an ethnographer to observe and record *"the imponderabilia of actual life"*, the intention being "to grasp the native's point of view ... to realise *his* vision of *his* world", and to show how the observed society and social institutions function together as an integrated, organic whole. In the same imperial era, Radcliffe-Brown (1922: 189) established the comparative fieldwork method, one which compares the different contexts of a custom in order to abstract its essential significance, anthropology as "the theoretical natural science of human society".

This British social anthropology, which stressed the connectedness between individuals, was established during the last decades of British imperial rule, "rooted" – as Talal Asad (1973: 16) trenchantly observes – "in an unequal power encounter between the West and Third World .... that gives the West access to cultural and historical information about the societies it has progressively dominated". So too, its underlying tenets were rooted in Enlightenment ideas and ideals, namely "the belief that people [can] comprehend and control the universe by means of reason and empirical research" (George Ritzer 1996: 10). Yet, social anthropology is by no means colonialism's handmaiden. Anthropological knowledge of colonial peoples does implicate anthropology in the colonial process, making the subject useful for colonial administrators, and a threat for anthropology's colonial subjects – many of whom underwent decolonisation in the 1950s and 1960s. Nevertheless, Kuper (1991: 119) rightly declares that social anthropology can also play a key – if uncomfortable – role in challenging and unsettling the assumptions of colonial regimes, colonial social structures and colonial policies through anthropological studies of colonial settlement and administration. This book – essentially an experimental ethnographic building block – attempts to contribute to the few studies of this kind.

If British social anthropology should retain a sense of uncomfortableness because of its colonial birth, I maintain that it should also contain a certain degree of uncertainty in its coming of age. This is because anthropologists gaining a picture of life abroad should neither be sure of their material or the native's meanings, nor should they be certain of their theoretical approaches and elaborations. As Michael Jackson (1998: 12) notes, intersubjectivity – the connection between self and other by rules of reciprocity, empathic bonding, synchronous interaction and mirror-imaging in intimate inter-personal worlds – is always ambiguous. And as Edmund Leach (1982: v) once wryly remarked:

"[A]mong social anthropologists the game of building new theories on the ruins of old ones is almost an occupational disease."

Throughout the history of British social anthropology in the twentieth century, anthropologists have been approaching their subject and their subject matter in different ways, revising theories and reinterpreting ethnographic material, jostling and competing with each other for dominance and disciples. Leach was guilty of his own criticisms when, in the 1960s, he began importing his own variation of structuralism from France.

In my mind, this construction and reconstruction of British social anthropology has been complicated further by the transatlantic influence of American symbolic anthropologists David Schneider and Clifford Geertz and their own seductive re-examination of anthropology's epistemological base. Both Schneider and Geertz subscribe to a meaning-centred approach to the study of culture and kinship. Like Malinowski, Geertz's (1993[a]: 24) aim is to gain access to "the conceptual world in which our subjects live". For Geertz (1993[a]: 5, 6, 20, 15), this is achieved by "thick description", by "guessing at meanings, assessing the guesses, and drawing explanatory conclusions from the better guesses": concomitantly, all anthropological writings are second and third order interpretations – only the "natives" make first order interpretations of their culture. In practice, Geertz (1993[a]: 448) *interprets* great significance in the cockfight in Bali for example, claiming that it gives him access to – a way of reading – Balinese culture: the cockfight functions as "a metasocial commentary [...] a Balinese reading of Balinese experience, a story they tell themselves about themselves." However, "there is only the constructed understandings of the constructed native's constructed point of view", criticises Crapanzano (1992: 67). Thus, I would argue, it would appear that social anthropology, in Britain and in America, is compromised by uncomfortable theories and methods, no matter the era. Furthermore, the ethnographic results of the anthropological discipline, marked by the anthropologist's individual participant observation, are themselves distrusted by the natives subjected to the anthropological gaze as well as by other anthropologists reading the results of one anthropologist's experiences. And finally, social anthropology is compromised by its epistemological uncertainty: whichever theoretical paradigm it embraces to process "local knowledge" (Geertz 1993[b]), the paradigm contains its own inherent shortcomings and limitations and is eventually superseded by another totalising grand narrative in an artistic, (social) scientific revolution (cf. Kuhn 1970).

From functional to structural to semantic/semiotic and symbolic/interpretative anthropology, entering the grand game myself, I might add my own criticism of Geertz from my post-modern "position" in the new millennium. I maintain that Geertz's interpretativism is quite contrary: it acknowledges that "[c]ultural analysis is intrinsically incomplete" (Geertz 1993[a]: 29), implying that there are endless levels whilst nonetheless presenting and analysing "the Balinese cockfight" as a generic cultural symbol amongst a homogenous Balinese people (see also Crapanzano 1992: 68, 64). Furthermore, it does this at the same time as distinguishing the order of interpretations – first for the native, second for the anthropologist (Geertz) interpreting the native, third for the anthropologist (Crapanzano) interpreting Geertz.

Always eclectic and literary in his writings, Geertz has been associated with "[t]he literary turn in contemporary anthropology" (Scholte 1987: 34, 34) – one which "deals with the textual and literary issues of ethnographic writing, production, construction, description, legitimacy, and authority". This "turn" is the result of struggles to fathom the native's meaning in the field, and the anthropologist's meaning in his or her text. Its focus on reading and writing in anthropology arose from a general reaction against structuralism, the ideas and ideals of the Enlightenment and sharply delineated boundaries, preferring blurred textual "genres" (Geertz 1993[b]: 20) instead. Structuralism – as a form of literary criticism – analyses languages and texts according to the arbitrary, but structured, relationships between signifiers ("apple" sound image) and signifieds (apple concept) which Saussure (1988) found constitute the linguistic sign. Post-structuralism stresses the signifier – rather than the signified – in this structural relationship, with the result that the "truth" of the text lies not behind or within the text, but in the reader's productive relationship with the text (Sarup 1993: 2–3). In other words, the reader responds and performs *with* the text; without the reader there is no text. But, in the extreme opinion of Jacques Derrida (1993: 3-5), the linguistic sign is completely uprooted as signifiers float free from their extra-linguistic referents – meaning, therefore, is endlessly deferred. Such thoughts lead to a textual double – "deconstructive" – reading of texts for the post-structuralist who recognises and appreciates the tension between the reader of a text's *push* into their own frame of reference, and the *pull* of the writer's attempt to impose ordering strategies upon the text (Peck & Coyle 1989: 166).

This crisis of certainty over the ability to write accurately for the reading – to represent and transfer meaning – has been promoted by an amorphous diversity of postmodern theories in the last two decades. Two well-read postmodernists are Jean-Francois Lyotard and Fredric Jameson, both of whom make different claims about their (anti-)theory which I go on to cannibalise for my anthropology of impressions. Economically, according to Jameson (1984; 1991), we are in the last phase of capitalism – society is post-industrial and capitalism is multi-national. Aesthetically, the commercial frontiers between high culture and popular culture have been effaced: in art, pastiche effaces parody as Andy Warhol's "Diamond Dust Shoes" replaces Van Gogh's "A Pair of Boots"; in literature, Italo Calvino (1992) writes novels about writing novels, diffusing the narrative in all directions; and in photography, Sherrie Levine gains fame by photographing other people's photographs creating perfect copies, imitations mocking, blurring, and destroying the original – the result, a deceptive substitute, a simulacrum. In language, the signifying chain has been snapped (a point I contest). And in architecture, the Pompidou Centre reveals its innards, and the shopping mall has become the tourist attraction. If modernity is the questioning and criticising of our ability to build grand theory, write universal history, discover eternal truths and differentiate between the real thing and a representation of the real thing, then post(-)modernity is an anti-modernity and not just a hyphenated follow-on ph(r)ase. As John Urry (1994: 85) explains, "[p]ostmodernism problematises the distinction between representations and reality", confusing the "real thing" original with the "better than the real thing" experience. Or, more famously, as Lyotard (1992: xxiv) declares, the postmodern condition is an "incredulity toward metanarratives", a rejection of Enlightenment ideas and ideals in a world which has changed from a world with an industrial *mode of production* to a technological world where computerised knowledge – a consumable end in itself – has become the principal *force of production*. This depthless world of simulation and hyper-reality, voyeurism and relativity – perspective without privilege – is much too complex and fragmented for any reductionist, essentialist or universalising social theories or philosophies.

As theory or anti-theory, postmodernism/s is/are complex and ambiguous, though well suited to social anthropology. Pool (1991: 310, 312) has argued that many critics have been using the term postmodernism wrongly; also noting that there might even be "as many postmodernisms as there are authors who write about postmodernism". As a "textual turn", postmodernism is a concern for the representation of the "other" through the writing of ethnography. It therefore includes a great variety of writings written between Said's (1991: 272, author's emphasis) exploratory question in 1978: "[h]ow does one *represent* cultures?"; and Geertz's (1995: 130) reminder in 1995: "[t]he representation of others is not easily separable from the manipulation of them." Neither Said (1991: 272) nor Geertz deny the possibility of representing others, but they do insist that the representations are subjective, "embedded first in the language and then in the culture, institutions, and political ambience of the representer". These issues were taken up in two potent volumes from 1986, *Writing Culture* and *Anthropology as Cultural Critique*, collections of papers that respectively argue that "ethnography is in the midst of a political and epistemological crisis: Western writers no longer portray non-Western peoples with unchallenged authority" (Marcus & Clifford 1986: inside front cover), and that as such, ethnography should be eternally "experimental" (Marcus & Fischer 1986). Linked with these experimental ethnographers are other innovators such as Clifford (critic of the West [1988]), Rabinow, Crapanzano and Dwyer (reflexive and reflective ethnographers of Morocco who challenge the "monologics" of the author's text [1977; 1980; 1982]) in North America. Amongst the British ethnographers we should include Rapport (1987) for his reconstructive conversational journey around a Canadian city, and Strathern (1991: xvi, 26), mentioned above, for her theorising upon the writing of anthropology and the representation of societies from a "postplural perception of the world", one which draws upon Stephen Tyler's (1986) concept of the "emergent mind" of the "author-text-reader".

In Stephen Tyler's (1986: 123-137) opinion of what, for him, constitutes a postmodern ethnography, evocation rather than representation is the key: "cooperatively evolved" with "perspectival relativity", "fragmentary" and temporary – "without the illusion of the transcendental", ethnography should evoke rather than represent because descriptions of reality are illusory imitations. Perversely, such "writing at the limit" (Tyler 1986: 137, 136) can "never be completely realised" in ethnography, for we depend too much upon the text and the anthropologist. In a post-modern, post-Saidian and post-Geertzian era, all we can do now is to keep using ethnography as a "meditative vehicle" (Tyler 1986: 140), and to continue in our experimental activities and our re-examination of the "many aspects of our representational praxis"

– as do the contributors to Allison James, Jenny Hockey and Andrew Dawson's (James & Hockey & Dawson 1997: 13) volume *After Writing Culture* (see also *Siting Culture* edited by Olwig & Hastrup [1997] on the question of the location of culture in a mobile, postmodern world [see also Gupta & Ferguson 1997; Wagner 1981; Amit 2000]). But, crucially, for me, we are accepting – after Tyler – that we are writing illusions, persuasive fictions (Strathern 1987: 256), anthropological impressions. These evocations – rather than representations – accept and encourage the reader's different engagement with the text. Perhaps, then, there is a compatibility of fit between an uncomfortable and uncertain (anti-)discipline and an uncomfortable and uncertain (anti-)theory.

FROM IMPASSE TO IF ... THEN

In this section, I would like to concentrate upon the positioning of the investigating anthropologist now under investigation. What happens, for example, when the anthropologist compares two widely disparate and seemingly incommensurable world-views – belonging to either *natives under investigation*, or to *investigating anthropologists*, for instance – when reading and comparing ethnographies? Here I suggest that one utilises the challenging features of the variety of postmodernisms which make up an investigative tool kit for the eclectic range of ethical, epistemological and even ontological uncertainties thrown up by anthropologists. This section is then followed by sections examining its implications for reading and writing in general, and for writing and reading this book in particular.

Richard Shweder (1991: 20) considers the first problem of incommensurable native world-views when examining Hindu and Protestant psychologies. Reviewing the anthropologist's position, Shweder (1991: 42) found that many anthropologists sustain a "Nietzschean null-reference argument" – the assumption that "tradition-based reality-posits are imaginary phantoms of mind". Take, for example, Schneider's examination of the criteria and reference points for defining kinship – whether it should be according to the various native beliefs about the supernatural, or some observer's beliefs about the scientific facts of biological relatedness (Schneider 1965: 85-86):

[m]an's beliefs about ghosts and spirits must be wholly formed by man
himself. Whatever unity there is to man's beliefs about the supernatural
derives, therefore, from the nature of man himself and not from the
nature of the supernatural.

This led him to the eventual conclusion that "there are only
cultural constructions of reality" (Schneider 1976: 204):

The world at large is not, indeed it cannot be, independent of the way
in which his culture formulates his vision of what he is seeing. There
are only cultural constructions of reality, and these cultural constructions
of realities are decisive in what is perceived, what is experienced, what
is understood.

Schneider was reiterating Berger and Luckmann's (1971[1966]:
13, 30, 134) original thesis about the importance of looking at
what people understand to be "real", and how that is recognised
for its independence. In other words, society has both an objective
reality and a subjective reality: society has objective facticity
and subjective meaning as concrete people make social objects
and define society in ways which are objectively open to fathom.
For Schneider, this meant acknowledging the native beliefs in
the supernatural as demonstrably real even if the supernatural
itself is not real.

Shweder does not see this as a satisfactory solution to his
question. He does not accept, as some anthropologists do (see
Lindquist 1995: 8-9), that different people attend to the same
reality in different ways, with different cultural models fixed upon
the same reality. Nor does Shweder subscribe to Ernest Gellner's
(1993: 54) averred faith in the ideal of truth and "[t]he existence
of trans-cultural and amoral knowledge". Shweder seeks a different
solution to the problem of universal concrete approaches and
relative shifting positions; between the poles of an objective and
external reality and subjective multiple realities; or, as Allan Hanson
(1979: 516) clarifies, "objectivism [that] makes truth and knowledge
contingent solely upon external reality, [and] relativism [that]
holds them to be contingent upon ontological and epistemological
standards."

This problem is critical to anthropological studies: the route
of all analysis is split between an underlying premiss that there
is a "natural" external bed-rock reality which is glossed over by
humanity's (ignorant) traveller's tales – reducing, in my opinion,
anthropology to the study of human emulsions; and an alternative
haemorrhaging pathway built upon the shifting (and shifty)

postulation that reality is multiple, itinerant and contingent upon people's predicates. The latter results in uncomfortable and uncertain anthropological methods and results but does not rest upon facile distinctions between representation and reality. Along with Shweder and the American philosopher Richard Rorty (1997) – who has declared that it is not possible to operate any independent criteria for assessing the nature of reality – I favour the latter; in other words, an anthropology which is inquisitive, responsive and receptive to an uncomfortable inquiry inclined towards contradiction and criticism.

Shweder's (1991: 29, 66) solution to the relativist/universalist debate is to accept that there are "multiple objective worlds": it is possible to have knowledge of the world even though that objective world is subject-dependent and "multiplex". For Shweder (1991: 29), "[t]he fact that there is no one uniform objective reality (constraint, foundation, godhead, truth, standard) does not mean there are no objective realities (constraints, foundations, godheads, truths, standards) at all." This kind of objective relativism, "post-positivism" in Shweder's (1991: 60) words, allows him to retain the accomplishments of normal science alongside the idea that nothing exists independent of our theoretical interpretation of it.

What remains is the ethnographic problem of describing, comparing and representing these multiple objective worlds, particularly if "the objective world is incapable of being represented completely if represented from any point of view, and incapable of being represented intelligibly if represented from all points of view at once" (Shweder 1991: 66). In answer to this problem, or impasse, Shweder (1991: 64) suggests that we "view the objective world from many points of view (or from the point of view of each of several prejudices), but to do it in sequence" and "feel eager to move on to some other world-view". In this book I do just that: my approach is both problematic and "perspectival" – I present my range of impressions of Montserrat gleaned from a diverse group of people. Where I differ from Shweder's postmodern realism is in my collapse of the subjective/objective polarities. For me, these realities are subjective insights and objective truths at one and the same time, depending upon whether they echo the observer's perspective or the native's perspective. Thus, though we cannot escape from subject-dependent and culture-dependent claims, I argue that with our sense impressions even Shweder's "multiple objective worlds" represent a subject-dependent position, one more in line with *multiple subjective worlds.*

In my attempt to circumscribe loosely this strong relativity, the work of American philosopher Nelson Goodman is of some use. Goodman argues that world versions are so disparate that they cannot be reduced into one true version or reality; that it is inappropriate, for instance, to reduce the art world to the world of physics. A "rightness of fit" criterion is thus more in keeping with the diversity of world versions: "a statement is true, a representation right, for a world it fits" (Goodman 1978: 132); or as Goodman (1978: 2-3) poignantly poses, "[i]f I ask about the world, you can offer to tell me how it is under one or more frames of reference; but if I insist that you tell me how it is apart from all frames, what can you say?" The anthropologist's task, then, is to translate rather than to terminate these realities; to "comprehend in general 'other minds'" (Overing 1985: 1); to encourage what Paul Hirst (1985: 88) bills as pragmatic points of contact, "bridgeheads" of communication. By extending Goodman's notion of irreducible world versions to the world-views held by different people on Montserrat, my impressionistic anthropology entertains all, but without entailing an "anything goes" relativism because of the constraints put upon it. The result is an IF ... THEN anthropology: a perspectival anthropology of impressions which does not begin its investigation with an *a priori* stance towards reality.

Anthropology is thus about the various experiences of realities the anthropologist can reflect and reflect upon. They can be individual or collective social realities which are recorded according to the impressionistic experiences of the anthropologist. The anthropologist writes these realities; he "'inscribes' social discourse; *he writes it down*" (Geertz 1993[a]: 19, author's emphasis), and tries to express and translate what he understands the natives to understand. The result is that a plurality of impressions, perspectives and interpretations are put on record, though none of them are as original, sacrosanct or true as Geertz would have us believe.

In addition to the problems associated with representing and writing realities, there is also the problem of assessing what is written. Is it possible to have a good or a bad impressionistic postmodern anthropology in terms of writing and analysis, or does it escape "systematic modes of assessment" like Geertz's (1993[a]: 24) interpretativism? My answer is that an ethnographic recording can only be judged to be faithful, aesthetic or consistent according to whether or not it fulfils the writer's intentions and the reader's apprehensions. The standards are relative and dependent upon the shifting variables – the IF which precedes the THEN. Only a phenomenological presuppositionless anthropology pays heed to our experiences and understandings. This anthropology-without-starting-points resolves the problem of seemingly incommensurable world-views – belonging to either *natives under investigation* (see the following chapters in this book), or to *investigating anthropologists*.

Regarding the latter, my theoretical suggestions break any impasse arising from reading and comparing opposing anthropological work. Consider the individual and joint work of Cohen and Rapport (Cohen & Rapport 1995) by way of illustration. Based upon fieldwork in the English Dales, Rapport (1993; 1994; 1997[a]) propounds a zealous and transcendent individualism and individuality, declaring the biological body to be the repository for the singular human subject. These assumptions are echoed in Cohen's (1987; 1995) work about the self-conscious self which derive from his fieldwork in the Sheltands. Their "Western" assumptions run counter, however, to Dumont's (1970; 1986) suggestion, itself based upon Indian ethnography, that we can treat the individual as a concept situated within a modern, dualistic Enlightenment tradition. To this, Cohen (1995: 14) responds with the criticism that Dumont denies the concepts and values of individuality to non-Western cultures. Reading their opposing ethnographies and this intractable dispute, the reader is not able to confer or deny individuality, but they are able to examine an anthropological argument as to the innate versus the learned perception of ourselves (anthropologists) and others (natives) as individuals. Cohen and Rapport take both the individual and individuality as given universals for all people, whether Western or non-Western. Accordingly, Dumont's work on South Indian culture is wrong because it is in conflict with Cohen and Rapport's initial premiss. Dumont's argument, however, is valid and rational according to its own premiss, but these initial premiss are incommensurable with Cohen and Rapport's.

I believe that there is a danger for anthropologists, such as Cohen and Rapport, who accept as universal and discrete various concepts such as the individual and individuality. Anthropologists are especially well positioned to raise questions and problems rather than dole out answers and circumscriptions. Cohen and Rapport take for granted the individual and self, and hence the body and attentive mind as a bio-dualistic starting point for anthropological analysis. This is despite numerous anthropological and philosophical writings to the contrary: Dumont's work with its emphasis upon society as opposed to the individual; Leenhardt's (1979) anthropological discovery that the Canaques of New Caledonia had no individuated notion of the body prior to European contact; Nietzsche's (Lash 1995: 271) writings about the body as a political structure of competing organs; and Synnott's (1993) study of changing Western perceptions of the body (Greek tomb of the soul, Christian temple, Enlightened individual, Cartesian machine, existential self, medical cyborg). In other words, Cohen and Rapport are guilty of ethnocentric (pre-) judging. Unlike Cohen and Rapport, my uncertain and uncomfortable anthropology accommodates incommensurable beliefs and perceptions, whilst denying universal categories and foundations.

By accepting the demise of grand theory within the social sciences, I am not constrained to Procrusteanate ethnographic impressions to fit functional, structural–functional, structural, Marxist or preconceived paradigms. Nevertheless, my anthropology still seeks Malinowski's holy grail – the native point of view. And my purpose is the same as Leach's (1986: 52) when he wrote that:

> [s]ocial anthropologists should not see themselves as seekers after objective truth; their purpose is to gain insight into other people's behaviour, or, for that matter, into their own.

I too seek first-hand observations and local explanations of exceptional and everyday interaction through traditional long-term participant observation. This is the only method which affords one the opportunity to examine the context of people's actions and the relationship between their notions and actions (Holy & Stuchlik 1983), the ability "to elucidate the meaning of social situations" (Burgess 1993: 2), the chance to "attempt somehow to understand how it is we understand understandings not our own" (Geertz 1993[b]: 5). Like Geertz (1993[a]: 24), I desire "access to the conceptual world in which our subjects live so that we can, in some extended sense, converse with them." This exercise involves translating insight for the reader (Leach 1986: 53), "comprehending the cultural translations of ourselves and of others" (Parkin 1982: xxiv), learning a foreign culture like learning a foreign language (Malinowski 1982[1929]: xlvii). Yet this has to remain a tentative and uncertain pursuit full of qualifications, not least because – to fine-tune these wry old game-players' games – meaning is abstruse, elusive, uncertain and inchoate. Meaning resides somewhere between the native's acts, the scribe's hands and the eyes of the beholder. It relies upon the changeable and interpretable Saussurean connection between the sign and the signified – a coil of communication which, for me, elongates with the poetics of metaphoric evocation and contracts with the attempted one-to-one correspondences of representation.

READING AND WRITING IMPRESSIONS

In this section I will show how writings – including anthropologists' ethnographies and my anthropology – are impressionistic and how they can, therefore, be read. This section thus naturally leads on into the final section on writing and reading this book. I open this section by briefly looking at several different "versions" of the coronation of Ras Tafari in Ethiopia. Reading the British expatriate travel writer Wilfred Thesiger's (1987) work, we learn that Haile Selassie was crowned Emperor of Ethiopia on 2 November 1930 in St George's cathedral, Addis Ababa. This "supreme moment" became an historical event which Thesiger (1987: 92) was proud to witness. Thesiger's account of the coronation is a translation of his experiences from the realm of his perceptions and impressions to the realm of representations – a logocentric and ethnocentric exercise in endeavouring to record an accurate account of events, as all writing is. Reading this mention of Thesiger here in my text is a reference and a paraphrasing of Thesiger, the reader's reading of Thesiger and my written reading of Thesiger. From this I, and you the reader, might form different impressions of the coronation. This is inescapable by nature of our different reading context, knowledge, experience and word associations and has implications for the reading of all texts.

According to reader response theory, the text is "the site for the production and proliferation of meaning" (Rapport 1994: 24). Yet reading the text does not give us the second or third order interpretations of an event that Geertz would lead us to believe. I would suggest that they are different readings entirely rather than readings of a different order. Each reading is an active and creative undertaking, one which transforms both the text and the reader. This is because, according to Iser (1988: 216, 214), the text is "inexhaustible" in that it "needs the reader's imagination" for it to be realised. Furthermore, "a text's unity lies not in its origin but in its destination" opines Barthes (1988[a]: 171). In other words, for Barthes, texts are multiple, fragmented and contesting, yet no matter how heterogeneous they are, they are all focused and united at the place of the reader. This, however, depends upon the assumption that the self is united and not fragmented; singular and not multiple. It also reifies the reader and the reading process which I seek to keep open and uncertain. *Contra* Barthes, then, I am persuaded by Iser (1988: 227) who declares that "[e]very text we read draws a different boundary within our personality, so that the virtual background (the real "me") will take on a different form". In this way it is possible to read and interpret an account in many different ways: it can be an ethnography, a work of fiction, a text giving insight into the writer such as Thesiger or into a social practice such as a coronation tradition. In short, the writer's and reader's impressions are endless.

There is a certain degree of indeterminacy in the multiple readings possible from the text. In other words there are many weak links in the chain of representation from writer's reality to reader's reality. The imagination "fills in" the indeterminacy in the mind's eye based upon narrative cues and mental clues. The cues are Barthes's (1988[b]: 173; Barthes 1988[a]: 170, author's emphasis) "avenues of meaning" where "every text is eternally written *here and now*" for the reader. Overall impressions appear from a synchronicity of reading; or, as Iser (1988: 224) explains, the text becomes the reader's present. It is in this "here and now" of my readings that the author(s) communicate(s) various meaning(s), establishing a connection between writer(s) and reader(s) along a vague but mutually understood and implicitly agreed-upon semiotic coil, upon an impressionistic consensus of meaning. In sum, then, I am suggesting that the text and the self can be both singular and plural, that a book such as this should not be treated just as a total repository for the text: the text "becomes" by being read – activated – by the reader.

Can these senses be trusted? For the postmodern anthropologist investigating his or her subject, there is no true impression, though it is through our perceptions that we lead our lives. It is important to retain a degree of uncertainty, an inchoate space for indeterminate and uncertain readings and impressions, even should I share with my readership the constrained and ethnocentric point of view which views the author as united individual, representative author, mental controller of a physical body living in a modern and progressive society. Many of us are conditioned to read as individual-subject-author representing individual-subject-object. In our situation it is likely that we all share what Rapport assumes to be a universal individuality, that which I hesitate to objectify and universalise.

Furthermore, even the historical fact that "Haile Selassie was crowned Emperor of Ethiopia on 2nd November 1930" is open to scrutiny – a notion entertained by post-structural theorists such as Robert Young (1992: 2) who subscribes to a heterogeneity of histories rather than any "arrogant and arrogating [evolutionary] narrative" of Western history. When the philosopher Deleuze (Young 1992: 82) famously asked "where is the battle?", he answered himself back, describing "the battle" as a phantasm, an incorporeal cloud hovering over the individual actions in the field. Likewise, when I think to myself about the coronation of Ras Tafari and ask "just where is the coronation?", my reply is that what is called the coronation consists of a vast heterogeneous array of actions none of which constitutes "the coronation" as such; each action fragments according to diverse movements, shifting meanings, realities and varied intentions of the spectators, writers and the Ras. History – for which we can also substitute other concepts such as race and gender – becomes relative, partial and lacking in essence.

Evelyn Waugh (1951: 84) shares our cultural and literary communality. His account of the coronation validates my impressionistic supposition as he attends to different events and interactions in his humorous endeavour to represent what was, for him, the reality of the coronation, a "preposterous *Alice in Wonderland* fortnight". Read together, the Thesiger and Waugh versions of the coronation do indeed show themselves to be writings of at least two respective overlapping realities. For Waugh, the coronation celebrations were a week long series of events beginning with the Emperor's partial unveiling of a statue of a horseman. And, adding to the complexity of the coronation, Waugh (1951: 93) notes that the coronation – a closely guarded state secret day by day – was covered by the world's journalists who had to file all their reports of the coronation ahead of the occasion so that their reports hit the headlines on the day of "the event". The result was that they guessed at its location (the city cathedral) and content (a crowning obscured by incense).

Such coronation versions were later used by the Jamaican Rastafarian preacher Leonard Howell as evidence of the guests' homage to the "King of Kings, Lord of Lords, Conquering Lion of the Tribe of Judah" (Owens 1984: 15, 18). For Howell, Haile Selassie was Christ returned to earth once more; the Son of God on earth who would repatriate the black man out of Babylon back to the promised land of Ethiopia. For uttering such claims Howell was arrested in Jamaica by the British colonial forces in December 1933 and sentenced to two year's imprisonment for "sedition and blasphemy" (Owens 1984: 17). Howell gives us another reality of Ras Tafari's coronation.

These three realities are not mutually exclusive or necessarily incommensurable with each other. They frequently overlap as well as contest each other. For Howell, Thesiger and Waugh there is a coronation consensus in that a coronation took place. So there is some degree of inter-subjectivity between their subjective worlds. This tentative inter-subjectivity I am referring to reveals just what is lacking in Shweder's schema of multiple objective worlds: Shweder explains incommensurability at the expense of looking into inter-subjectivity. Waugh and Thesiger, nevertheless, enjoyed a different coronation from each other, and all three have widely diverging meanings and significances for the coronation. If the coronation is to have any reality beyond Thesiger, Waugh, Haile Selassie and other participants, it has to be recorded and framed, and then read by others. The native insights sought by the anthropologist are thus multiplex, mobile and metamorphic – local rather than global. As a postmodern anthropologist, I thus simultaneously entertain the realities of the writers, however incommensurable Thesiger and Howell's realities might be with each other; the one British, colonial and Christian, the other African, anti-colonial and Rastafarian.

Such native worlds and realities are created and constructed from different levels and from different locales, from Rapport's individual villagers to Leenhardt's collective islanders. They can be extended in these places as people build on the ramifications of their world-views and realities, some of which may subsequently converge with each other (Christian with Christian) whilst others may diverge as incommensurable native realities (Christian and Rastafarian). "IF ... THEN" we are to speak of grand truths then we must write that they are local rather than global. Ironically, from the anthropologist's perspectives, realities are universally subjective and locally objective in that the native realities of the British villager and the West Indian Rastafarian are each true but only for each other. From the observer's allegedly comparative and panoptic vantage point – Schneider's stance – these insights and realities are often treated and collated as belief systems and as social constructions; short-sighted convictions overlaid upon an objective reality. In this academic preface I have maintained an argument against just such an approach – against an anthropology as paint stripper (a null hypothesis study of the different ways that people attend to the same reality).

WRITING AND READING THIS BOOK

As suggested above, care and attention has to be given to reading and writing in general, so let me finally pay attention to the processes of writing and reading this book, first to myself and then to the chapters in this book. Both the writer and the reader undertake active roles in the production and consumption of a book. For Leach (1984: 22), "we can read a text with the set purpose of discovering projections of the author's personality, of finding a record of how he or she reacted to what was going on". This means that this book can be read variously as an ethnography, as fiction, as personal travel writing or more, depending upon the "reading culture" or consciousness of the reading audience. Howell (1994: 327), along with many other anthropologists, would like to keep a distinction between anthropology the discipline – anthropological texts and ethnographies – and other disciplines' texts. She does this by invoking the work of Stanley Fish (see

Chapter 2), by noting that anthropologists have a "reading culture", one which is ostensibly distinct from other genres and disciplines: specifically, "[a]s practising anthropologists we all belong to one or another interpretative community whether we acknowledge this or not". Naturally, I disagree with arguments for such an inflexible discreteness in anthropology or the interpretative reading community. I prefer to see blurred genres of writing rather than ordered, divided and delineated groupings. I, the writer, can only exert some mild and distant influence over any reading of this text.

To foreground any reading of this study, I should like to situate myself and my writing. It has been written from the academic Oxbridge of the north, St Andrews University, by a product of British public school training. It was at school that I was first introduced to the diversity of roles and positions in the school – the informal as well as the formal nature of school rules, the need for diplomacy when dealing with housemasters and the hierarchy of prefects. But it was on a year-long foreign exchange to a private school in Canada that I really formed my anthropological interests. I held an English Speaking Union scholarship to a school also founded in the Victorian age and upon Victorian principles, also with a school chapel and school prefects and school houses, Shakespeare in the classrooms and rugby and football and rowing outside. Yet for all such overt similarities, inside, there were many small but very distinctive differences which first set me off thinking comparatively and writing ethnographically. The school rules and the drinking laws were very similar but they were interpreted very differently – to the letter, in fact: preparing for a school expedition into the Amazon Basin, Canadian parents refused to sign consent forms allowing their children to drink wine rather than contaminated water should the need arise.

When I began studying social anthropology at St Andrews, I realised that I had been "doing anthropology" whilst I was in Canada – namely, living, observing and comparing and contrasting the cultures of two educational institutions. In their own ways, these are brief edited segments of personal events which have contributed to what I consider to be my individual make-up and academic interests: concerns such as to be comparative, evocative and sensitive to textual and social subtleties. When it came to post-graduate anthropology, I sought one of the last surviving British colonies, an English-speaking field-location where I could test the new post-colonial literature scene where assertions were made between writing and social formation through the analysis of non-Western and Commonwealth literature by literary critics such as Said (1991), Bhabha (1994) and Spivak (1990) – all declared from their university positions in Western countries. I wanted to go a colonial place to test their post-colonial readings of people's lives based upon literary stories. It was in following such lines of inquiry that I stumbled upon Montserrat where I chose to undertake the fledgling anthropologist's traditional year of participant observation (see the next two chapters).

Stressing the participant side of this anthropological formula, I "did anthropology" on Montserrat by joining in as much as possible (see the next chapter), and by writing extensive fieldnotes at the end of the day or the next morning, detailing as closely as possible the events and interactions of the day. As far as possible, I would try and follow-up on the events or issues as they arose, sometimes carrying a scrap of paper around with me to remind me of what I was considering to be noteworthy material, or as to what I was looking into that day. When I left what I had notionally circumscribed as "the field", I had approximately half a million words and numerous sketches in a collection of journals, similar to the ones I had written in whilst at school in Canada and on some of my travels around the world. I also had a large number of interview tapes, videos, newspapers, poems and books collected from my time on Montserrat and from some brief visits to neighbouring islands. When it came to writing about Montserrat, here, I made use of all of these materials as well as what Simon Ottenberg (1990: 144) would refer to as my "headnotes". By this, Ottenberg means the anthropologist's incorporeal property in his head – their vivid memories, impressions of the days in the field which are cued by the fieldnotes or other lodestones such as a certain smell, taste, sound, sight or feel. Crucially, Ottenberg continues, because these headnotes – an adjunct to fieldnotes – are carried in the head, they are susceptible to change, decay and revision over time. For Ottenberg, the Afikpo of Nigeria, amongst whom he worked, have changed from being democratic when he was happily married, to being quite undemocratic and at times downright autocratic following his unpleasant series of broken marriages. From this observation, Ottenberg (1990: 146) concludes:

> [i]n short, as my own life unwinds, I naturally see and reflect upon Afikpo
> life differently. I am constantly reinterpreting Afikpo, ever looking at
> my fieldnotes in different ways. [...] My headnotes and my written notes
> are in constant dialogue, and in this sense the field experience does
> not stop. Things that I once read in my fieldnotes in one way, I now
> read in another. Evidence that I thought excellent, I now question.

I share such a relationship with my headnotes, my fieldnotes, and this text here – all of which I wish to acknowledge in the indeterminate and inconstant processes of writing and reading this book.

Indeterminate and inconstant, the writing and reading of this book is in keeping with the uncertain and uncomfortable theorising mentioned earlier. My writing is necessarily framed with a start and a finish, but I also deconstruct myself as I go along; if I were a painter, I would be painting the frame as part of the picture. Following this voluntary academic preface, the chapters are written so as to encourage a consecutive reading with the introduction of many characters in the first chapter. But there are also readings which can be made with or without attention to the sequence of chapters: chapters can be read alone or in a different order to that recommended here. Furthermore, the series of volcano updates – chapter prefaces – at the beginning of each of the chapters are chronological and tell their own story, interruptions which remind the reader, during their readings of the book, of the writer's positions when the book was written. Significantly, when reading this book, you will find no pictures or drawings. The reason for this returns us to reader response theory, back to Iser (1988: 219) who favours the creativity involved in reading a word-painting as opposed to the "immutability" of passively viewing a pastel-painting: I thus take from Iser the need to produce a book without pictures, a book of creative impressions.

In this way, the writing of this book shares an affinity with the paintings done by Impressionists such as Cezanne and Monet who painted their perceptions of reality rather than any representation of reality. Different canvases: similar impulses, in effect, to challenge the doctrine of realism – that "[o]bjects existing outside the mind can be represented (reproduced by a concept or work of art) in a way that is adequate, accurate and true" (Appignanesi & Garratt & Sardar & Curry 1995: 13, authors' emphasis). If we apply the artistic Impressionists' theoretical approach to ethnography we get what John Van Maanen refers to as "impressionist tales" (1988: 101, 103, 104). These are evocative and sensuous ethnographies which belong to the confessional subgenre of ethnography. These impressionist tales are "striking stories, not luminous paintings" which aim to draw the reader into the writer's worlds by dramatic recall, by slipping cultural knowledge to the audience "in fragmented, disjointed ways", appealing to the audience to read with the spirit of the tale in mind and not just the literal words that comprise it.

The following impressions of Montserrat do not seek to be true and accurate representations for the reader. Illusive fictions – after Tyler, Marcus & Clifford and Strathern; uncertain anthropological impressions – after Firth, Geertz and Fernandez: these chapters can be read as valid according to their "plausibility and credibility", as Martyn Hammersley (1993: 73) would have us assess and read all ethnography. Though I take note that the reader's readings are open and indeterminate, and thus liable to great degrees of variation and levels of appreciation, I also admit that I do not know the reader who may well be an anthropologist, a reader interested or concerned with Montserrat and those who are – or have been – living on the island, or Montserratian themselves. What I would like to state to any anthropological reader is that this monograph is more an ethnographic building block than a comparative and generalising work; it is not my intention, here, to concentrate upon comparing Montserrat with other islands in the Caribbean, with other British Dependent Territories or many other anthropological monographs. This is an ethnographic building block about Montserrat and postmodern ethnography. Hence the absence, in this book, of the customary literature review in favour of the readers' and writer's impressions – the former in this academic preface, the latter in Chapter 1.

Finally, after such a lengthy theoretical academic preface to this book, let me sum up its nature and chapter content. This text is clearly written in a fashion which "stresses the interaction of reader and text as productivity" (Sarup 1993: 3). It is explicitly uncertain and uncomfortable. It follows Barthes's death of the author thesis up to a point. It also leans in the direction of Derrida's separation of signifiers from that signified. And it engages with postmodern artists' attempts at non-representational art. This text, however, stops short of Barthes's, Derrida's and Impressionist artists' conclusions in that I maintain that the text may be stretched away from the creator as it is read by creative readers – but is not read into infinity: semiotic meaning is elongated, by metaphor for instance, but it is not separated; the canvas is never closed to interpretations of reality. This book, then, is a rejection of grand theory in the Social Sciences. It begins by interrogating the nature of social anthropology, both its theoretical and methodological assumptions. It then goes on to establish an anthropology which is partial and relative, uncomfortable and uncertain, and impressionistic. The substantial chapters in this book support this impressionistic anthropology by referring to an ethnographic encounter with the competing and highly contested realities expressed by myself, some Montserratian poets, some calypsonians, some development workers, some local Montserratians, some tourists and the Montserratian Government and Tourist Board.

More precisely, via the anthropologist's impressions, Chapter 1 introduces the reader to the place and people of Montserrat. In Chapter 2, I comment upon the construction of Chapter 1 before going on to filter Montserrat through poets' impressions of the island and islanders, namely through the poets of the Maroons Creative Writers' Group which is led by Sir Howard Fergus. In Chapter 3, I go on to show that impressions of Montserrat, despite their highly contested nature, can be held not just singularly – as in the case of individual poets, but also plurally – as constellations such as in the contrasting world-views of Montserratians and development workers on Montserrat.

Chapters 4 and 5 continue my ethnographic impressions of Montserrat by presenting, respectively, the labours of several calypsonians on Montserrat who seek public recognition for their work, and union leader Chedmond Browne's struggles such as maintaining the trade union workers' employment at Plymouth Port. The last chapter – Chapter 6 – recedes (ethnographically) from Montserrat: It considers the competing impressions and controversial histories of St Patrick's Day, an annual celebration and commemoration on Montserrat. The contentious content of the last two chapters in this book affirms and reinforces the need for my theoretical approach to Montserrat. They also comment more directly upon the notion of the "Black Irish" of Montserrat which is an ethnic category introduced from the start of the book. Finally, the conclusion to the book sums up the aforementioned chapters and makes general comments towards establishing a reflexive and sustainable postmodern impressionistic anthropology.

In this book there are only a few modest textual experiments within the text: shifts in tone, degrees of personal involvement and changes in narrative style and flow. These strategies can also be found in other ethnographies such as Anna Tsing's *In the Realm of the Diamond Queen* (1993), a feminist informed ethnography of marginality amongst the Meratus Dayaks of Indonesia – a humanistic tapestry of Shamanic tales, romantic poems and transforming songs showing how an isolated community links with the wider nation-state. Our craft is similar though the narratives, poems, songs and conversations are different. Tsing's work is framed around the words of an eccentric informant Uma Adang. My work is situated "before the volcano", but framed around the eruption of the volcano: ethnographic present and ethnographic artifice together is my way of playing with the convincingness of the readers' text. Tsing's aim is "to develop a different set of conceptual tools for thinking about out-of-the-way places" (1993: x). My main preoccupation is to create "subject-centred" impressions of people on Montserrat (cf. Jackson 1998: 58); and to do this by evoking partially as opposed to representing wholly, by accepting the indeterminacy of this text from which the reader will flesh out their own reality. Thus, it is not here but in the following chapters that I narrate a series of ethnographic examples in which I see different individuals evoking, representing and worldmaking their realities. So, let me begin Chapter 1 with my personal arena of investigation, my traumatic social world evoked hereafter, my own impressions of Montserrat ...

Date: Wed, 19 July 1995 10:51:23 MST
From: Global Volcanism Network
Subject: Soufriere Hills, Montserrat

The following report from the Smithsonian Institution's Global Volcanism Network on 19 July 1995 is preliminary and subject to change as additional information is received.

Soufriere Hills, Montserrat, West Indies
16.72 N, 62.18 W; summit elev. 915 m

The Associated Press reported a "full alert" on the island of Montserrat Tuesday (18 July) after a light ashfall. The Director of an Emergency Operations Center told AP that no mass evacuation was planned, but two schools had been set aside as refugee centers for those living near the volcano who wanted to evacuate. The Synoptic Analysis Branch of NOAA saw no evidence of a plume on satellite imagery.

The following information is from a telephone report to GVN on the morning of 19 July from Richard Robertson at the Seismic Research Unit, University of the West Indies, Trinidad. Based on his conversations with Montserrat residents, this eruption appears to have been a small phreatic event with minor ashfall being spread around the island by local winds. The UWI maintains two seismic stations on Montserrat. Seismicity has been elevated for the past three years, and an earthquake swarm was recently recorded. William Ambeh and Lloyd Lynch have been dispatched from UWI to confirm the activity. They will prepare a report for the GVN Bulletin upon completion of their investigation.

Soufriere Hills volcano has grown on the N flank of the older South Soufriere Hills volcano at the S end of Montserrat Island. The summit area consists primarily of a series of lava domes emplaced along a ESE-trending zone. The youngest dome, Castle Peak, is located in English's Crater, which is breached to the E. Block-and-ash flow and surge units associated with dome growth predominate in flank deposits. The capital city of Plymouth lies on the coast, ~4 km W of the summit.

An active fumarolic area, named Galways Soufriere, is located on the S flank of Soufriere Hills. There have been no reported historical eruptions, but some undated deposits and the cone have a young appearance. A radiocarbon date of ~320 BP from a pyroclastic-flow deposit is significantly younger than other radiocarbon dates from the volcano, but could result from the latest activity of Chances Peak.

Ed Venzke – Global Volcanism Network | Phone: 202-357-1511
Museum of Natural History, MRC 129 | Fax: 202-357-2476
Smithsonian Institution |
Washington, DC, 20560 | Internet: mnhms017@SIVM.SI.EDU
USA

MONTSERRAT PLACE AND MONS'RAT NEAGA

Heat. Hot. It's damn hot. It was so hot when I went to bed last night and it's hot even now. Another morning to plug and unplug the fan as I walk around my apartment with the sweat glistening down my awkward body. It hits my skin when I disturb the lizards by winching up the shutters. They were built and bred for this place, not me. And the light needles my eyes so I have to frown at everything like a frustrated anthropologist.

But I am frustrated! 7.40 a.m. and Jed's playing a scraping ragga version of "Redemption Song" down below me. He's screaming the words, macheting a carcass in his yard, pinning the meat to the wall of his little wooden house caught between the new Government Philatelic Bureau (run by the former Chief Minister) and my apartment, an appendage above the Emerald Cafe. (Both myself and the Cafe belong to Pippa Irish further down the street so I can't complain when Jed sets up all their metal chairs outdoors at 6 a.m. – more scraping.)

Jed's wife must have already heard her Morning Service programme and left for the hospital. The children, Micky and Nicky, have already been punished by their policeman father. Micky hoses himself and finishes dressing in the yard before going to school. He sends the kittens and chickens in all directions, spraying the air whilst singing and wining his hips to himself. Nicky plucks strands of mango from between her teeth and throws them over the galvanise walls. There they land on no-man's land to further the battle between rubbish tip and garden allotment.

The music is loud but when I open the shutters overlooking the road, Neil Diamond's *"America"* shakes me even more awake.

Doc must be on a day-off. It's his favourite song – it must be to be so loud at eight in the morning. He doesn't like Jed, a fat policeman who doesn't know how to box. Doc likes to play louder music than Jed because Ninja, Doc's dog, was poisoned by Jed. Me, I think it was the AUC medical students, Americans up on the hill who used to meet Ninja behind The Green Flash when the toilet was occupied. At any rate, Jed likes dogs, he has some tied up with the goats, up above Doc's, at the abandoned hotel. You know, the one that was blasted by the hurricane.

No one minds the music except for me. Doc's girl Lou-Ann is a bit deaf cos Vicki suckled her on dance floors before she took to sitting out on the porch and watching the American doctor students drinking down the road. Vicki keeps the music on all day whilst she makes clothes. That way people know she's in and they can lime on her porch. She daren't touch the stereo without Doc's permission, and he's not going to start speaking to her.

Doc's out by the road in a shell suit and singlet and his goalkeeper's bandanna that stretches down his back to keep off the sun. He's scratching the weeds away from Ninja's memorial pile with his machete, worrying Ant's donkey, forcing the ground lizards to scuttle under his house, and throwing karate kicks at his friends driving down the hill to work. An ordinary morning. Nice to see – Doc in the garden and at last watering some of the cacti on the porch, Vicki waving to her friends walking to the market. She's got her hair, she just relaxed, wrapped in a blanket, and she's just sitting with a thin wrap around her torso. She's a butterskin as the Antiguans say, a redskin as they say here. She's a Browne from the north where they all have clear skins, and she always tells me that she's one of the Montserrat Irish. Some say Doc's lucky to live at his girlfriend's – such an attractive, light-skinned woman, especially with him being so black. Interesting that Lou-Ann's just brown. Ridley and Leon, Vicki's teenage sons from elsewhere and another time are more like their father, not that he acknowledges them. Sad really, Doc also has two other kids from another time. There's pictures taped onto the wall of them. They're at school now and he sometimes sees them as they walk up the hill to their grandmother's where they live.

Anyway, Vicki's shouting up to the branches of a huge breadfruit tree arching out above their house. It covers Chef Tony's car park for the Cafe. He says he's poor and that as a whiteman I should buy him out, though he's got a Mercedes which he parks opposite the Cafe gates, at the foot of Doc's porch, rather than at his customers' car park. Ant, his odd-job man, cleans the car every day. But, in this case, Ant's picking breadfruit out of the trees. Sometimes I wake up in the morning when he throws breadfruit onto the galvanise outside my window. Today, his shoes are at the bottom of the tree and he's heckling the schoolgirls walking up Wapping to town.

"Wha! Gal, leh me teach you wid me tung!"

"Wotcha. 'Come betta dan dat' Ant, ya raz-boy."

"Aiou. You a one fuking hard gal, fuking hard ya hear. Any more you mothers-cunts like she?"

Banter, but the girl has the better of Ant who doesn't like to be reminded of his dreadlocks that were shorn off when he went to jail. He was framed for raping his girlfriend who moved in with some policemen. Maybe they poisoned Doc's dog, saving their bullets whilst on the stray patrol?

Bang – Bang – Bang

The metal door reverberates. It could be anyone and I'm not ready for them yet. Doc could be angry about something from last night? Down the stairs, outside, by the side of the road, a grin and a goatee beard are pointed at me. Ant's still barefoot with a pair of trousers tied up at the waist, a torn shirt open to his navel. His hand's on his belly, stroking it in pain. He's sweating and puffing on a fag.

"Ooh. Got anyt'ing fu me stomach mon? 'E hurt bad bad. Me need somet'ing warm." Ant implores me, begging for a drink.

"Wha, but it's only eight o'clock. A wha' kinda t'ing is dis ya?" I practise my dialect and Ant cackles through his teeth.

"Aiou, boy, you's Mons'ratian. Jus' some rum an' ice?"

Doc must have told Ant about the new bottle of rum we started last night. But "once in de morning" is "once every morning" with Ant.

"Me got na rum."

"Wha, you finish de rum like dat? Wha' 'bout me, mon? Aiou!" Ant leaves for his breadfruit, knowing full well that I won't be shifted so early in the morning. We both prefer a lie to the coarse truth.

Doc sees me topless by the door and waves at me with his machete. I have to go across.

"Hey Doc, how you doing?"

"A wha' you say?"

"Huh?"

"A WHA'YOU SAY?"

And what do you say? I try out, "I'm fine. Me chill! You rub up?"

"A'right Jono. The boys say they like las' night. Angel pissed man, pissed. He just sit dere an singing. Teknikal choose 'e song. Eh, 'A News Dem A Look'!"

"Great, tell 'e 'to go and read a newspaper' then!"

We laugh at the joke from last night and I take my leave, feeling self-conscious.

"A'right Jono, me check you later."

"Yeah, yeah, yeah." I imitate Doc.

Back upstairs, I continue to prepare myself and work out a rough path for the day. Slow after last night's singing at Doc's. I set straight some fieldnotes from last week, jot down events from late last night and leave for my own wanderings and wonderings around the capital.

"A'right John."

"A'right."

John is busy at the top of the street, leaning against a wall. Every day John leans and watches down the road. Later on he'll follow the shade to the bottom of the street where it joins the road south. There he'll spend the evening looking up Wapping. He's there every day, wearing the same shorts and shirt. He only begged from me the first day he saw me. Thereafter we just say hellos for the first time each day and, should I pass him later in the day, he'll just pretend to be looking in the other direction. He has a war tattoo and a peace tattoo on each forearm, and he lives with his old mother. Though in his forties, his mother tends to his needs. Today, two American tourists, on their way to investigate the Emerald Cafe, or just off-track, are asking him if they've given him enough money.

At the bridge – my favourite view of the island. The bridge divides Wapping from Plymouth. Underneath the bridge runs a large river-bed, a ghaut where goats graze and rubbish is dropped. Up on the right, if you follow the ghaut, there's a green mountain shaped like an old volcano. It was a volcano, and most tourists describe the vegetation on it as 'verdant'. That word now makes many Montserratians cringe. The term is appropriate, but when it appears in every description of the island – and now in all the island tourist adverts and on the lips of all the Montserratians abroad who describe the island that they belong to – it becomes worn and clichéd. The grasses are a bit dry and patchy from the unremitting sun, but there's still that emerald tint about them, the rhododendron bushes and tropical trees. "Emerald" is another of those well-worn words. There are other hills and mountains to the north but Chances Peak is the highest, the one with the Cable & Wireless mast, and the one everyone associates with the shape of the island.

To the left the ghaut reaches the sea, passing through some broken-up old boats, and you can just see the new jetty for cargo ships and the occasional West Indies Guardship permanently stationed in the Caribbean by the British. In front is the new Plymouth Prison, the old colonial fort. Outside, the prisoners chop wood and line up for manpower services around the island.

On the way into Plymouth centre there is the garage, Texaco – "the Star of the Eastern Caribbean". The Wash Bar – "now serving goatwater, souse and conch". The stone slabs of the market. The Pleasure Palace Bar "in action". The Bird's Nest Bar. Squeakies Supermarket – "ask if we can do any better". The Taxi-Memorial Stand and dominoes zone. The Wharf, jetty and Seamen's Union. Liat – "Land In Any Tree" – Airlines. The Post Office and its disabled inhabitant Thesman. Wolfe's Diving Shop.

There are passing hellos, nods and papal flicks of the wrist. I disappear up past the new Bank of Montserrat, the Montserrat Chamber of Commerce, Lloyd's Shipping and Insurance, Wall Shipping and Trucking, Cork's Pharmacy, the Heliconia and Tradewinds Real Estate, to get to the Royal Bank of Canada. I have to avoid the taxi drivers who are determined to drive me up to "AUC School". At the bank, the doorman welcomes me to his air-conditioned building. There are about five active counters and two or three closed with "Please try the next wicket" signs. All the cashiers have some words with the customer before getting the money from the one dispenser. The queue's long enough to give me time to look around at the builders, Cable & Wireless personnel, the man who deposits all the Texaco cash throughout the day, some old ladies with brown bags of old notes and a few taxi drivers. Dey say Mons'rat taximen so fas', dey make money 'fore dey learn fu sign fu um.

After my withdrawal, on the way out I pass Doc sitting in the shade of the bank where the buses pick up for the south of the island. He was just sitting with a Carib, just watching the street-life. He just stared at me without any recognition. I smiled and waved to him, but people are just like that sometimes. Vicki tells me that he's often like that. Moody. He hasn't spoken to her for two weeks now. But there's no reason. Friends, girls and children come and go, only his poetry stays with him. Dare say I'll be one of them going someday. Teknikal's scared of him and his strength. Only Ant and Fab have known him from school when they used to throw stones at each other. They're all from East, Harris village, "the wise men of the East" people call themselves from there. Vicki, she's from the city, never been to some of the villages in the East, up in the Soufriere Hills below Chances Peak. The squats – where Ant's built a shack without water and electricity – are too wild for her. No sir, she never go country.

On the way, passing the Evergreen is like running the gauntlet. A large tree – blown over in the hurricane, now growing sideways – marks a junction for cars, a shaded circle for pedestrians, an arena of observation. Ant's washing a car outside the Evergreen Bar, next to the MNT and some of the firemen are sitting on a wall focusing upon Caribs and country-girls visiting the town. Everyone's gaze follows a white-person and I don't always recognise the faces I know amongst the squatting drinking men with gold chains, rings, studs and teeth. If I miss someone, they could come after me to know why me dis dem. If I stare too hard or too long then I could feel the wrath of a vocal Rasta.

Above the East Indian Supermarket, the Library – temporarily located since the hurricane and until the new British development building opens. There're already fears that no black consciousness books will be bought by Britain – the donor of books and building. What would Cheltenham's Women's Guild be doing with second-hand jumble sale copies of Black Power Movement literature?

The front room librarians are flicking their nails and flicking through copies of *Ebony* and *Essence*. There's no one else in the library at the moment – school children will be in the temporary corrugated classrooms which were erected four years ago after Hurricane Hugo, nicknamed "the furnaces from Britain". This place is often used as the courting house for the older students on special projects, but they only come in after 2 p.m. when school finishes early due to the heat again.

I return some Len Deighton spy novels – second-hand copies donated to the library by expat residents – and some Walcott poetry – Caribbean literature bought by the library. Lorna is engrossed in conversation in the back chambers with Sarah and Amy. She's talking about the Governor, a ceremony ...?

"... services they wanted. This is exactly ..."

"Hullo, Jonathan, h-how you been man?" Amy diplomatically interrupts Lorna.

"Good morning ladies," I address the three librarians.

"T'ought you bin an' gone off island dere." Sarah joins in.

"Wha. Dis boy travels far an' wide through the islands. We were just making plans for the handing over ceremony your friend the Governor insists on." She giggles.

"No friend of mine thank you very much," I rejoin.

Lorna kicks me from her chair by the door, "So what about those breakfasts on the veranda. La-de-dah, tea and civil service development planning?"

"Yeah, and don't forget the swimming we do in the pool each morning. He floats and I pull him."

"Aiou! Jonathan, what a cheek 'e got on 'im, Sarah," gasps Amy.

"So tell me why your Governor has to have a big ceremony every time he does something, or the Red Cross or Police Commissioner. Why don't they just do what we do; do the job and get on."

"Lorna, my we look so busy. Is that *Good Housekeeping* there? It's good public relations, of course."

"Humpf. Dependency colonialism if you ask me."

"Did I?"

As with Pippa, Doc and others on Montserrat, when we meet, Lorna and I have established a pattern to our verbal relationship. She plays the ignorant informant and casts me as the complicit coloniser. At the end of each week of these exchanges we then we go to shows together and she insists that the coloniser pays for her – she does drive us though. We're very close: I helped her with archives and projects and she lets me tape interviews, deliberately contradicting her stories and beliefs that I've come to know from her. This is all part of our relationship with each other, one characterised by affection and exasperation.

As for Amy, I'd love to interview her. A published writer and poet, she organises the Writers' Maroon meetings for Sir Fergus, she edits all manuscripts with keen eyes and ears and was forced – so she tells me – to buy her British Dependent Territory (BDT) Nationality when Thatcher introduced the new laws. She's always worked on Montserrat but her family comes from Haiti and Antigua so she lost her British passport along with everyone else in the colonies with the 1982 House of Commons Nationality Act. Only she had no automatic right to a new passport. It's probably for this reason that she's so anti-nationalities. She refuses to tell me "who she is" or "where she belongs" or "if she's Montserratian". "What is dis 'Montserratian'? I'm me. I'm not a geography." She goes on (and I agree with her though I don't want to influence her comments by saying so), "but what is it to be British?" Identity's as awkward to identify as ethnicity, and here people seem to be twisted and hijacked by semantic pirates. There's little use in this but for knowing how "Montserratians" discriminate and reify distinctions. The others in the library are proud "to be Montserratian" where they were born amongst extensive family networks, where they were taught and learned together, and where they will be buried where their ancestors toiled and died and were killed.

Lorna mentions a Voices concert at the Vue Point Hotel – $20, the same routines as other concerts, so it's obviously a fund-raiser targeted at the "snowbirds" here for Christmas and the new season. I slip away with a reminder that I'm one of the judges for the school's story-telling competition.

Lunch is a roti – a kind of chicken piece wrapped in a pancake made with soaked peas – at a fast-food by the Evergreen. There are lots of pictures of foods to look at but none of them are ever offered; pizza, roti, chips, rice, Johnny cakes and chicken are the mainstay. Public rounds of courtship continue at the Evergreen with school kids, road workers and office workers all eyeing, judging and rating. It feels like first-year university in the Students Union but, here, with no university and no public funding; there is no "student" category, except for that closed medical community on the hill.

"Radio" creeps past the outside tables. No one speaks to him but everyone looks. One of the best calypsonians on the island, notorious for his veiled criticisms of society. He stares ahead of himself, sits mumbling in corners and is oblivious to the world he once portrayed and characterised so eloquently. His dreads are a shock, a mane growing out and upwards *en masse*. The Rasta-ruffians can no longer understand him, but everyone can recall some of his lyrics.

Walking towards the Evergreen is Chedmond Browne on his way home; clear-skinned, grey-bearded, shirt, jeans and working boots, carrying copies of his newsletters rolled up in his hand. A few men stop him and argue. He starts slapping his *Pan-Afrikan Liberator* into his palm, the baton of a riot police officer. They stop talking when I draw near. He greets me with a curt nod, gives me a copy of the paper and waits for the money. I ask for two, one for me and one for Pippa. He doesn't believe that the second copy's for a Montserratian, telling me that it's for my friend the Governor, or for some of the expats to read and burn. I think he's joking because he refuses to sell his copies to any white people on the island. He knows that some of the expats' black friends buy copies on their behalf and that a copy of each edition, along with all local newspapers, is sent back in the diplomatic bags to be read and analysed at the Foreign & Commonwealth West Indies British Dependent Territories Desk. That's why some of the comments are extreme or confusing – they're written not for other Montserratians but to create an impression in the mind of the Foreign & Commonwealth Office analyst who informs the Minister who informs the Prime Minister who informs the Governor who informs the local Government who informs the Montserrat people and newspaper writers. Thus, an open letter to John Major titled "The Black Condition of White Colonialism", or "Governor's policies rely upon dependency" are more than just frustrated criticisms. They can be massively calculated long-term strategies pitted against those of the Foreign & Commonwealth Office (rather than some short-term recommendations to an incumbent Government).

Swiftly, I ask him a question, "Can I drop by and return some of those books sometime?"

He shrugs, "Anytime, you know where I am."

Cheddy seldom sleeps, plays countless games of chess against a computer each night to improve his powers of concentration and reads late into the morning to improve his mind so that he can teach others about the oppression suffered by "Afrikans" on

Montserrat and around the world. He's the head of the Seamen's Union which the Governor has decided to break. He represents several hundred illiterate workers; that's why he's always out on the streets talking about his newsletter outside bars, on street corners and at the Evergreen.

"Okay, thanks then." I leave, working out a night when I can listen to his five hour soliloquies without losing or forgetting any of his words. Maybe I can tape him and we can go through the theories and perspectives which he used to broadcast on the radio (until the Governor censored him under an Act of Sedition, one usually used against Germans in times of war)? Not tonight though, there's a Maroon on which I can't miss.

Amy told me back at the library about the meeting tonight, so I'll skip some work on local calypso up at ZJB Radio and go get some exercise.

Down in Wapping, I pass John, Jed's now silent house, the flock of chickens which live, feed and are killed on the Wapping Road, the car park with the Governor's white *de luxe* Range Rover and chauffeur – or is this one his wife's? – and the same tape recording blaring from Vicki's house. I wait for the traffic to die down to open my door and climb above the noisy Cafe.

There's been no time for exercise this past week and the weekends are my most busy time when people and friends are not working "nine to five" at their jobs. I take off up the hill for a brisk run in the afternoon. John follows me with his eyes, confused; Ant shouts some encouragement about catching some girls in front of me. I leave behind the fictions and confusions of life and climb the left side of the road, passing some British road signs, the Hotel which Jed uses and other derelict house boxes.

I reveal my idiosyncratic body to Montserrat; brown calves, starched thighs, peeling forehead, blinding white shoulders. I glisten past the huge, new Pentecostal Church with three-hour long services, a bridge with a graffiti name leading to "This Holy Mount Zion", the sentry at Government House, up to the American University of the Caribbean (AUC) campus – medics in condos dissecting imported cadavers. There I get a few cautious waves from white North Americans who misplace my name but recognise my colour as belonging to some other class cohort – waspishly suffering along with them the disadvantages of affirmative action.

Down the other side of Amersham Estate, past the back of the school, another granite-built windmill resisting the end of slavery, another plantation house, some new houses with goats on the lawns and dogs in the driveways, satellite dishes four metres in circumference. Steep, steep roads above Plymouth and a pale sea. No other islands visible today.

Over-grown car wrecks litter the sides of roads. They remind me of the artificial reef the Governor built offshore by dumping over 100 cars in a line. Mothers sit with children on their porches as I run down to Kinsale sea shore. A village a mile south of Wapping, named as a reminder of an Irish home the inhabitants once possessed; here too, the site of Fort Barrington marks the Anglo-Irish troubles and the problems with European integration which are played out along the sharp edges of Empire. Niggy's is a jazz bar: Niggy, married to a whiteman, sings along to backing tapes. Moose's is a sea-food bar and restaurant on a wooden jetty, an evening retreat for tourists and expats and AUC students and businessmen, but not for anthropologists on tight budgets.

Back to Wapping up the southern island road, sea to the left and a beach shelf of black sand. Past the bus shelter which bounds the two areas, the old Yacht Club opposite the Inn; I've arrived at Sugar Bay; the fork to Captain Weekes's and the town docks, or to the bottom of Wapping – the Governor's cliff, Zacky's Hangout Bar, a collection of houses receding into the cliff-side, the old Pentecostal Church which used to lock the congregation in, the Oasis outside restaurant, Irish's Funeral Home and White's Pest Control. And then the one-way Wapping road between stone houses; Pippa's long house, the Cafe and my apartment, Jed's and the Philatelic Bureau on the left (before the bridge), one of the Weekes's old family homes, now leased to Michelle's (expat) hair salon and The Green Flash Bar, with two North Americans in their twenties – Dan and Jan – with matching his and hers nose-studs, and Abdul Weekes's new-found mosque above. An empty plot of land, Vicki's house, a small deserted concrete office and Chef's car park.

Tap – Tap. I enter my landlady's house. Polished floors, antler coat-racks, French prints, Sally struggling to lift herself from a wooden bench by the yard window.

"What you make me move for? Why you knock and get me up each time?" She curses me.

"Oops, sorry Sally, I'm just used to knocking."

"I see ... said the blind man."

Sally resettles herself in the gloom and wafts away mosquitoes, real and imaginary.

"Pippa's upstairs, sleeping probably. Would you just look at that kitchen. I try my best but I can't follow after her with my hip the way it is."

"I think I'll just leave her then. Is she okay now after I forgot to put Beau back on the chain?" I hadn't forgotten. "Pee-Pee" Beau, Pippa's black stray dog, "a thoroughbred Montserratian dog", needs at least an hour a day off his metre long chain, if only to wash his semi-circle of territory.

"It's a state in the kitchen and you can smell him on the chain outside. Put him in the garage at night and he makes a mess outside my window, leave the garage empty and The Green Flash people make a mess in the gutter and leave their filth everywhere. I don't know."

Last night must have been annoying for the two of them. Pippa sleeps during the day to make up for the noise during the night. Sally maintains the hours she kept as a seamstress – early to bed, working by 6 a.m., resting for breakfast and lunch and mid-afternoon and working into the evening. Now into her late eighties, Sally no longer has any clients or apprentices to sew for.

Pippa must have heard me with Sally. She opens her shutters and calls down to me as I leave, giving me five minutes to change and to meet her for one of her periodic spins in the car.

Ant, Vicki and Lou-Ann, John and Chef Tony, all talking around Doc's porch, watch me return to my apartment.

I wave to Lou-Ann who doesn't always recognise me. She pokes her tongue out at me and twists her body from side to side.

"A'right, Jonathan," calls Vicki.

Ant, faces me and salutes me with a tumbler full of rum and coke.

"Jonathan, whiteman, times is trouble see, look at dis empty place. When you going to buy it from me?" calls Tony.

"Chef, me got nut'ing, nut one damn t'ing ya hear." And I disappear behind my door faster than Lou-Ann can check the road and come across to play.

Ten minutes later I reappear, but this time I am only subjected to inquisitive stares. The gates are open to let the burgundy banger go. I guide Pippa in her exit onto the one-way lane, facing the entrance of The Green Flash. We motor down to the junction, cut across some earthy no-man's land, bang the exhaust and pull over so that Beau can catch up with us.

"Get off! Get back, I swear ... "Pee-Pee" Beau, me loves you but if you don't return to the house this instant me tan you' hide wid me boot, so help me I will." Pippa slips into dialect when provoked or when joking. She kicks the dust near the dog. Beau backs off, waving his tail at this attention he's getting. I hang the exhaust back onto its coat-hanger ledge under the tail of the car. We motor off, chased by an excited dog, watched by an inscrutable John.

Pippa hits the gas and we soon leave the dog behind us.

"Jonathan, check fu see dat dog out de way."

"He's standing in the middle of the road, panting an' watching us."

"Good. He'll not need to walk then!"

"Since when have you taken him for a walk?"

"Tchups! Watch you' rent boy, it doubles when it's overdue."

It's a shame I don't have it with me to throw down on the dashboard.

During all this, we pass familiar sites – the back of the prison, the jetty, War Memorial, Evergreen turning, Ram's huge supermarket, another Texaco, the place where buses start to drive to the north and the old Anglican church and beach cemetery on the road out of town; past school, the sports grounds, Shell station and industrial complex of Lover's Lane, the MNT Museum, onto the runway.

"So, where are we going then?" I ask, at a later stage in the proceedings than usual. But, as a friend, companion, gate-keeper, landlady and aunt, I've come to accept these things from Pippa, to expect and to let these things happen to me. I must be a much nicer person – for all this acceptance – than before.

"The Montserrat runway. You know why it's called that?"

I do: for the sake of an ethnographic answer, and for your sake, I could say I don't, but that would be untrue; Pippa could remember her telling me how the runway got its name when we were last on it; and it doesn't make the slightest bit of difference what I do or don't know when it comes to Pippa deciding to explain or show something to me.

"Something to do with Liat suddenly dropping out of the sky, running out of petrol during the ten minute flight from Antigua, or maybe something to do with a motorway development project assigned by the Foreign Office to make Montserrat like Guadeloupe," I reply cleverly.

Pippa snorts. We swerve. Our speed settles on a jerky 30 mph after the earlier burst.

Pippa wags a finger in the air: "You young t'ing, you t'ink you white people can come and tell us what we want. Us dat live here. On my Montserrat. Baah! Look, look, see dat junction we passed, up to the museum. There's been some nasty accidents there in my time."

Is this another of Pippa's *non-sequiturs* which I've now come to expect? Is she continuing her stream of opinion? Is this a veiled warning to me, to the expatriates? Is there going to be another St. Patrick's Day rebellion?

We both start laughing. Pippa tells me about some accidents she's been in, how her father always rode a horse around the cotton estates on the island, and that the car needs its exercise in fourth gear or else serious problems can develop.

"The only straight road on the island. You can let her rip. But why didn't Britain put in any pavements?"

"No idea," I shrug awkwardly in the car – but I'm happy with my interpretation of Pippa's accident descriptions.

"Anywhere else and it wouldn't have been allowed. Standards you see, standards. Britain would not build a road like this, especially if people need to walk along it to get to town. It would be illegal. So, Jonathan, why build it here?"

As white token – representative coloniser – I have no idea. I'm concentrating upon watching the one-legged man who rides his donkey along the road each day, and the field with grazing donkeys which distracted another villager who couldn't control his passions. These were the stories related to me by an expatriate couple who regularly wrote home to their children about life and retirement on Montserrat.

Long after the turning off to Foxes Bay, the road rises to the Cork Hill junction. I've only ever turned left here, to continue on the road to the north of the island. We do that and follow a winding descent into Belham Valley. There's a view of the centre of the island on the right, green hills all covered in thick vegetation of young trees (the old ones were thrown down in the last hurricane). There's a plantation house on the rise of a hill with a vista of the valley and the sea. The Hollanders' own Waterworks – one of the last of the plantation estates (2,000 acres) in the Caribbean to retain family control since colonisation of the island in the seventeenth century. It is said that the Hollanders own land from one side of the island to the other and that many of the expat houses are on leased land; Montserrat may be only just over seven by eleven miles, but there are over 100 miles of roads covering only some of the pear-shaped 120 miles of surface area. The Hollanders show tourists around their estate, explain the sugar process, serve lunch to the tourists and let them admire the views and location of Air Studios where the Rolling Stones, Sting, Stevie Wonder, Paul McCartney and others used to record their albums in splendid isolation, on an island where bodyguards become obsolete; where Midge Ure can visit a bar for a quiet drink with the regulars. Each Montserratian has their super-star story, most of them describing the casualness of relations which they detail to excitable foreign fans.

Above the golf course is the main congregation of expatriate villas and luxury condominiums with pools and verandas, American and Canadian flagpoles, and self-labelled houses: Crowe Hall, Dutcher Studio, ASDIP (A Splendid Day In Paradise), Stern Villa, and a few pseudo-Irish/West Indian names – Killarney, Finnegan's Wake (a writer's residence), Ras Retreat, Pippilo Condo. These last few names don't go down well with the Montserratians, many of whom have equally luxurious mansions though few are able to rival the Mars Bar family's summer retreat on the top of one of the hills.

"Jonathan, you na piss wid me? You wid me or you asleep?" I stop gazing around the island and turn and look at Pippa.

I think about cracking the joke from the television, "no, I'm with the Woolwich", but there are no Building Societies on Montserrat and there is no such commercial in the people's consciousness.

We turn left at Belham Valley Bridge where the island roads meet. The centre of the western side of Montserrat? The approach to the north? Salem City lies stretching out on the other side of the valley. It grows to incorporate the expat ghetto as well as local areas, Lower and Upper Frith's. The few areas which are mixed are when a wealthy Montserratian moves to the coastal villas built for expats and the AUC students rent cheap housing in the middle-income belt of houses.

We pass alongside the golf-course on the left and on the right I spy Mrs. Harris's home. Living under a white shadow, Mrs. Harris has a three-room prefabricated wooden shack planted down next to the golf-course, like an illegally parked trailer-home. She lost everything in the last hurricane.

"Look up dere Jonathan, dis is where an expat sold his house so he didn't have to live next to a black family," Pippa tells me indignantly. An unlikely interpretation of events, but rumours are born this way and are carried through the long grass like the dengue.

At the top of the hill, we pass lots of land barely developed, standing vacant next to villas which have been occupied for years. Here lives the Police Commissioner sent by the Foreign & Commonwealth Office, the other Technical Co-operation Officers (TCOs), and the seasonal "snowbirds" migrating from Canada to pass their winter. The former Governor's widow, and other past Administrators' descendants all maintain a residence on the island here; they are respected throughout the community and find it so difficult breaking away from such situations.

The luxurious villas suddenly change into prosperous residences and into then cheaper houses. We motor down through Salem conurbation, home to the Killer Bees female cricket champions, past Desert Storm – the roadside bar, and back down into Belham Valley, past Buffonge the dentist/Government Health worker's mansion next to the Hollander's secluded turning, past the up-market restaurant Ziggy's, and back up the hill to Cork Hill. Past Woodsville apartments – "condos with class", up past the churches – "think salvation", the "Keep Montserrat Clean" painting on the road-siding, the Rotary sign – "Don't Ask Why", and the Montserrat Water Authority billboards – "It is illegal to make unauthorised connections to water pipes", and – "It is illegal to fell trees within 30 m of a water source."

"Next time, Jonathan, when you more awake boy, me show you up Isles Bay, those houses are mmsstt," she smacks her lips and performs a slow U-turn across the track. "An' de drug barons. Expats doan like house bigger dan dey!"

Wapping is the same as when we left it, but each time I leave it mammoth changes in my experiences and knowledge of Montserrat occur. I want the neighbours to share this.

We reverse and turn at great speed into the garage.

The dog is back on the chain, but Sally has moved from the bench to the kitchen. She has done Pippa's washing up and is reheating a thick stew – a broth of boney goat meat, plantain and pumpkin. The sauces are delicious and it makes a change from tuna pasta or beef hoof or souse (pig's tail). Any thicker and it would almost pass for traditional goatwater.

I ask if there's to be a wedding for all this goatwater.

Sally chuckles and Pippa leaves for TV and solitaire upstairs. I daren't play a quick game of Scrabble with Sally without Pippa: Sally takes so long figuring out her moves that she forgets that it's her turn. Either that, or she can't read the letters and uses the wrong ones by mistake.

Pippa's started making a habit of eating upstairs at a later time so she doesn't miss the OJ trial updates, or the live Crossfire TV discussions from Washington on Montserrat Cable. She'll probably use her kitchen upstairs for the evening until she's forgotten that she forced Sally to do her washing up downstairs. Sally mentions all this to me whilst asking about what I saw and did with her younger sister. She's almost housebound except for some slow wandering up the middle of Wapping road with her walking frame and when Pippa feels like driving her about the island.

"I don't like it. I'm not hanging my washing out for everyone to hear if you know what I mean. This goes no further. But I'm not happy with this constant clearing up behind her. She can manage the stairs, so let her use her own kitchen. But don't come leave everyt'ing down here."

"I know, I'll get the plates. Here, let me help."

Sally continues admonishing Pippa and after a few sentences I'm not sure if she's mistaking me for her dear sister. "I don't know. I'm still new to the place. Pippa moved me upstairs to have my floor varnished. She never moved me back. I had to creep me t'ings down, bit by bit."

"Oh dear."

"I never grew up here. One night when I was a young girl I visited my grandparents up in Dagenham. It was separate from

Plymouth then. I fell asleep and spent the night there. I stayed
and they looked after me and brought me up ever since. So I've
always been a visitor here, you see."

"How many were there in the family at that time?"

"Well, there were nine of us in all. I had five brothers. You
know Red from Trinidad ..."

"Oh yes, the one that visited and fought the Germans."

"That's right. And there's Sidney up the hill. You know him."

"He's got the dogs? Drives real slowly."

"Yes siree. We were a big family with our parents, the Estates
to manage and the maids looking after us. There was always
somebody cooking and somebody washing for the family. There
simply had to be. Everyone was out working and in those days
it wasn't like now. None of that's left anymore. In those days
people weren't scruffy. You couldn't be. Red dressed for work in
a suit, starched collar, ties, waistcoat, a proper jacket and hat.
Everyone tipped their hats in those days. If school kids didn't
they'd get respect beaten into them. None of this cheek nowadays.
No sir. Ssttsstt. Look at that Lou-Ann girl: brought up backwards
like her. Can't speak nor eat. No manners. Damn cheek. Do you
want some more?"

"Mmmm. That was lovely. But really, no more. Maybe later?
Thanks though." I decline another helping.

"Humpf. Damn neaga food dis – aiou, the black man's palate!
Heard you next door last night. The noise was so bad I went to
the bedroom upstairs and came down at three. They'd quietened
down then but one awful smell of drink on the road. Saw your
light on earlier when I couldn't sleep."

"Sally. I was not at The Flash last night and you didn't hear
me. I was over at Doc's, that was why it was so late."

I try my best to dissociate myself from an aspect of Wapping
life which plagues the Irish household. I find myself observed
at all times; put into groups; interpreted by people; deliberately
cross-examined and riled to have my reactions weighed and tested.
Diplomatic truth is the only way forward. People know other people
all too well, despite miscommunications. Kindly picking me up
at the airport on the other side of the island when I first arrived,
Pippa went on to pick me apart on the drive to Plymouth: she
bargained with me over rent; she refixed prices and tested my
determination before accepting my genuine interests, my

anthropological and literary studies, my sympathies and concerns with local people. And then Pippa held dinner parties to introduce me to her friends, oriented me around the streets of Plymouth, filled me in on the unofficial histories of the island, the gossip, the cuisine, the class–race–colour divisions; and she refused to be interviewed but insisted on telling me her stories. Every day I heard more and more about her youth, the coming of the white residents, the end of the cotton days, the labour unions, adult suffrage – the horrific tail-end of slavery – her work for the West Indian Commission, the racism she experienced during her visits to Canada and Great Britain (*"when it was great"*), her love of royalty and British administration (*"when it was administration"*), the all-night picnics on the beach, and all her rosy-coloured memories of an island-life coming to an end.

I became her irksome son, her secret confidant, her brother in the extended family, her companion, her lodging guest, her very own *savant*. I brought her all the gossip from the streets; the expat intrigues, *faux pas* and stupidities which were only guessed at by Montserratians, guessing through a veil drawn between public interactions and private personas. And I grew to love her, a mentor through Montserrat, an impossible subject, a mother, a sister, a critic and a special friend who let me be all my relations with her and gave me others besides.

Sally is full of reminiscences tonight, so I do the dishes and spare ten minutes for some dominoes before the Maroon at half-seven.

Sally continues to talk through me. Swatting at mosquitoes, she continues, "if I had only been brought up here, then I wouldn't feel such a stranger." She finishes by smoothing her skirt and examining her domino pieces.

"Why don't you just tell her, speak to her about her mess you keep having to clear up?" I ask, indignant on her behalf.

"I know. I know. But the Bible says that you should do all that you can to keep the peace in the house."

"Are you at peace?"

"Ttcchhaa!"

"Well then. Not doing anything doesn't give the house peace. You live here too." These are old discussions so I feel free to give advice. "How long have you been here then?"

Sally sighs. "I don't know. Forty years I suppose."

Sally shrugs and sits in her wrinkles of skin. Concentrating on the game, she misses my recoil. Forty years she's lived here. I wasn't expecting such an answer. Four years. Six years at most. But forty! I can't comprehend that length of time. She's lived in Wapping almost twice the number of years that I've lived my life, and she still feels that she doesn't belong. If she's a visitor, then where does this put me, or Dan and Jan above The Flash? Jan refers to herself as a Montserratian because she was born here, but she's transitory – from Canada. Do you have to lead all your life almost exclusively in one place to be at home? Montserratians move around the island, but they retain family areas: Ant moved back to Tuitt's where he grew up; back to where his cousins and brothers and sisters and girlfriends and children all live. His girlfriend and children live with his brother and brother's girlfriend and brother's children. That's belonging. Me, I must be just an inquisitive interloper.

All this races through my head from a chance discussion and complaint about the dishes. I beat Sally at dominoes.

"Lucky neaga-man," mutters Sally.

Feeling flattered by a back-handed compliment, I excuse myself, pass a deserted Cafe and porch, return to the apartment, pick up some poetry I've just come across and a poem I've written myself. I leave Wapping for the Library again, leaving Mersal to open The Flash and to set the music rolling for her expatriate managers.

From what I remember, the Maroon itself, that night, went on for a few hours. It finished with one of Dr Fergus's poems. Afterwards, Josh – who works in airport customs almost alongside Doc – criticised me in public for not interviewing him as a performance poet. I mentioned that last week had been busy for me, what with all the steel pan bands and cultural events going on around the island.

Josh made the most of this: "Jonathan, you'd be at the War Memorial if there was a pan beating there."

Josh raised some smiles from his audience and his target: "A sardine pan!"

We depart in laughter, Josh bent low, his body shaking and his throat cackling at me.

The rest of the evening in Wapping was busy and noisy: that night, Victoria beat Micky around the head with her saucepan;

Vicki watched taxis dropping the AUC students off outside The Green Flash, and kept an eye on her Lou-Ann and Chef's Natalie until the restaurant closed at twelve-thirty in the morning. I was kept awake by the students chanting "Bye, Bye, Miss American Pie" and "He is a penis, he is a horse's penis, he – is – a – hor-se's – penis" in-between refrains from Grease, Queen's Greatest Hits and a mix of Asian-American rave: all favourite imported CDs the students bring down from their dormitory rooms.

The local Montserratians stood at the doorway, watching, looking in on the Americans. On Friday nights the back of The Flash is turned into a joint for barbecue and reggae, limbo and wining, drinking and flirting. There, tourists, locals, Americans and Rastas can all rub, wine, grind and jam for as long as they like. For those tired of the alien music and dance, the American tracks play at the same volume in the front bar, a doorway away. If there aren't enough students to keep their music running, they congregate in the street to drink outside Sally's bedroom window.

Twenty dined at Tony's till eleven o'clock. By midnight the students, and drunk tourists, dominated The Flash: thirty dancing, drinking and playing dice with some expat residents; forty outside, north of the Bar, facing twenty Montserratians sitting and standing, spectating and encouraging inter-ethnic brawling between Asian-Italian-Jewish Americans. After an exam, the entire AUC cohort stays down on the street till 3 a.m. when Pippa finally persuades the police to turn the music down, or the groups split between the Yacht club and The Green Flash. If there is no exam, the students are gone by half-twelve and the locals take over. That's what happened last night until The Flash closed at two in the morning and individuals dispersed by about three.

A typical Tuesday for Wapping, Pippa, an anthropologist, the Maroons creative writing group, Vicki, the students, Ant and John.

CaribTalk
The on-line beach bar

2nd Edition July 22nd, 1995
2nd Revision July 28th

Montserrat

Subject: "Volcano Update for 7/26/95"
From: John C.V. Ferguson

This update is current up to 7/26/95 and is based on newswire reports from Reuters on 7/25 and the Associated Press on 7/26.

The full reports can be read on the clarinet newsgroup:
news:clari.world.americas.caribbean

Reuters reported Tuesday that Governor Frank Savage made a radio address urging residents to remain on alert. Seismologists reported "four small earthquakes and three small eruptions Monday night" in the Soufriere Hills where 3000-foot Chances Peak is located.

AP reported that local banks ran out of U.S. dollars and the passport office ran out of passports Wednesday. Montserrat Aviation Services manager Sarah Silcott said LIAT ran eight chartered flights Tuesday and Wednesday in addition to four daily flights to Antigua. Montserrat Airways said it is booked up for the next two weeks. Several businesses were closed Wednesday in Plymouth, the capital.

Scientists, seismologists, volcanologists, and geologists from the UWI in Trinidad, the U.S. Geological Survey, France and other countries, are responding to a call by local officials to come to the Caribbean island to monitor the situation and advise accordingly.

It was also reported today that "in view of scientific reports evacuation of the population at risk is being considered."

The Caribbean Disaster Emergency Response Agency (CDERA) was reportedly co-ordinating with regional security system for mass transportation of civilians and with international donor agencies, if needed.

Neighbouring governments in Antigua & Barbuda and St. Kitts & Nevis were contacted and identified as possible hosts for potential evacuees.

The situation in Montserrat is indeed tense.

John

"Barbarian" Montserrat:
Expressive poetry from Howard Fergus and
his Maroons

Montserrat is a small island, so small that social relations are
dense and communication often has to be guarded, muted and
indirect (Skinner 2001, 2002). Poetry is one strategic means of
indirect communication (see below). Calypso is another (see
Chapter 4). Whether poets or calypsonians, these artistic social
commentators can often be critical without being criticised, express
themselves without being socially compromised, and even influence
society with impunity. In this chapter I make an examination of
Howard Fergus's literary expressions and role as a "barbarian"
writer on Montserrat. First, however, let me zoom in, expand and
comment upon the Maroons meeting referred to at the end of
the last chapter to give you a more detailed impression of "the
event".

A token Maroon

*The library tables have been pushed together. Sir Fergus sits com-
fortably at their head in an open African top. You know, the ones
without collars, buttons only down to the chest. His top and his sandals
are a sight which contrasts with his usual suit and tie he wears at
his University of the West Indies (UWI) Adult Education Centre where
he teaches history and represents the University and the arts on the
island. At other times, as Speaker for the House of Parliament and
as Deputy Governor when the British Governor is off-island, Sir Fergus
is dressed much more formally. Sir Fergus is with his long-standing
literary friend and editor, Amy.*

"Haahaarr! Jonathan. You early mon." Amy greets me.

Sir Fergus turns to see who enters the library, sees it's me, nods and turns back to Amy.

"Well I believe he don it mon. Easy. Why 'e run down de motorway den, eh Sir Fergus?" *Amy continues her conversation with Sir Fergus.*

"Well, everyone I hear this story from, they all say that it's a conspiracy. First Michael, then Tyson and now OJ."

"Right. Soon dere no black stars 't-all."

I pick up that this must be the OJ case in Los Angeles again, avidly watched on Montserrat, debated, picked apart, advertised on T-shirts, polarising black/white communities.

Devilishly, "What about you Jonathan, as our token spokesperson, what do you think?" *Sir Fergus asks me.*

"Me? I don't know this person. Never heard of him. Is he important? I mean, it's just one case."

"Hhmm." *Sir Fergus gives nothing away.*

"Black but comely", *is how Sir Fergus describes himself in one of his poems. Others have described him as having a velvety skin, Nubian black, close-cropped hair, a strong chin, handsome and smooth. I'm in the middle of a series of interviews with him during which he reads his poems and talks me through them. We've known each other for a while but each time we meet the ice needs to be reheated before he opens up to me, speaks freely and reveals his poetic loves.*

Maurice wanders in. We greet him and he mumbles, "Irie", *shyly at the concentration of attention.*

Maurice sits at the opposite end of the table, well away from us, muttering and mumbling unintelligibly to himself. He brings out one of his many notebooks he's always filling with Rasta verse. Lean, as most Rastas are, in a tracksuit, a bandanna curled around his neck and another with the stars and stripes around his forehead to keep his dreads out de way. Maurice is a constant smoker with a toothless grin; a drinking Rasta who often just stands in the corner of The Flash waiting patiently.

"A'right daddy," *I get from him.*

"How's things?" *I follow up.*

Nervous again: "Oh, you know, t'ings is not too bad you know. Saw you in town, Skinner. Wa me wan fu say ... power in de place ... America is de land fu dis you know."

He's lost our attention so Sir Fergus continues his open conversation with Amy: "So I'll miss the next developments whilst I'm away."

Amy marks down the dates that there will be no Writers' Maroon because Sir Fergus will be off-island.

Josh enters: a lively customs inspector at the airport in his twenties, a performing poet and costume designer for clothing and festivals.

"Good evening."

We all greet him. Although dark outside, it is only now that he takes off his shades.

"Thought you were going to ring me," *he complains in my direction.*

I give him no reply bar an eyebrow flash which is returned.

Sir Fergus convenes the meeting and asks Maurice if he has anything to share with us. We all know that he writes poetry throughout the day so he gets coerced into a reading and stumbles over his lines: "Dis one is 'Care', 'No Care'."

Amy recognises the poem because she keeps his filled notebooks for him. She interrupts, "Aahh. Dis one's 'No Care'. Okay Maurice."

"Let's hear it then," *requests Sir Fergus firmly.*

'No Care'

Man dem a run
   dem a run
man dem a run
   dem a run
soldier a come
     dem a come

Maurice stops to look around.

"Come on then. Is there more?" *Sir Fergus asks curtly.*

ono a stan before dem
now dey reach
before de feast
no mercy
   no mercy
mankind ina fear
cause dem a rip and tear
dem have no care
cause security no sincere
no recovery
   no mercy
     no mercy

Maurice finishes his reading. We're not sure of all the words. Josh is smiling. Amy is encouraging him. Expat Barbara arrives quietly and sits down. Sir Fergus lays his hands on the table before him and asks for an explanation. Maurice shrugs and looks down at his bum-

bag around his waist. Sir Fergus is annoyed that Maurice is so unforthcoming.

Amy lightens the situation: "Dere was dis rhythm to de firs' stanza – dem a run, dem a run. Boy, dat really come through man." She adjusts her head-tie and sits back.

"But he can't explain any of it," says Sir Fergus. "Maurice, it needs some more reworking on it. Right." Maurice's piece is dismissed. "Josh?"

A broad smile, "Sorry I'm late, I'm on the last flight shift at the airport. I came as soon as I could. I didn't have time to bring anything. I've only got these squiggles." He holds up a notebook open to a page of female figures draped in evening-wear designs.

"Barbara?"

"I've only just come tonight, we're planning our trip through Asia. We leave in a few days."

Josh and Amy exchange "how lucky" glances.

"Jonathan?"

"Well, I've got two things."

"Good. Let's hear them then."

"I came across 'The Star-Apple Kingdom' *by Derek Walcott. Um, there's a line here that's really caught my attention and reminds me of what we were talking about last time. It goes like this: 'I had no nation but the imagination'. It's from a long poem that's, well, all about a West Indian sailing between the islands, kind 'a like a modern Odyssey."*

"Yes, that's what 'Omeros' is about. Go on."

"Well, he brings up many issues in a clever way and sets you thinking about them. This line really sums up what we were saying about what poetry is, you know, when you mentioned how creative it is, expression, looking at things in an intriguing way, sort of ..."

I'm a student back in a tutorial. I have everybody's attention so I continue. I long ago gave up the distant observer role-play: say something and the conversation would go in that direction; if I said nothing then the conversation was finished. It is almost religious: give, and you will receive; take, and your grabs will be at straw men. You cannot attend and hold back in a small group and expect acceptance and co-operation. You would get suspicion and mistrust instead. People know these things, and they don't mind if I open up to them. We exchange and connect, argue, and disagree; but if they feel a distance, a dis-respect, an arrogant reticence, then the shutters are wound down and our selves become identity's hurricane shelters.

I get caught up in myself and introduce the poem I read: "There's this wonderful bit about the revolutions around the islands, the importance of history ... "

. *"Oh wow, let me see that! I love the power of the machine gun gutturals." a-dZiko had slipped into a seat without my noticing her.*

"Just wait till you get to her caesarean 'stitched by the teeth of the machine guns'!" I reply, giving her my photocopy of the poem.

Whilst a-dZiko sits chewing over the images, Sir Fergus distributes copies of one of his poems which came out of his "in progress" file.

"As you know, I like to get up at 4 a.m. to start my writing for the day," Sir Fergus informs us. "Well, we've got the new national song and we're changing the name of the airport to W.H. Bramble in honour of our first Chief Minister, that great man. Now, all this will take place on National Achievers Day which will no longer be called August Monday: you will all – except Jonathan who is new to us – know the significance of the Emancipation commemoration throughout the Caribbean. We will all be marking this, our present Chief Minister has decreed, in a number and variety of ways. One of them, The Montserrat Reporter *mentioned, will be by marking his State grave with the island's official emblem. Now, with a day of local celebrations, ceremony and Montserratian awards, everyone singing our new National Anthem, I find it particularly ironic that the headstone will have the symbols of an Irish harp and a mermaid engraved upon it ..."*

"Does that mean we won't sing 'God Save Their Queen' no more?" asks Josh in mock confusion.

"Quite. It depends upon the sense of occasion. You know that I don't like publishing in the paper – they always make mistakes and never send back the proofs – well, this time the poetry disease overran my body ..."

Josh chuckles and looks for support at the long-standing joke about the poet's affliction.

"... and I penned this piece. Could you tell me what you think of it? You all know the headline from The Reporter, *even Jonathan.*

'A Question of Emblems'

"The Lady and the Harp for Bramble"
The Reporter said
an old custom heroes having

Sparkling maidens as their medals,
resurrected for the dead
But why a white ghost weeded green
for Bramble scourge of the Great House
who broke slave middens down?
Planters black and white
made a better choice in a broad field
day or night black things were nice
has their uses slaking thirst

So a local bird for Bramble
mango bosom heliconia lips or oriole
the companion of our hero
must be unrepentantly creole.

There. ..."

MY TOKEN TUESDAY – AN ACADEMIC COMMENTARY

Social anthropology is not, and should not aim to be,
a "science" in the natural science sense.
If anything it is a form of art.

– Edmund Leach

In this interlude I shall make some comments about how I cope
with the indeterminate nature of writing and reading the previous
chapter. Here, I explain why my introduction attends to my literate
impressions of Montserrat rather than an historical, political,
comparative or economic review of the island. I consider, further,
the writing of Montserrat when I continued this chapter with an
introduction to Howard Fergus and his work and world. My
intention is to build Montserrat from a diversity of impressions,
experience-near, "thick" accounts, reflective and humanistic. All
of these impressions of Montserrat are filtered through my own
approximations of Montserrat. Some chapters in this book, however,
seek other people's approximations of Montserrat. The first chapter
– one Tuesday on Montserrat – is from my perspective: the partial
point of view, position, experience, reality of the anthropologist;
just one such example of a version of reality which I have lived
by. It is written as my introduction to Montserrat the place –
Montserrat the island, and to the people of Montserrat, locally
known as "Mons'rat neaga" and sometimes known by tourists and
travel writers as "the Black Irish of Montserrat", an exotic tag and
epithet which has had dramatic implications in its use (see Chapter

6). I have tried to bring the immediacy of the fieldwork experience to the reader of this text, yet at the same time I hope that my impressions of Montserrat, and the way that I present other people's impressions in this book, are read with authority but not authoritativeness. Anthropology is an uncertain and uncomfortable discipline after all, and so the anthropologist's ethnography should be "emergent and intermediary" (Fernandez 1983: 325): it should therefore retain some of the ethnographer's diffidence and confusion in the field.

The reading of this book is of equal importance to its writing: it should be evocative and constructive, and engage with the narrator in order to construct in the reader's mind portraits of Montserrat, Wapping, an anthropologist and a landlady. These portraits will be individual to the reader who is forced to flesh out the sketches visible on this textual canvas. The result is a partial glimpse of a day of fieldwork by an anthropologist collecting and connecting and writing up diverse realities. According to Strathern (1991), my connections are only "Partial Connections"; according to Rapport (1993: 191), they are multiple and multifarious as each individual muddles through their social life. In the end, the text, then, is but a small part of an illusionary journey "through various 'positions' that have recently marked changing anthropological approaches to writing and representation in ethnography" (Strathern 1991: xiii).

If these social connections are only fleeting and partial, and social life is in a constant muddle, then the mode of investigation and presentation here has to cater for all too human characters, inconstant individuals with fickle personalities and inconsistent practices. For me, isolating, capturing and delimiting their identity is like cupping a soap bubble between two hands – it is the wrong approach to adopt when scrutinising and observing an Arielesque subject which reverberates about the island. Respecting this in the sculpting of the text, we get impressions which are created and fashioned, not carved and stamped. Why? Because people defy the scientific and the rational. People are unreasoning and unreasonable; people are religious and superstitious; people's lives are a muddling-through; people's actions are a muddle of inarticulate habit and convention; people's minds are distinctly non-rational. This "*non*-rational", Richard Shweder (1984: 28, author's emphasis) characterises as a central tenet of anthropology's romantic rebellion. Clifford Geertz, David Schneider, James Fernandez and Sir Edmund Leach are (and were) just a few of the practitioners.

Unbounded individuals, open communities, interpretative-processual cultures – these are the constituents represented by Shweder's romantic anthropology and my impressionistic anthropology. My impressionistic anthropology is also characterised by an absence of knowledge-bytes in the text. This is not done to complicate the presentation of experience, it is done in recognition of the rise of the story and the fall of the fact in anthro-biography – Fernandez's (1986: xv) "an-trope-ology", Geertz's (1995: 98, 166–168) "indisciplined discipline", my postmodern stage with blurred boundaries and backdrops. Both Geertz and Fernandez impress us with their rich imagery: culture as spider webs of significance, humans as spiders suspended in the webs, the world interned upon the back of an elephant – in turn resting upon the backs of numberless turtles, for Geertz (1993[a]: 5, 7, 24, 20, 17, 10, 27–28, 5); "culture" as inchoate – "the dark at the bottom of the stairs", for Fernandez (1986: 214–238, 17). Theirs is symbolic anthropology *sans* structuralist strategy. With Fernandez, however, anthropology re-turns full circle: culture theory revolves around problems of meaning, yes, but we must also note the inchoate-ness of meanings guessed and interpreted – interpretations grasped or forever unfathomed. Adding sophistication to Geertz, we have returned to sensitive interpretations resting upon the backs of numerous interpretations; each, Strathern (1991: 8) reminds us, to be examined and compared "for their resonances and effects ... for their aesthetic impact". This is all in keeping with Leach's (1986: 52) art–social anthropology, with its objective, "to gain insight into other people's behaviour", often gained by use of the artistic technique of making the strange familiar and the familiar strange; see, for example, the literature of Tolstoy (the world narrated through a dog's eyes), the poetic art of the Russian Formalists (Shklovsky 1988), or, closer to my Scottish home, the "Marsian poetry" of the Scottish poet Edwin Morgan (1985). The danger which comes from examining Difference, Exoticism and the Other is in their accidental inversion as lectures become side-shows of native rituals, and the insensitive writing and reading of ethnography leans towards objectification and alienation rather than subjectification and connection (Miner's [1956] example of the backwards "American" turned into the "Nacirema" tribe is now the classic example).

What I have done in the previous chapter is present an introduction to a place with some of the people passing through; a sampler of scenes, a variety of events of interaction from life's insouciant *je ne sais quoi*, ethnographic impressions which retain the vignettes, emotions, relationships and memories which are often academically edited out. We thus have a muddling-through Montserrat, a narrative slice and cross-section made from a composite of days, both synchronic and diachronic in time, processual. This introductory personal narrative of experience is preceded by a lengthy Academic Preface (pre-text) without mention of Montserrat, a table of contents, and a brief report extracted from the Internet. Likewise, this chapter is also preceded by a volcano update received on the CaribTalk Newsgroup of the World-Wide Web which I subscribe to through this computer. The table of contents and the Academic Preface prepare the reader for the ensuing text, but the two chapter prefaces do not. They are not reading or writing junctures but reading and writing dissonant spots akin to my references to the computer I'm writing this text upon. These moments of discord jar with the immediacy of the text, confusing the reader's reading reality. Each chapter is preceded by such a rupture. They are reports taken from the period of writing this text, reminding the reader that this is a retrospective text; that it is being written from the safety of the university home and that it is only by literary artifice that we continue to dialogue and connect with my experiences of Montserrat (see also Dwyer 1982: 263, 265). These chapter prefaces also rationalise my departure and evacuation from the island. They form a narrative within a narrative: they are a post-fieldwork narrative within a text which constructs and analyses "the field" location.

Chapter 2, this chapter, also begins with the anthropologist's tail-end impressions related from the token Tuesday; here, an expansion upon the Maroons' meeting which Fergus uses for inspiration and as a workshop for his poetry. This written reality finishes off the day and links the two chapters. Neat? "A bit too neat," as the anthropologist and textual analyst's voice of Vincent Crapanzano (on Geertz, for example, 1992: 60–69) would "immediately" tell you. And what about the rest of the text you have just read and paused over? In sympathy with Roland Barthes (1988[a]: 171), this text so far "is made of multiple writings, drawn from many cultures and entering mutual relations of dialogue, parody, contestation". It is not by mistake that the text in the first chapter is the reader's first acquaintance with Montserrat (the place), Mons'rat neaga (the people), and myself (the anthropologist) – not the Academic Preface. It jumps right into a day from the anthropologist's perspective, with the anthropologist in the thick of social and colonial relations.

The limitations of the text, in its evocation of daily affairs, are ironically apparent in a form of loss: the loss of rhythm in the American students' songs is a small loss. But the tone of all conversations are lost and can only be grasped at by the anthropologist with his partial understandings and limited recall: the loss of Maurice's Rasta accent spoils his rendition of "No Care"; the uncaught winks and twitches and non-verbal communications from long-standing relations between the writers at the Maroon cannot all be mentioned; the force of the quips shot back and forth along Wapping lose their timeliness. These losses, however, is not necessarily a problem for the imaginative reader. For the reader, there is no strict accuracy in the descriptions of people and places. There is an indeterminate space between the reader's and the writer's realities which can be encouraged by the writer – I, the author with my authorial eye, creator of text and Montserrat, both commander of – and commanded by – the nature of this writing–reading enterprise.

I, the native writer, can only ask for the reader to read imaginatively and to tolerate the different dialect spellings, the confusions, the unknown and unexplained – the indeterminate in the text: from untranslated dialect to my adoption of the loosely defined term "neaga". These examples contrast with the explanation of what *roti* is and the mental rationalisations behind the naming of the "Montserrat Runway", explained for your sake in my acknowledgement of the reader in the text. So too, the reader should approach the text like a novel, allowing the subtle time and narration shifts from the immediacy of an eyewitness account on the streets of Wapping to the contracted and expanded memory of a Montserrat Writers' Maroon. These shifts and ruptures in the textual fabric of time and space can be handled by the reader whose response to a text is highly creative and flexible. Similarly, there are moments in the text where dialect creeps from the speech of my friends to my own introduction of Montserrat (take for example my untranslated, almost parable-like, use of Montserratian dialect to comment upon the taximen: *"Dey say 'Mons'rat taximen so fas', dey make money 'fore dey learn fu sign for um'"*). If the anthropologist is lost and confused whilst muddling through the field then so too the reader should sometimes be lost and confused. Acceptance of all these writing and reading observations bring to social anthropology a fresh wind to stale reeds, reads and readers.

In my attempt at ethnographic realism, local words lie read but undefined, they are treated as comprehensible, just as the anthropologist – Strathern's (1991: 1) "fieldworker, writer and author" – finds them. Some are treated *au naturel* as I burst upon them in my postmodern, un-*rouge*-d – untranslated – unanalysed text; a creole narrative where the context of use gives the word its meaning and builds comprehension: the anthropologist picks out the sense of words, translates them, tries out expressions and familiarises himself with etiquette and the situations for using dialect until the cultural mantle, a Montserratian scaffold, becomes a (second) coat of skin. Eventually, the anthropologist becomes a racial zebra, Edward Bruner's (1993: 7) "Arab Jew" ethnographer, accepted by both blacks and whites, a token for both, the *"lucky neaga"* in a game of dominoes. It is the anthropologist – blurred and confused signifier/signified in the field – who alone, back home, sees the sense behind the dialect joke; the sacred significance of land features on Montserrat; and the importance of the small "g" in "Great Britain" and the reclaiming of the "k" in "Afrikan" – foolish, incomprehensible and deliberate typographical errors which are laughed at as the errors of the colon:ised.

In a traditionally constructed ethnography, Chapter 1 would have begun with a description of the island – Montserrat: 39 square miles in the Eastern Caribbean where 10,000 people live on a pear-shaped, tear-shaped island. Instead, in this ethnography, we have the impressionistic gaze of the narrator evoking a living there, a working text based upon his cognised impressions of Montserrat. In a traditional ethnography, a map of the pear-shaped island is expected, with crosses marking the airport, Plymouth town and the anthropologist's Wapping. But visualising this,

presenting an image rather than evoking an image, is to constrain
the freedom of the text, dominating, framing and forever freezing
the island's outline as a part of the reader's reality (Iser 1988:
219). The lack of images, the flexibility in the writing of dialect,
the raw and unexplained ethnography, all are in accordance with
my impressions of Montserrat. They are what I found during my
work and life there, where there was no uniformity in writing dialect,
where expressions common to some were unheard of by others,
where even the name of the island was political and subject to
change – variously, named "Alliouagana" by extinct Amerindians,
named "Santa Maria de Montserrate" by Christopher Columbus,
named "Montserrat" by British settlers, named "Colony of
Montserrat" by estate agents, "Emerald Isle" by travel-writers, "Black
Ireland" by some East Coast American tourists, "British Dependent
Territory" (BDT) by Margaret Thatcher, "British Overseas Territory"
(BOT) by Robin Cook.

My strategy of indeterminacy is necessary because, to
paraphrase Barthes (1988[b]: 173), "the text is open to infinity",
there are multiple readings, meanings and interpretations possible:
this "plurality of the text", this "opening of its "significance", means
that all the reader can do is locate some of the ethereal "avenues
of meaning". Whether reading for character, reading for location,
reading for escapism, reading for theory ... Chapter 1 – indeed
all the chapters – have been created with such beliefs in mind;
reading, writing and ethnography, all are subject to Barthes's
(1988[b]: 173) pronouncement that "no reader, no subject, no
science can arrest the text". Thus, all we can do when reading
and writing is to look to "the forms and codes according to which
meanings are possible" (Barthes 1988[b]: 173). For me, once these
forms and codes are learned in a rudimentary fashion, they become
personal, experiential and subjective. They share reader response
correspondences just like the constellations of impressions which
I consider in the next chapter; diverse "interpretative impressions",
to rework Stanley Fish's (1988: 327) notion of an "interpretative
community" whereby the interpretation of a text lies with the
individual or group deploying similar or different understandings
underlying their reading and writing. I have therefore constructed
Chapter 1 so that it is full of immediate impressions and vignettes,
encouraging a sensitive type of reading. The chapter can be read
as a story with characters drawn, outlined and left to be fleshed

out by the reader. The chapter might be read as an anthropologist's impressionistic experiences. Unfortunately, the chapter could also be read and mined for concrete pointers, demography, geography, history, pre-volcano social structure. If I did succumb to write that the population of Montserrat is 10,000, then the reader would be tempted into treating this information as a factual statistic, a faceless byte of information, a synchronic snapshot of an island from a reified text. For me, this would be an ill-fated consequence of a particular reading of the chapter, one which fails to appreciate the fluidity of knowledge and the possible application of postmodern theory – and Deleuze's pronouncements – to indigenous Afrikan or indigenous European Montserrat. Knowledge depends upon context and position: the population of Montserrat, for an illustration, depends upon the timing of the population count as well as the politics of inclusion and exclusion of categories such as inhabitants, visitors, tourists, migrants and "snowbirds". The Government popularises the 1990 census of 10,000 BDT citizens. Pippa's Montserrat, however, contains, at a guess, 7,000–8,000 residents and a society population (those she knows) of 3,000–4,000. Tony and Doc, no doubt, know fewer people, but different people; and the anthropologist knows only several hundred people on the island.

So, the claiming, ordering, "factoring", event-making, tailoring of processes; the analysing, figuring and re-figuring, claiming and colonising of experiences and interactions are all problems associated with reading, writing and representing. We constitute – and thereby colonise – by event and fact. Resisting this activity, the rest of this chapter takes a poetic turn with an examination of "barbarian" poets and their barbed poetry, paying particular attention to Howard Fergus, Maroon poet leader. Fergus's impressions of Montserrat, like my own and those in subsequent chapters, are arbitrary in the sense that they may just as well have been impressions gleaned ethnographically from the politicians, economists, farmers and unmarried mothers on Montserrat. I picked upon Fergus's Montserrat because it is a well-documented literary Montserrat, one easily privileged and also very well known about the island. The style is literary criticism.

"BARBARIAN" FEATURES

> *I am trying to fit in*
> *When you see me icy grin.*
>
> — *Benjamin Zephaniah*

Through my written impressions of Montserrat, we have already heard some of Fergus's poetry and the social and colonial context of its creation. This is how Fergus comfortably expresses himself. Poetry is his passionate outlet. It is through poetry that his voice is heard. At this point in this chapter, I would like to suggest that Fergus's poetry belongs to a genre of "barbarian" poetry, and that Montserratian Maroon cries of freedom can be heard alongside Scottish literary cries for devolution and independence, and Nigerian chants for mental decolonisation. Once I have identified "barbarian" poetic features, I shall then spend the remainder of this chapter situating Howard Fergus in such barbarian company. The "barbarian" term possibly comes from the title of a volume of poetry published in 1979 by the Scottish poet Douglas Dunn in 1979. In *Verse*, a poetry journal, Dunn defined his use of the word, referring to "barbarians" as "people who contest the Establishment and the degeneration of the State" (Smith 1992: 85). Images of Empire and the colonial condition abound in Dunn's *Barbarians*: there are references to the now "dead imperia"; "drowned Britannias" which harnessed the Scot to the aggrandising Imperial enterprise; and now the Scots are thrown aside and left as *teuchters*, England's colony in the north, just as Montserrat, Gibraltar and the Falklands are "England's" colonies in the south:

> They ruined us. They conquered continents.
> We filled their uniforms. We cruised the seas.
> We worked their mines and made their histories.
> *You work, we rule*, they said. We worked; they ruled.[1]

Robert Crawford (1992: 281) notes that this "barbarian literary attack" against the men at the centre of English cultural power is "one which appropriates the weapons of the dominant culture". To continue with Dunn, it is an attack aimed at subverting "[a] culture of connivance".[2]

The prosaic attack by the provincial, foreign – alien and alienated – tribes of barbarians, brings together the poets and critics and provincial spokes-people from the margins of Great Britain: Yorkshire exile by dialect, Tony Harrison, author of "Them

& [Uz]" and "The Rhubarbians";[3] Oxford educated "black" West Indian and "potential Afro-Saxon", Edward Brathwaite (1970: 37); "Irish" poet and Nobel laureate (1995) from Northern Ireland, Seamus Heaney; and "Black British" Rasta poet, Benjamin Zephaniah, author of "Us & Dem".[4] Dunn's "barbarian" term may be extended to include not just poets resident in the British Isles, but also those of the Commonwealth, as well as writers such as Kenyan writer Ngúgí wa Thiong'o (1993: 438) and Nigerian writer Chinua Achebe (1993: 429) – the former resentful of the English language imposed upon his native Gikuyu, the latter celebratory of the creativity and freedom available in bi-lingualism (Skinner 1994: 74). To this list of "barbarians" we can also include East Indian "exiles" in Britain, David Dabydeen and V.S. Naipaul amongst others. In sum, we might note that, more generally, the term "barbarian" can be applied to any agitator marginalised from the metropole whether colonial metropole, political metropole or cultural metropole.

To give some examples, British-born poet Zephaniah feels as much out of place in his British environment as "a red hot Eskimo", "[a] city dwelling peasant", "a African".[5] The poet and writer Fred D'Aguiar, who was also born in Britain but was then brought up in Guyana, considers home "always elsewhere".[6] D'Aguiar tries to feel at home in Britain, but feels that he is not being made to feel at home in Britain such as when arriving at Heathrow airport:

> my passport photo's too open-faced
> haircut wrong (an afro) for the decade;
> the stamp, British Citizen not bold enough
> for my liking and too much for theirs.[7]

D'Aguiar now oscillates between work and life in America and Britain. He has become a barbarian commuter, following examples set by West Indian island-boy Derek Walcott (St. Lucia and Boston), northern-lad Tony Harrison (Nigeria and Florida), and Ulsterman Seamus Heaney (Professor of Poetry at Oxford and Harvard). These international pariahs have learned to profit from their margins and outraged sense of exile, becoming an "establishment of the unestablished" with positions at key universities in the world; Dunn is now Professor of English at St Andrews, and Zephaniah was recently shortlisted for the position of Professor of Poetry at Oxford. These barbarian poets have, in fact, joined the ranks of the elite exiles led by notable literary critics such as Gayatri

Spivak (Andrew Mellon Professor of English at Pittsburgh), Homi
Bhabha (Chester D. Tripp Professor in the Humanities at Chicago)
and Edward Said (Old Dominion Foundation Professor in the
Humanities at Columbia).

The barbarian poets and writers can be identified for their
marginal and often colonial or neo-colonial obsessions; their
concern with the use of dialect rather than standard language;
and their literary resistance to the dominance of the metropole:
in effect, theirs is "the Empire writes back" genre (Ashcroft &
Griffiths & Tiffin 1989), one of play and parody, a celebration
of creolisation and hybridity from *Barbarians* to "Rhubarbians"
– "Them & [Uz]" to "Us & Dem". All these barbarian writers and
poets from the Caribbean womb, the African birth-mother and
the European dominatrix are barbarian by birth, breeding or both,
and *Decolonising the Mind* (Thiong'o 1991) is their intent, especially
so for Thiong'o who refuses to continue writing for his English-
speaking international audience in the language of neo-colonialism.
These writers are "barbarians" according to Dunn's definition and
my extension of the term, and the rest of this chapter will go
on to show just how Howard Fergus and his work fits into this
expressive and evocative category.

CALIBAN'S COLONY – HOWARD FERGUS'S "BARBARIAN" WRITINGS ON MONTSERRAT

> *Take it easy, stranger man*
> *In your imperious drive*
> *To build an ivory wall*
> *In my black sand*
>
> – *Howard Fergus*

Barbarian poets have a variety of writing strategies to choose
from. Applying Michel Pêcheux's (1982: 156–157, 159, 215) theory
of discourse to their work, we see that they can resist the dominant
"colonial" discourse emanating from the metropole by either opting
to turn their backs and do something different (dis-identifying),
or by turning back the offending discourse (counter-identifying).
It is difficult to give examples of dis-identification, perhaps
Thiong'o's refusal to continue to write in the English language
can be counted as one. Walcott's (1990) epic Nobel prize-winning
verse "Omeros", a version of Homer's travels set amongst the

Caribbean islands, is perhaps an example of counter-identification. Other examples of counter-identification include Caribbean and Latin American reworkings of Shakespeare's (1984) *The Tempest* such as José Rodó's allegoric *Ariel* which brings about the dénouement of Caliban (Brotherston 1967; see also Retamar 1989; Mannoni 1990; Bloch 1990; Fanon 1991; Bhabha 1991), or Fidel Castro's speeches which cite the demise of Prospero at the hands of his emancipated servants, and the above quotation from one of Fergus's poems which articulates a threatened black Caliban forced to threaten ivory expats.

Dunn's barbarian response to the Oxbridge literary metropole is to use his native cunning and connivance:

Drink ale if you must still,
But learn to tell one good wine from another –
Our honesty is cunning. [...]
Carry your learning as does the mimic his face.[8]

These savant skills of concealment and patience, Naipaul's (1969) mimicry and Bhabha's (1994: 93–101) "sly civility" occur in contradictory colonial situations such as that found on Montserrat. The smallness of these "island universes" (Dolman 1985: 41) forces an ambiguous relationship between the colonised and the coloniser who is simultaneously father and oppressor, figure of authority and target of resistance. The key question Henry Louis Gates (1991: 470) raises, then, is whether or not the former colonies can ever achieve the economic, psychological, and cultural independence of the post-colonial? One answer to this question lies with an ethnographically tried-and-tested – rather than literary critical/ cultural studies (see Miller 1994: 1) – examination of a Montserratian "native" point of view of Montserratians, one of which is articulated and expressed in the poetry and writings of Howard Fergus, professional poet, literary historian and commentating campaigner.

FERGUS, THE PROFESSIONAL POET

Montserrat is Howard Fergus's home and literary resource. Montserrat's principal historian and poet, Sir Fergus is also Senior Lecturer – indeed, sole lecturer – in the University of the West Indies at Montserrat's Adult Education Centre. In 1995, Dr. Fergus, formally known as The Honourable Dr. Howard Fergus, OBE, BA, MEd, PhD, was made a Commander of the Order of the British

Empire (CBE) in the New Year's Honours List by Her Majesty Queen Elizabeth II for serving as Speaker in the Legislative Council for 20 years and as Acting Governor for 19 years. In 2001 this title was upgraded to Knight Commander and Dr. Fergus became Sir Fergus, the first knighted Montserratian. As an island official – Speaker of Montserrat's Legislative Council, Sir Fergus maintains a strict impartiality towards local political concerns; his is the neutral voice presiding over Government debates. In addition, as the appointed Acting Governor of Montserrat when the British Governor is technically off-island, Sir Fergus moves from his academic office in the UWI Adult Education Centre to take over the diplomatic office at Government House – the Governor's official residence with an Administrative wing staffed by Montserratian and Foreign & Commonwealth aides. There, he changes position from critical academic – or neutral Government Speaker – to Queen's representative in the colonies, a position which he uses to the advantage of local Montserratian British Dependent Territory Citizens (BDTCs).[9] On top of all this, several evenings a week Sir Fergus serves as a Pentecostal Church Elder.

As I mentioned earlier, only very early in the morning does Sir Fergus find time to write his poetry. And on Tuesday evenings, particularly during the winter season, Sir Fergus calls his Writers' Maroon where he can test his verse. This term, "Maroon", is historically understood throughout the Caribbean to refer to a runaway slave, someone who actively fought against slavery (Mullin 1992: 44). On Montserrat, however, a maroon is a local affair at which a person – such as a future tenant seeking help in the construction of their house – will seek labour from friends and neighbours, repaying them by way of food, drink and goat-water (Fergus 1992: 57). It is a social event similar to that which the anthropologist Donald Donham (1981) found amongst the Malle of Ethiopia. This value-laden but ambiguous title for the creative writing group is known and shared by all on Montserrat and reflects the social engagement of the work of the poets and writers, previously known as the Alliouagana Commune – referring to the Amerindian name for the island and to a solidarity of purpose. That purpose, Fergus admits, is to achieve sovereign status, self-determination and social development on Montserrat, to break the debilitating psychology of dependence bred by a life-time of political, social and economic colonialism. For many

Montserratians, economic independence is a pre-condition for political independence; not for Fergus who believes in the creativity of the human spirit and political independence before economic independence. First, Fergus wants Associate Statehood, then full local control. The cultural activities held at the University Centre encourage local artists and scholars to share insights and to promote learning around the island. These activities are the social and cultural means towards political ends.[10]

Only now, whilst approaching retirement, has Sir Fergus broken into the Caribbean poetry anthologies (Burnett 1986: 276–277) and the Caribbean Examinations Council syllabuses (McWatt & Simmons-McDonald 1994: 103). In total, he has published at least seven volumes of his own poetry (Fergus 1976; 1978[a]; 1980; 1987; 1993[a]; 1995[a]; 1998[a]). He has edited several volumes containing poetry written by himself and other Maroons (Fergus 1984; Fergus & Markham 1989; Fergus 1990; Fergus & Rowden 1990; Fergus 1998[b]), nearly all of them published through his Extra-Mural Department at the Adult Education Centre (Fergus's PhD is in Education from the University of the West Indies). Clearly, Sir Fergus holds a key poetic position on Montserrat: his prolific publishing profile – recycling his poems in the newspapers into collections and then into single volumes – is a practice which over the last twenty years has resulted in a distinctive island record on a par with his collection of historical pamphlets and books (1975; 1978[b]; 1983; 1992; 1985; 1994; 1996), and radio programmes such as "Tours Through Montserrat's History".

Fergus utilises the strengths of poetic expression and his own early memories to represent a history that is both literal and literary. Below is an example of one such elegiac portrait:

> Ripe men call him "Bruk-Up"
> Cause his walk was like the canter
> Of a lame and skittish horse
> But young ones loved to watch
> The rhythm of his body
> Moving like a concertina[11]

Along with the other members of the Maroon who are writing poetry, Fergus writes about life, people, personal experiences, memories and situated observations. Bruk-Up is a Montserratian figure whom Fergus captures and keeps alive, nurturing and teasing out his impressionistic life-thread. I would argue that it is possible to read these miniature profiles to build an humanistic and anthropological understanding of the island and islanders. Indeed, because Fergus and the other writers on the island have continued to write through, and about, the end of the cotton industry; the struggle for adult suffrage in the 1940s and early 1950s; the struggles for independence; and the devastation of recent natural disasters (hurricane and volcano [Fergus 1989; Fergus & Markham 1989; Fergus 1990; Fergus 1995[a]]), their poetry has become a colourful history of Montserrat in itself.

Fergus's poetry, amongst others, is more than just an "event poetry", a chronicle of events in verse, for in it we have references to islander feelings and sentiments. Fergus articulates himself through his poetry. "Footprints" is one such poem, one which can be read as an excursion into the world of Fergus's Montserrat in the late 1970s, an era of troubled allegiances and causes with political and cultural colonialism running alongside social, cultural and racial resistance:

> Planted in these Montserrat sands
> Are footprints many nations beat
> My blood burns but I know not where
> To plant my schizophrenic feet.[12]

Fergus's identity and allegiances, like those of many on the island, are torn and troubled in the Caribbean maelstrom of British colonialism and history, African ancestry, Amerindian mythology and North American sphere of influence. But he does not shy away from the problem of identification. He faces it on his own terms, in keeping with his "British" education: though dealt mental blows by "Teachers yoked / in whitewashed collars / choking minds of ebony",[13] Fergus endures his education so that – like Caliban who once faced Prospero with the words, "You taught me language; and my profit on 't / Is, I know how to curse" (Shakespeare 1984: 39, Act II, Scene I, l.365–366) – he might later use it to set himself and his fellows free.

Fergus admits to his hijacked, barbarian mind – one which accepts the Queen's Honours, but when in London declines to attend the ceremonies; one which teaches West Indian and Montserratian history to foster national identity, but sprinkles the lessons with Latin phrases from when he both learned and taught Latin on the island; one which enjoys to dance to local tunes but also one which hums along to English nursery rhymes. Fergus can do little but live his part as a colonised barbarian:

Shod in Shakespeare's socks [...]
a cultured curio of the tribe[14]

Fergus reacts to his colonial personal history not by agitating on the streets but by expressing himself and Montserrat's colonial condition through his poetry. Poetry is Fergus's modern-day maroon means to change Montserrat's possible colonial future. This is a successful technique on a small island, living in a muted society where you repeatedly interact with the same people year after year and so have to guard your words carefully. Though some Montserratians are suspicious of their man of letters, Fergus's writings have brought him respect and symbolic capital. With muted means, he skilfully maintains his variety of positions, offices and uniforms. Whilst Cheddy – with his *Pan-Afrikan Liberator*, an unmediated outlet – has been known to make enemies by confronting rivals on the streets and readers in their homes, Sir Fergus's diplomacy and recourse to the media have at least established and maintained his reputation. Foresighted rather than forthright, Sir Fergus has influenced many and, in so doing, he has alienated few. Should Montserrat achieve independence, Sir Fergus has the potential to become the governor-general of the island, leaving his literary campaign to history.

FERGUS, THE LITERARY HISTORIAN

Without a doubt, Fergus's maroon poetry is barbarian poetry, but some of it is also a literary history on a par with his histories of Montserrat. Some of his poems are chronicles, his recording and shaping of the island's social history and the historical memory on Montserrat – conspicuous literary commemorations. In March 1995, for example, the High Court was opened for its new legal year with a church service. For the first time, in full court regalia, Justice Neville Smith, court officials and advocates marched from the Court House to an Anglican Church, all escorted by a Royal Montserrat Police Force guard of honour. After prayers and blessings, the administrators of justice were escorted back to court where legal proceedings began.[15]

The following week, Howard Fergus published a poem in the newspapers, "When Justice Came To Church", poetically prying

into the affair, punning with legal terms, probing at the religious
and secular tension on Montserrat:

> Justice went to church on Monday
> in rank order on me Lord's day [...]
> The message from the cloth was pre-
> meditated but no crime. The law
> was put on trial for mugging
> mercy, no bail for the innocent [...]
> they settle out of court with heaven[16]

Fergus goes on to conclude the poem on a reflexive note, showing
us that he is fully aware of his ambiguous position on the island
as poet, academic observer and commentator, but also dignitary,
distinguished guest and participant:

> I hope his Lordship does not indict me
> for contempt. I will plead innocence
> and retain a Queen's big wig to cite
> poetic licence, licence to indite[17]

Other social, political or even religious occasions are often marked
with a poem; "Easter" is another example which was published
during Easter 1995 on the front cover of *The Montserrat News*.[18]
In addition to these "historical poems" which appear as regularly
as though Fergus were a court poet, or as though Fergus's most
candid voic : can only be channelled through the medium of poetry,
there are his prose historical accounts of Montserrat to consider.

"Dr. Fergus" – as he is still generally referred to on the island
– became Resident Tutor at the Montserrat University Centre,
moving from his position with the government as Chief Education
Officer. He took over from his colleague, and friend, George Irish
in 1973. Whereas Irish (1985; 1990; 1991; 1993) had promoted
social, cultural and national awareness through drama, journalism
and the labour unions, Fergus concentrates upon (his) writing
– his-story. Following on from Irish's (1972: 14) *Alliouagana Voices*,
a work which publicises the rediscovery of the Amerindian name
for Montserrat, Sir Fergus (1975) began publishing histories of
Montserrat with his History of *Alliouagana: A Short History of
Montserrat*. This account opens with an historical poem –
"'Dedication' for Heroes of St. Patrick's Day (1768)" – to the
"martyrs" of a failed slave insurrection which was due to take
place whilst the Irish planters on the island celebrated St. Patrick's
Day, an event which Fergus wanted to mark with a national
commemoration (see Chapter 6):

To heroes
Who conspired to squeeze
The juice that sate
Thy fatsome enemy
You were betrayed by brothers black
But you escaped
Your slavery.[19]

The historical account which follows the poetic opening begins with Columbus naming the island after Santa Maria de Monserrate, a monastery near Barcelona, and goes on to give a brief overview of the island's history from its colonisation by Protestant settlers and Irish Catholic refugees fleeing Oliver Cromwell in the seventeenth century, right up to its status as "The Anglo-Irish Colony" (Fergus 1975: 3, 7) in the 1970s. The pamphlet documents the rise and fall of the sugar and tobacco industry, and its replacement in the nineteenth century by the production of lime juice and cotton. By the twentieth century, both industries were in decline. According to the history in the pamphlet, they collapsed after the Second World War, mainly due to the actions of the newly formed Montserrat Trades and Labour Union (1946), a successful social protest movement which led to universal adult suffrage on the island in 1951, and Montserratian William Bramble's election to the Legislative Council, previously a monopoly of plantation owners. Fergus concludes the political and historical pamphlet with the poem "Epilogue" which contrasts with the formal and traditional opening "Dedication" with its use of "dialect as malt" as Crawford (1993) would say, with its use of rich Montserratian expressions and images, and Rastafarian references to Jerusalem, Babylon and social upheaval:

Cut down cow-itch, nettle and 'cassia tree
Spray modern massa mangy sheep
Kill pink ball worm
Mek new Jerusabylon
De First, third, world.[20]

Besides this history of Montserrat, and several other historical/biographical pamphlets about the island and her population, some of which I shall refer to in the next section, Fergus has two more recent publications which are international in scope and in press. For the Macmillan Press, Fergus (1992: 14) wrote a brief guidebook for tourists to the island in 1983, describing the place as where

"Afro-Irish combines [...] with a 'New World' interpretation", taking issue with the social anthropologist John Messenger who has argued that there is a significant legacy of "Irish retentions" on the island such as a Black Irish ethnicity and "linguistic patterns, systems of values, codes of etiquette, musical styles, smuggling and an Irish recipe for stew". Of more significance is Fergus's (1994) *Montserrat – History of a Caribbean Colony*, an extension of his tourist publication with Macmillan, his historical pamphlets and radio broadcasts. This scholarly book spans the entire history of Montserrat: from Alliouagana Amerindian settlement to British slave colony; the years of Irish and African emancipation; the twentieth century struggles for trade unions, universal adult suffrage and education for all; and the hurricane and volcano natural disasters which have plagued Montserrat at the end of the twentieth century and the start of the twenty-first. Given Fergus's barbarian bent, attention is also paid to the independence issue, some constitutional changes imposed upon Montserrat by Britain in 1989, recent natural disasters and their socio-political consequences, and to the role that culture and the arts have to play in developing Montserrat's cultural and national identity. A review of this book by Chedmond Browne in his *Pan-Afrikan Liberator* quotes many sections in pursuit of Fergus's "independent-Montserrat" platform. Fergus has unearthed the tormented legacy of slavery and colonialism so that it may be confronted and finally laid to rest. This is because, in Browne's words, "[w]e will not begin to make a sensible approach to solving our current problems if we have no foundation knowledge of their causes".[21]

FERGUS, THE COMMENTATING CAMPAIGNER

Though cautious and diplomatic in person, a great deal of both Fergus's prose is full of topical social commentary and strong recommendations for political change. Fergus's (1978[b], see inside cover) Macmillan history of Montserrat is built upon his earlier political treatises such as *Montserrat: The LAST ENGLISH COLONY? Prospects for Independence – Two Essays on Montserrat* (1978) which is dedicated "[t]o the Montserratian proletariat" and demands independence for Montserrat by first elaborating upon the investigations of the United Nations Colonialism Committee and the United Nations Decolonisation Mission (committees which assess colonies to see if their mother country is encouraging or enabling them to gain their independence). The pamphlet is also part hagiography as it goes on to celebrate the achievements of William H. Bramble, who – via the Montserrat Trades and Labour Union – led Montserrat for eighteen years (1952–1970) and became the first Chief Minister in 1961. Fergus (1978[b]: 5) is critical, however, of Bramble's rejection of an offer to move towards independence with associated statehood for the island in 1967 on the grounds that "the English budgetary dole [... was] indispensable to his island's economic survival". This argument is still supported in many sectors of Montserratian society – part attributed to psychological self-criticism and part to a lack of confidence. According to Fergus (1978[b]: 7):

> [s]ome leading members of the business community make capital out of the colonial status. They highlight it as a guarantee of a stable socio-political climate in order to encourage business. The implication here is that a government which derives its authority from Westminster is superior and more acceptable than black indigenous rule. This is another version of the self-distrust and dependency syndrome which is endemic to the colonial condition.

There is thus a political tension on the island ranging between the extremes of dependency and decolonisation or, more personally, between the British appointed Administrator (now referred to as "His Excellency The Governor") and the locally elected Chief Minister. In this tense tropical climate, Fergus (1983) developed his initial devotional study of his mentor, Willy Bramble, with another history of the man, *WILLIAM HENRY BRAMBLE: HIS LIFE AND TIMES*. In this account, Fergus (1983: 4, author's emphasis) called for a new postcolonial pride in the nation and the celebration of "indigenous" as opposed to colonial figures:

> Caribbean children of Bramble's day and after, sang the glories of Hawkins, Rodney, Nelson, and Napoleon. With the advent of the statehood era in the 1960s, Caribbean man has attempted to identify national heroes as part of his search for meaningful independence. This is reflected *inter alia* in the renaming of airports after local figures and the building of heroes' parks and monuments. Montserrat's airport still carries the name of a colonial British Governor, Sir Kenneth Blackburne, but then, Montserrat is still a British colony. It has not, however, escaped the new national pride which is surging through the Caribbean. Its outstanding figures must therefore be researched and studied. This essay is a contribution to that research. It is ultimately a part of the process of moulding the Montserrat national *persona*.

Approximately ten years later, whilst I was on Montserrat, it appeared that Fergus's calls for an assertion of national identity had at last been heard: since 1985, St. Patrick's Day had become an established national holiday; in June 1995 the winner of the national song competition was announced – Denzil Edgecombe's "*Montserrat – My Country*"[22] and not Fergus's "*Motherland*" – which was "expected to replace the British National Anthem at appropriate occasions and events";[23] and in August 1995, the Blackburne airport was to be renamed after Bramble after a campaign lasting more than 10 years. All that was left was for Fergus (1985: 64; see also 1994: 266) to continue to campaign for Bramble to be celebrated on the Caribbean-wide 1st August Emancipation Day, a day which Fergus wanted to turn into Montserrat Heroes Day. It is no wonder, then, that when Fergus heard that the government were going to mark Bramble's grave with the island's official emblem – the Irish Lady Erin and her Harp – he responded by first writing an article against these colonial emblems on the gravestone,[24] and then following up his prose campaigning with poetry by publishing in the following week "A Question of Emblems" in a rival paper.[25]

Just as Fergus is able to write his history of Montserrat, he is able to write the future of Montserrat, campaigning with prose and poetry, and often a combination of both. Clear illustrations of this are the poetic opening and closing of *History of Alliouagana* (1975), or his poetic Appendix in the Bramble pamphlet, "A Song for Willie Bramble" (18 verses, 74 lines), a poem which argues for the immortalisation of Bramble in Montserrat's history, placing him alongside Nincom Riley, a literate slave who read the emancipation proclamation to his fellow bondsmen:

> Hurrah for learnéd Riley!
> He read our parchment liberty
> But lowly Willy Bramble toiled
> To wreck the yoke of slavery.
> No hurrahs for Willie B
> No pen and paper freedom traced
> He stripped the legal subterfuge
> From slavery's chameleon face.[26]

Elsewhere, Fergus is more controversial, such as in his poem dedicated to Caliban, "This Land is Mine", which I quoted at the start of this section on Fergus's barbarian writings (see also Fergus's [1994: 16] *History of Montserrat*). The poem was printed in the local *Montserrat Mirror* in 1976,[27] and caused a commotion amongst many expatriate non-belongers – those who "bang water" to Montserrat (a term which refers to those who are not born on Montserrat and have travelled across waters to gain "belonger" status on the island by marriage, settlement or social acceptance) – who continue to denounce him as a racist to this day.[28] This shows that his historical and poetic commentaries certainly do more than record the antagonisms of Montserrat society. They play their own part in the making of some antagonisms. Another poem which reveals Fergus's (1994: 217) literary manifesto, his stewardship of the Montserratian "journey from slavery to emancipation", constitutional and psychological independence, is "Ruler and Compass".[29] A powerfully anti-colonial poem, this is barbarian poetry baring its teeth, a mocking rhyme about imperialism, colonialism and an independence of thought:

[...] Britain rule the waves
and baa baa black sheep
have you any news
yes yes H.E. but no views[30]

Britain rules the high seas, but not the thought waves. Echoing the barbarian barbs of Dunn and Bhabha, sly civility strikes back at the "[c]ivilised servants" of Westminster with their "Oxford smile" as they "divide and rule / [...] with ruler and compasses only".[31] It ends, "[t]he points of the compass / are daggers at [the] brain".[32] And yet, in stating this, Fergus (1994: 266) is using poetry to demonstrate the thesis behind his prose histories, namely that "Montserrat can be colonial in constitution, if it thinks it has to be, without being crassly colonial in identity and mentality".

Finally, one of the most recent of Fergus's contemporary natural disaster anthologies records the ongoing slow eruption of Chances Peak which started in July 1995 – a publication which contributes to a growing disaster literature on the island (previous collections were published in response to Hurricane Hugo in 1989). In *Eruption – Ten Volcano Poems,* Sir Fergus (1995[a]) describes the scenes of evacuation in the north of the island, the waiting for the volcanic eruption, the work of the volcanologists, the fears and prayers for the future and, strangely, how repetitive and similar the situation is to other past calamities. As "[c]hoppers paddle / through our skies cutting through the Queen's / peace and tourist paradise",[33] and Montserratians evacuate to the north of the Belham

Valley safety line, Fergus belittles his Government and the Governor's invocation of colonial emergency powers during natural disasters:

> We have come by faith just beyond Belham river
> in obedience to God, Government
> and the Governor's emergency powers
> which do not govern earthquakes and volcanoes[34]

In this barbarian poetry, there are parallels with the Hurricane Hugo natural disaster in 1989 which also set back the independence movement and left the Governor ascendant whilst the elected Chief Minister of Montserrat was relegated to coping with the morale of the islanders (see also Fergus 1996; 1998). Certainly no one can govern the natural weathers which buffet the island, not even His Excellency Prospero, but, more positively, neither can hurricane nor volcano stop barbarian Caliban from writing and righting his Montserrat.

NOTES

1. "Empires" (Dunn 1986: 109, l.16, author's emphasis).
2. "The Come-on" (Dunn 1986: 99, l.26).
3. "Them & [uz]", "The Rhubarbarians" (Harrison 1984: 122–123, 113–114).
4. "Us & Dem" (Zephaniah 1992, 44–45).
5. "As a African" (Zephaniah 1992: 28, l.20, l.23, l.28).
6. "Home" (D'Aguiar 1993: 14, l.10).
7. "Home" (D'Aguiar 1993: 14, l.13–16).
8. "The Come-on" (Dunn 1986: 100, l.42–44, l.49).
9. Interview between Jonathan Skinner and Sir Howard Fergus, 4 July 1995.
10. Interview between Jonathan Skinner and Sir Howard Fergus, 4 July 1995.
11. "Bruk-up" (Fergus 1978[a]: 28, l.1–6).
12. "Footprints" (Fergus 1978[a]: 41, l.17–20).
13. "Blessed" (Fergus 1978[a]: 46, l.5–7).
14. "Blessed" (Fergus 1978[a]: 46, l.23, l.28).
15. Anon., *Montserrat Reporter*, 10 March 1995: 1.
16. "When Justice Came To Church" (Fergus, *Montserrat Reporter*, 17 March 1995: 8, l.1-2, l.9-12, l.16).
17. "When Justice Came To Church" (Fergus, *Montserrat Reporter*, 17 March 1995: 8, l.25–28).
18. "Easter" (Fergus, *Montserrat News*, 13 April 1995: 1).
19. "'Dedication' for Heroes of St. Patrick's Day (1768)" (Fergus 1975: 1, l.18–24).
20. "Epilogue" (Fergus 1975: 66, l.22-26).
21. Browne, *Pan-Afrikan Liberator* (October 1994: 8).
22. Edgecombe, *Montserrat Reporter*, 30 June 1995: 1.
23. Fergus, *Montserrat Reporter*, 30 June 1995: 1.
24. Fergus, *Montserrat Reporter*, 30 June 1995: 1.

25. "A Question of Emblems" (Fergus, *Montserrat News*, 7 July 1995: 13).
26. "A Song for Willie Bramble" (Fergus 1983: 51, l.28-39).
27. "This Land Is Mine" (Fergus, *Montserrat Mirror*, 2 July 1976: 4).
28. Interview of Dr. Fergus by Jonathan Skinner, 4 May 1995.
29. "Ruler and Compass" (Fergus 1989: 17–18).
30. "Ruler and Compass" (Fergus 1989: 17, l.24–27).
31. "Ruler and Compass" (Fergus 1989: 18, l.32, l.35, l.45–49).
32. "Ruler and Compass" (Fergus 1989: 18, l.50–51)
33. "Volcano Watch" (Fergus 1995[a]: 11, l.63–65).
34. "Volcano Watch" (Fergus 1995[a]: 9, l.11–14).

Volcano Island Call

A DUNDEE couple living on a Caribbean island hit by fears of an impending volcanic eruption have managed to contact their daughter in Aberdeen to tell her they are safe and well.

Terry and Iris McLeod have lived on Montserrat, where Terry is employed in the Overseas Development Administration, for a year and a half.

Over the last few days they have transformed their home in the north of the Montserrat into a temporary refugee camp and feeding and watering station to help hundreds of people fleeing the Chances Peak volcano, which experts fear may be about to erupt.

The mountain, whose last major eruption was over 100 years ago, has been spewing dust and debris for about a month, forcing many of the island's 11,000 inhabitants to seek sanctuary in the north.

The McLeod's daughter Kirstin, Kirkton Road, was understandably concerned until her parents telephoned on Thursday night to reassure her.

"Mum and Dad say they've turned their house into a refugee camp," said Kirstin yesterday. "The situation doesn't seem to be too bad at the moment, although Dad said that in the main town of Plymouth the ash was so bad you could hardly see six feet in front of you."

"They don't believe they are in any danger, and plan to stay on the island until the worst is over."

(Anon., *The Courier and Advertiser*, 26 August 1995: 13, no other references available.)

CONVERSING MONTSERRAT: TWO PLACE-SETTINGS

EVOKING TWO CONSTELLATIONS OF REALITIES ON

DEVELOPMENT AND DEPENDENCE

In this chapter I will demonstrate the inter-subjective possibilities of the postmodern impressionistic anthropological analysis which I briefly mentioned in the Academic Preface and Chapter 2. I do this by evoking two place-settings – two dinner parties at which the guests discuss their differing world-views on the development of Montserrat. I juxtapose two conversation-narratives from development workers at one dinner party, and from Montserratian British Dependent Territory Citizens at another, to show the diverse realities which people inhabit and the various Montserrats they evoke. Sometimes these worlds and Montserrats collide against each other and sometimes they overlap and merge together. These various conversations about Montserrat – dinner-party commentaries about Montserrat – are the focus of this chapter, the aim being to reveal two loose constellations, one orienting itself around the development workers on Montserrat, and the other orienting itself around the Montserratians themselves. Both constellations are a collection of personal realities: they are indeterminate Shwederian extensions of Stanley Fish's (1988: 325) "interpretative [reading] communities", and Nigel Rapport's (1993: 80) loops of thought – "world-views", diverse, multiple, and partial. My juxtaposition of these two conversations also affords me the opportunity to develop the anthropological argument that in order to enable effective development work it is important to be aware of indigenous world-views and indigenous responses to development, what the indigenous people consider requires development, and how the development work might best suit the needs of the indigenous. Thus, this chapter concludes that development work is intrinsically linked with the anthropological enterprise, an enterprise which seeks to uncover – in this case – both individual and group convergent and divergent realities.

Such personal and diverse – individual and group – realities are particularly identifiable on small islands where even the opposing "belonger" and "bang water" constellations mentioned in the last chapter are clearly visible. Small islands are enclosed microcosms of life where interactions are multiplied as the same faces are met throughout the working day and relaxing evening; where the clefts and divisions running through society polarise social relations between "networks" (Boissevain 1974: 24). Thus, it is in a village in the Yorkshire Dales, or on a small island in the Eastern Caribbean, that actions can be observed to have consequences which ripple through the community and, in this case, development projects can be observed to have wide-ranging consequences – reactions and responses to them which are often not predicted or considered; reactions and responses which also reveal the multiple realities on Montserrat.

Particularly critical of the merits of development work, Mark Hobart (1993: 1) writes:

> [g]ranted the vast sums invested in trying to find a solution to what is described as the problem of underdevelopment, by the criteria of the development planners matters should be getting better rather than worse. Instead it would seem that development projects often contribute to the deterioration.

This is Hobart's conclusion following an assessment of the impact of technological expertise used by development workers in underdeveloped countries, an assessment of how the global, "world-ordering" knowledge from the over-developed ignorantly rides rough-shod over the local context of development. His anthropological approach varies with Rapport's theorisations upon the cognitive world which we, as individuals, inhabit; world-views which are the results of interpreting behaviour, constructing meaning; world-views, perspectives and positions created, adopted, sometimes forced upon people and sometimes collectively shared. The strength of a particular world-view comes from its Weberian power to carry sway over other world-views or individual positions, the development worker's views as opposed to the indigenous, for instance (see Riches 1985: 84). For me, though, what Rapport refers to as diverse world-views – views of the world – I reify and multiply as multiple subjective realities discussed in the Academic Preface, anthropological impressions which can be gleaned from conversation.

Implicit in this chapter is the opinion that development and aid projects are complicated and complicating activities. Explicit in this chapter are the attitudes, perspectives and world-views of development workers towards their development projects, their Montserratian co-workers, and their view of Montserrat from their villas' balconies. Explicit also are some Montserratian responses and reactions to the development projects, the project workers themselves, and the Montserrat to which they belong. The purpose of these conversations which I have placed together is not to polarise or further any animosity between the communities, but to reveal the contrasting realities, to promote increased awareness and consideration of activities – their consequences and possible responses and, above all, to further evoke some impressions of Montserrat. In other words, I am following Bryon Good's (1994: 140) evocative and anthropological mission "to retell stories in a fashion that will provoke a meaningful experiential response and understanding in the reader". An introduction to the projects and communities on Montserrat is followed by the two conversation-narratives with development workers and Montserratians.

THE POLITICS OF DEVELOPMENT ON MONTSERRAT

Attracted to research on Montserrat – the Emerald Isle of the Eastern Caribbean; the-39-square-mile, pear-shaped British colony, marketed by the Montserrat Tourist Board (Montserrat Department of Tourism 1993: 1) as "The Way the Caribbean Used To Be" – the anthropologist soon found himself adopted by Montserratians as well as the working expatriate population of development workers. The indigenous population of Montserratians far exceed the several hundred North Americans and British who have retired to Montserrat or maintain holiday homes on the island. Some of these homes are let to the 30 to 40 development workers with their families, the "professional expatriates" as they like to call themselves. These workers are contracted by the Overseas Development Agency (ODA) to work for between one and four years on island development projects.

It is the British Foreign & Commonwealth Office which tends to British interests overseas, often under the name of the Overseas Development Administration (ODA) – a wing of the Foreign & Commonwealth Office which runs Britain's programme of aid to developing countries. Many ODA workers are Technical Co-operation Officers (TCOs). Employed and salaried by the ODA, the TCO works on loan to the overseas Government. With the co-operation of the Government of Montserrat and the ODA, many TCOs receive perks such as a luxurious house with pool, a car, generous wages above local rates, tax concessions, and free shipping and flights to and from the United Kingdom. On Montserrat the TCO grouping is the most affluent and influential grouping on the island, consisting of the British Governor of the island at the head, the British Police Commissioner as his second, followed by a rigid hierarchy of TCO positions who are all above the site overseers and foremen from the international construction companies.

Ever keen to join in, interact, and possibly glean some insight into social relations and development, the anthropologist welcomes evening social events where people relax, drop their guard and speak their mind. Around Christmas time and the New Year, the anthropologist made himself very busy and very available.

DEVELOPING MONTSERRAT THE ODA WAY

The anthropologist, in his twenties and from a Scottish university, is adopted as a surrogate son and a surrogate Scot by the McLeods. Terry McLeod is a skilled architect now reaching his mid-fifties, very lively and very Scottish; when Terry was laid off from Aberdeen Town Council, he pulled some old contacts in the Foreign & Commonwealth Office made when working in the Seychelles and Fiji some twenty years ago. Terry tendered and won a two-year contract as Government Architect of Development Projects on Montserrat. As a wealthy TCO on Montserrat, living and working with the full co-operation of the Government of Montserrat and the ODA, Terry decided to bring Iris, his wife and sometime primary school teacher, with him.

Before leaving, the McLeods attended a residential course at the International Conference Centre at Farnham in Surrey where they were given a grounding in the practicalities of living and working abroad: they were told how to deal with culture-shock, the indigenous population and their customs; the social structure of the island was explained to them; and they were given information about fellow British expatriates, the British Governor, the British Police Commissioner and other British TCOs.

Tony Slade – retired head of a Yorkshire police force, TCO Police Commissioner, number two to the TCO Governor – is holding a New Year's Party for the TCOs on the island at his mansion which he rents from Paul McCartney's sound recorder; a sound off-shore, tax-free investment. Although not invited, the anthropologist has been coerced into gate-crashing the occasion as a member of the McLeod's household.

A wine bottle breaks into pieces which are swept up and thrown onto the lawn.

Though his white face is familiar about town, here, the anthropologist needs introducing: this is because he lives amongst Montserratians, next to a landlady who is always complaining to the police about noise from a bar which the expatriates frequent.

"Tony, come and meet young Mr. Skinner; he's from St Andrews." Terry practises his golf swing which he's learning at the island's exclusive nine-hole course.

"That's good, glad to hear it." In the same breath Commissioner Slade turns back to Terry. "Heather and I put in a full round this morning. It's the only time for some peace. They've even taken to ringing me at home when I'm off duty. They don't bother with the police desk anymore! I'm going to have to make an announcement; this can't go on."

More guests enter the house, skirting the wine on the floor. "Listen," continues Commissioner Slade, "got to man the reception. Is that a kilt you've got on, or are you a transvestite! Talk to you later, Terry."

The dining room's spacious, with modern chairs set around the sides of the room. People have congregated into groups – TCOs and their wives; eminent tourists visiting the island from the US; retired expatriates – "snowbirds" – with a house in Canada and a house on the island to migrate to over the long winter; and last and lowest on the protocol list are the team of British foremen and their lively cosmopolitan girlfriends – professional expatriates, these men work for international building corporations such as Northwest Holt: each completed building marks the end of a contract and the start of a journey to another building-site around the world.

"Come on, Jonathan, let's leave Terry to his wee business meetings, eh?" and Iris leads the young anthropologist in the direction of the drinks. "This is just so ... so ... absolutely marvellous. How can you manage all this out here, Heather? Here's a bottle for the collection."

"Glad you could make it," Heather answers in a Yorkshire accent.

Iris continues: "That walk you've arranged with Tony for the snowbirds. What a lovely idea."

Heather preens herself; "Thank you Iris, and would you be willing to sit in for an hour or two at the Red Cross stall next week?"

"Of course, I'd be only too happy to help. There is the bridge class, so Tuesday's out, and I just lend a hand at the National Trust, Friday afternoons, you know, but any other time would be fine."

"Right then, Wednesday morning it is. Lovely." Heather pencils Iris into her little blue notebook and the anthropologist starts to slip away to join other conversations. He turns to an interesting crowd of old, red-faced men in Hawaiian shirts, red either from the sun or from their gin and tonics at sundown.

There's a tug on his arm; Iris: "Look over there, that's Lee Farquhar, university student like you. He's just 'come on island'; doesn't know anyone; go and say hello."

On the far side of the room, the anthropologist introduces himself, stumbling over unrehearsed words, unaccustomed to the rituals of networking.

The reply is in similar fashion: "Oh, right. Lee Farquhar, bio-medical engineer seconded from Luton University Health Centre. Pleased to meet you. I'm at the new hospital next to the old Glendon site."

"Er, sorry, just what is bio-engineering?"

"Oh, erm, bio-medical engineering, well, you know, like, I was into cancer research, giving them radiation doses ..."

"Chemotherapy?"

"Yeah, sort of. Doing well with some patients, but they closed the wards so I applied for this – setting up, training, installing, maintaining the new hospital equipment. Lots to do, eh."

The anthropologist starts to pick up. "So, how's it been going then?" he asks, filling a hand full of peanuts, expressing a body-language of interest.

"Nightmare, absolute nightmare mate." Lee runs his hand through his hair, self-conscious but glad for a sympathetic ear as the anthropologist shortly discovers: "I just get here, right; spend a month in the only decent hotel, looking for a place to stay. Well, the buggers, they downgrade me so I don't get a car or an office, just housing allowance and a converted broom cupboard in the basement of the hospital, pipes running everywhere, leaks like nobody's business."

"Sounds pretty rough, I live in a noisy part of Plymouth myself, no hot water and stuff ..."

"Yeah, well, get a load of this: I'm in charge of a million pounds worth of equipment in British Aid. It's going to the new hospital. I have to set it all up, get it running and do the same thing in Anguilla at the same time. My boss says to leave Anguilla for now, they're not co-operating. But they haven't a clue here. One million pounds of equipment; that's a third of that cost every year in maintenance. I'm only here 18 months and what's going to happen after, eh?"

"Dunno. Sounds pretty expensive for here."

"Right. And I've got to train two of the locals in everything. They came from the social security office and believe me, they don't know shit. Fucking waste if you ask me!" He bristles, draws closer, and starts to confide in the anthropologist. "Racism, that's what it is, can't win you know."

The anthropologist looks confused but is still listening to him.

Lee explains himself, "Cos I got downgraded, they know I'm not that important. Their salaries are paid by the hospital and I can't do anything to them. Slim and Highman, biggest couple of dodgers. Turn up sometime in the morning, go away for lunch and only Slim comes back, Highman's away driving his taxi. Can't do nothing about it, you know, if I do I become the white slave master ..."

"Alright Lee. Arr, you must be the anthropologist whatever Iris's raving on about." Shaking hands: "Scott; VSO; do the roads; pleased to meet you." Lee and the anthropologist are joined by Scott, a tanned man in his early thirties, just starting to go bald.

"What's that about your hymen eh? Lost IT – oops – I mean HIM, again!" Scott's speedy comments draw chuckles so they continue – "Fucking hell! We did the road signs today. Bastards want them painted just like they take the corners. Only problem – none of them know how to drive. We just sat around with the bosses arguing. It just can't be the same with the runway next week. It just can't."

Scott pauses for some nibbles and Lee changes tack. "Look over there. She's alright." He gazes at the only black at the party, a young woman with long relaxed hair in a tight mini-skirt, holding onto the arm of a white man in the contractors' huddle.

"Dionne. Married to Graham – doing the computers at GHQ; two kids; leaving in April," Scott informs us through a mouthful of sausage rolls.

The anthropologist chips in, "Where's he going in April?"

"Back to London."

Lee: "Anything going?"

"Naw. Rough. Left his business to come here; the building wasn't ready. They move the computers in after 14 months in one of those Portaloos; he sets up the network and has to leave before it's running."

"Rough."

"Yeah, probably sleeping at his mother's flat again." They all look suitably downcast for a moment. "Look, I spy food, come on."

Wandering over to a large central table of chickens, pizzas, rotis, salads and samozzas, the anthropologist leaves their company as they queue ahead of him and discuss the next cycling competition on St. Vincent.

"... I think I can get the half-price tickets again. Should be about thirty quid and Sonya's coming as soon as she's finished her exams ..."

With a full plate, the anthropologist sits down in another corner of the room, a room now full of about twenty couples and floating individuals. The Governor's in conversation with another career diplomat sent out to Montserrat by the Foreign & Commonwealth Office. He's expanding upon his ideas for the development of the island, though he only has one and a half year's left out of the three to four year stint per location. Then he's rotated to another Embassy – the shrinking bastions of the British Empire.

"... Tourism. That's the ticket these days. Now when I was in West Africa supervising the VSOs out there, tourism was doing wonders to the economy. Of course, that's not your main concern is it Euan? Now if I were Reuben I'd push along with the airport extension, turn the centre of Plymouth into a tourist development area with nice little boutiques, a few cafes, restaurants and fast foods – for the less discerning Americans off the cruise ships. Oh, and with that new prison up on Amersham Estate, that'll free up the old one. The Trust can have that so long as it's a public museum ..."

"That was a lovely opening ceremony you gave at the Trust offices."

"You think so?" The Governor's pleased with this compliment. "Bit of bother with my name on the plaque – the newspapers got hold of it, colonialism and all that. Well, I think that a museum of waxworks of all the pop stars who recorded here would do the trick. There's even the old gallows, we could just leave them standing. There'd be entrance fees of course. What would Treasury coffers make of that?"

The Governor signifies that he's finished his comments, for the moment, and the man from the Treasury opens up: "Anything would do, but for the long term we need to establish tax paying for everyone, not just the civil servants. Their 60% of the GNP is nothing compared with what those retailers, businessmen and taxi drivers should be paying; no one else quite meets the tax bracket."

"Stiff resistance I suppose. Entirely understandable of course. The trouble is that they've never had to pay anything in the past."

"So they send me out here."

"Good idea though – give the Montserratians the roads, airport, hospital, prison and Parliament. Make a fresh start after Hugo but force them to collect revenue for their upkeep. Still have to drop the civil service numbers. Can we hold off on the completion of the prison and GHQ till local Government's passed the cuts?"

"Ooh. That's going to be nasty. You could be talking about up to 10 percent of the population."

"Hmm. I'll get back to you on that. I'll sound that out through the usual channels."

The anthropologist turns his attention to the other side of his plate which he's been ignoring. A slick, well-groomed man with his wife in an evening gown are picking over a vegetarian mix of samozzas and salad.

The three of them talk about the evening so far and the time zones between Montserrat and Britain. Then they get round to introductions.

"I'm sorry, I don't believe we've met before. I'm Francis Mortimer, this is my wife Hazel."

"Pleased to meet you, I'm Jonathan, Jonathan Skinner." The anthropologist feels embarrassingly like he's out of a Bond movie. "I'm looking at the literature on the island and how it fits in with life on the island, sort of context."

"Hmm. We're trying to decide how they make the vegetable samozzas. Hazel wants to try them out on the children."

"Lucky them," replies the anthropologist. "Are they here for the vacation?" The anthropologist directs the question, with his eyes, to the attractive Hazel.

She's shy and giggly. "I teach them Spanish, French and Geography and we have a tutor for the Sciences."

Francis is more measured and precise with his words: "We couldn't bear to part with them for boarding school." There's a pause for observation of people and each other, and then Francis volunteers his profession. "I'm with the UNDP at the moment; a town planner by trade, I'm designing and implementing the building restrictions in Plymouth and around the island so that, for example, no new building in Plymouth can be more than four stories in height – that's the height of Cable & Wireless – nor can it detract from the overall aesthetics of the historical core."

"You enjoy it?"

"There's a lot of satisfaction involved with preservation work though I'm meeting with a lot of resistance from the locals whose extension plans I have to sometimes turn down."

"Can't win can you Francis dear," Hazel sympathises.

"And once the legislation's in place?"

"Who knows? Maybe they'll need some qualified professional with a detailed knowledge of the building legislation to deal with the enforcement of 'the Terry'!"

"I always tell Francis that he's writing his own job description," Hazel titters.

On the same theme Francis responds that that joke would be inappropriate in real life.

"Hardly. Well, at any rate, there's always some work to pick up, some agency with funding. That's why one needs to be a familiar face around the island and the region."

Clearly Francis and his wife are here out of duty to his job and necessity for his future activities. They do not fit in with the other guests, as though they lost tickets for their favourite opera, but were happy to settle for a popular music hall performance instead.

Terry and the Governor pass by to refill their whisky sodas.

"... understand ... hold. If they behave like that then we have to treat them like children. Free the trade through the port, break that Chedmond Browne and stop his stupid rag. The next ..."

Terry halts the Governor. "Jonathan. I see you've met Francis. Hello Hazel."

Francis returns, "Good evening Terry, how are you? Our 'Frank'ly Excellent Excellency, Frank Savage."

"Just Frank here, please Francis. No need for formalities. Hazel."

"Frank."

They continue on their way, and on the same side of the room Mrs. Slade begins to play old popular songs on the piano. She needs no music but a pair of bifocals to search the keyboard for notes. Commissioner Slade lumbers over to the piano, as though trying to reduce his great height so that he doesn't stand out above the gathering crowd of male impresarios. The singing soon gives way to Terry and Iris's Scottish country dancing (broken up by GHQ foreman Euan O'Leary's drunken wheeling); disco takes over after midnight and the loyal toast to the Queen.

At the end of the party, the McLeods and the O'Learys help the Slades to clean up. As far as the Slades are concerned, the anthropologist is still not a TCO, and is only barely welcome. But what of the O'Learys' status? Virginie, a Glaswegian secretary, a friendly, pragmatic blonde, aids Heather with the washing up; Terry and Tony rearrange the furniture; Euan and the anthropologist stand in a messy corner of the room carrying out token gestures associated with the cleaning process.

"So where'd you learn to dance all that fancy footwork?"

"At university, teaching foreign students, we always had a ceilidh for them at the end of the course. I thought you were from Glasgow?"

"Aye, I am, but we never had no ceilidh in the Gorbals."

"I thought all Scots knew the dances. And you've even got a kilt on!" The anthropologist teases and baits the Scot with a grin.

"I'm Scottish by birth, British by conquest, Irish by choice."

"You're more Irish than Scottish? Is that what you mean?"

"Sort of. I come from all over and shouldn't be anywhere, not even here," he replies curiously. "My grandmother left Ireland for New York. My mother migrated the other way and met my father in Glasgow, at the old yards. I've got all the passports by convenience, but as a Catholic I'm a firm Celtic fan."

"And here?"

"Shouldn't even be here. None of us should – those that work for the companies, those of us expats who aren't TCOs," Euan replies with his nose waving in the air, an unmistakable reference to arrogance and assumed class distinctions. "Virg' does her bit at the Red Cross, a TCO wives' club. This means that grateful people invite her and me to their parties out of gratitude, but they don't know I'm not a TCO until it's too late."

"Forget it. I'm not a TCO myself, felt a bit out of place too."

"This place's died early, most of the lads crashed here after drinking 'Round the World' at the Nest; you should have heard the Commissioner with his revolver last year! They should be at the Yacht Club by now if you want to catch them."

"Naw. I'm sleeping over at the McLeods," says the anthropologist rolling his eyeballs.

Euan then goes on to tell the anthropologist about Montserrat: "Fucking artificial cesspit this place is if you ask me. No one does any work: if you tell them to do anything you're a racist; they have no experience of anything other than rebuilding their house after Hugo hit, but if they're doing a big job for us and we tell them the door they've put on is askew, they say 'It works, it's better than I have at home'. I mean, what can you do with that? They try their best but they've got no education, no training, the island's too small for any big experience and the standards are so low that they just don't understand the need for quality."

"Woaw."

The diatribe continues, "All the tools go missing, even between each other – they have to hide their tools whenever they take a break or go home, and that's if they've decided to come to work at all! So, all good experience for a builder to come and work out here for a few years, you know, to see how things are different."

"Do you like the place or the people then?"

"Some of the people are just brilliant! Couldn't do without them, in fact I'll take a team of the carpenters over with me to St. Kitts when we start work on a new bank there. They're from Trinidad, four of them; only the foreman's Montserratian. The rest, well, pigshit. We have to employ 70 percent local workers, so they give us those blacks from social security who wear sunglasses indoors, under Malcolm X baseball caps. Never trust a man who wears sunglasses indoors. Never."

"It is a bit strange. There's a number of workers from Montserrat then?"

"Too bloody right. They all call themselves experts, tell me they can do everything and we end up having to sack them for incompetence – laying drains in the wrong places, upside-down doors, sideways switches – and then they sue us for racist dismissal. We have to payout – a cut to the lawyer and enough to get them to leave island. Once I had to get $40,000 on a weekend. I don't know how I did it!"

The anthropologist has difficulty keeping up with the stream of sentiments and frustrations coming out of Euan.

"It all comes from this small place. I mean, what has it got going for it? Nothing! No raw materials, no resources, no manpower, no middle class, no educated groups; corrupt politicians, grabbing, grabbing, grabbing, it's becoming like Scotland. That's why I left. Never been back since working in South Africa. Once voted SNP, a sort of romantic nationalism protest vote in my youth. No. We're not helping this place, but hey, they're paying my bills. No; you can keep a colony going in the Antarctic if you keep pumping the money in. But, as soon as it stops then it all collapses. Best thing is to scrap this island, leave it like before it was discovered, no one here then – now you know why. $500 (EC) million on development. Do you know how much that is for less than 10,000 people, less than a town in Britain! That would cause a scandal, eh. But what do you see for it? A hospital, Government Headquarters (when that interfering prick Terry McLeod will let me get on with my work and stop expecting miracles with the workforce we've got), a prison for the rising drug violence and maybe a runway extension."

Nervously, the anthropologist looks around for his generous host for the rest of the night. "Watch it," he says, espying Terry clearing up nearby.

The ranting spell has been broken. Euan moves away, "Listen Jonathan, nice meeting you. I'm down at GHQ, drop in anytime. I've an office near the entrance – if that prick will let me keep it during the handover," he declares, pointing at Terry.

Three o'clock in the morning, Terry wants to drive home around the corner, past all the other expat houses grouped together. Iris wants a New Year's walk and for the sake of a New Year's breakfast by her, Terry and the anthropologist both acquiesce.

New Year's Day interlude

In the afternoon – the morning was slept through – there are hangover jokes and eventually Terry decides to drive the anthropologist back to Plymouth. On the way down he talks about how difficult it is "to work with the blacks", but that this island is the "cushiest number" they've had so far, what with all the perks. "I can't understand it, it's as though they're sucking us dry now because they were slaves then. It's not as though they're not better off here than if they were back in Africa. I mean, I know the place, I've worked there, I know these things. Believe me, they're lucky they're here. Right ho; and you're here too." They pull up in Wapping. "Cheerio the now. Anytime you feel like it, dinna trouble youself, just come by."

Terry drives off leaving the anthropologist, Jonathan, outside the road-side door of his apartment. Upstairs, above the Emerald Cafe, Jonathan sleeps until he's awoken by the sound of his name arriving through the windows.

"Jo-na-than. Jo-na-than." It's Jonathan's landlady calling from her bedroom window, inconveniently parallel with his.

Miss Pippa Irish – an effervescent spinster of seventy, a civil servant who gave the Government 'licks', a Sunday Methodist, a trusted member of every extended family on the island – is shouting another message over and through the heads of the guests at the Emerald Cafe. As usual she's confusing the guests.

"I'M HAV-ING A NEW YEAR'S PAR-TY AT SE-VEN O'-CLOCK. DON'T FORGET."

Cheekily, as befits the relationship of impudence, Jonathan calls back imitating her staccato shouts:- "O-K! HO-W COU-LD I?"

"GO-OD. YOU WI-LL D-O THE DRINKS," she reveals with a sly twist and a sneaky smile. Once more she's sprung the trap on the innocent anthropologist – Jonathan.

Pippa's soirées are friendly groupings of eight or so people including Sally – Pippa's elder sister who lives on the bottom floor of their large stone house, and Jonathan – purveyor of street and expat information, source of cultural amusement with his mistakes and *faux pas*, and who is her endless topic of conversation to her guests. Sometimes Jonathan spends evenings watching television on the edge of her bed whilst she reads his fortune in her worn cards, other evenings they duel over a Scrabble board, hurling lengthy expletives at each other. Tonight, Jonathan ends up buying ice at the supermarket on the seafront behind Pippa's old yard.

DEVELOPING MONS'RAT THE MONS'RATIAN WAY

Jonathan wrings his wet, numb hands, drops the 2-lb bag of ice cubes into a cauldron on the balcony, and is introduced to several of the early guests. Once more, one of Pippa's errands has forced Jonathan to miss the start of an event he wishes to delimit and observe from start to finish.

There's a small brown man with a beard sitting in an armchair. He has one of those recognisable faces so that Jonathan's annoyed that he's missed the general introductions with other people. Now it's too late, too rude to ask his name even from the sisters for fear of appearing to view all blacks as an amorphous and indistinguishable collection, when – so he's told – it's the white people who look all the same.

Serving out aperitifs, Jonathan meets all the guests and exchanges pleasantries with Ed Cork and – by intuition – his wife sitting quietly next to him; Mary from the Public Library where Jonathan often scans the local shelves; Sally sitting opposite the bearded man in aged silence; and the Zambiqués, the only black members of the party – dressed in bright African clothes they stand out amongst the local creole elite. *Though Pippa often boasted about the free society in the West Indies where, now, every person, no matter the colour or shade of their skin, was treated equally, I remember her telling me that thirty years ago only light-skinned West Indians could hold bank accounts. And I could not help but notice*

that despite the alleged colour equality on Montserrat, it was more
likely to be the members of old established families which emphasised
education, and could afford to pay for off-shore university learning
for their children.

Dr. Zambiqué's the island surgeon who left Nigeria with his
wife, Ubike, and five children. As usual, Mary is questioning him
about life in the unknown homeland that West Indians feel
deprived of. Leaving the two of them to iron out their conceptions
of history, development and civilisation, Jonathan turns to Ubike:
"Ubike, that's a wonderful hatwrap you have on. Did you make it?"

Smiling and full of humour, Ubike replies, "Thank you. Of
course. Jonathan, you think I would advertise some other person's
clothes?"

"How is the business going?" Jonathan smiles back and
remembers that sometimes Sally sews for Ubike, and Jonathan's
other neighbour takes measurement fittings for Authentic Africana
fashions.

"Oh, still a bit slow on this island. Orders picked up after the
Government House show; my designs still tumble out each day."
And Ubike beams at me.

Pippa, sporting a turquoise sarong, commandeers Jonathan
to lay out the dishes: macaroni, chicken, plantains, stuffing cake,
salad, garlic bread, carrots and ground coconut, Johnny cakes.
Lastly, she brings in the complete corpse of a baby pig, roasted
with a sugar-apple in its mouth. There are cries of praise for the
delicacy.

"Look at this little piggy straight from the market!" Pippa cries.
"It had to be done up at the baker's oven it's so big."

The family and friends tuck into the meal, sitting in a circle
of curious chairs. Dewburry and Sally are exchanging pleasantries
about St. Kitts where Sally lived with her husband for a year,
conceived, and then returned to Montserrat on her own. All other
conversation is addressed to the group in general.

Pippa: "I went to the Police Station to complain about the
noise down there," throwing a nod to The Green Flash bar. "Jonathan
was with me, so I introduced him to the CID Officer from London
as my cross." Her expression causes laughter to ripple out through

the group, including Jonathan who only just figures out the joke in time.

She continues, "Of course the man didn't know what to say, and he didn't know what to think. Aiou! He just left his mouth open. So I says to him. 'Young man', I say, 'Young man, do you think I came from the sea so long before your time that you think I am so old? Well, let me tell you something," she pauses midstream, "I may be a Montserratian, but I evolved at the same time as you, so if you please be good enough to not think of me as a fish and to close your mouth when I'm speaking with you.'" There is more laughter and Pippa stamps her foot several times in glee at confusing, embarrassing, criticising and silencing a policeman from London, all in one swift broadside.

"So you got one up on the Englishmen there. Why wasn't that the Commissioner though?" queries Mr. Cork.

"The Commissioner needs a mouthpiece to be heard," quips Pippa.

Mary turns the topic to colonialism – "why wasn't Winston promoted to Commissioner? There have been West Indian Commissioners in the past. Why not now? Get rid of Commissioner 'Revolver' Slade, I say."

"Arr, my dear, for that answer you must sound out and fathom Britain's 'hidden agenda.'" Sally remains silent but Dewburry answers Mary.

"Who knows what the end of Hong Kong will bring. We're already being bought out by South Africans disliking the demise of apartheid."

Mr. Cork brings his experiences to the friendly company: "I was up at Government House." The group goes silent with the invocation of the Governor's residence. Cork continues, "After the dinner we had drinks brought out to us, and the Governor and I talked about world affairs." Cork knows that he has everyone's attention so he casually stretches, elongating the moment. "I dare say, Montserrat's future was considered by both of us."

"And ..."

"Well, he asked me what I thought about the Chinese yellow people coming to the island, about how the locals would feel."

Mary sucks in her lips and utters an exclamation, "Wha!"

"I told him that WE would be gaining even greater pressure of competition with outsiders on an already small island. He said he would 'bear that observation in mind'. In mind for what I don't quite know. I was just thinking about how the Montserratians mind the whites just as much as any other."

"Tss. I must get an audience with this new Governor. David was such a friendly soul. Did you read his letter in the paper?"

Pippa's thoughts on the granting of a brief audience with the Governor, because she used to be a mighty civil servant, are dampened by Dewburry: "Not with this one. Surrounds himself with expats from the projects. This one'll leave the island not knowing a single Montserratian. You've no chance of an audience, he hasn't been here long enough to know who you are. They don't brief them like they used to."

"They don't send us the ones that they used to. No class any more. And they think we don't know it. Governor Dawkins still visits the island, sits and plays dominoes with the taxi drivers and he remembers every person's name when they say their hellos." Pippa passes any possible criticism of herself, from the uncomfortable truth that she is no longer granted immediate access to the Governor's ear, by unfavourably comparing the Governor with the last three or four who administered the last decade.

"Well," Cork starts up again, "I saw the new swimming pool up behind the House, next to the Administration building. It's all been nicely refurbished."

"At a price. One million pounds I hear!" Mary's educational hackles have been raised. "Why can't they spend that sort of money on the library, or education, or developing an infrastructure like the French do on Guadeloupe? There's no chance that Britain's to let us have independence if we're not even educated in the choice." She sits back in her seat, agitated.

"If they now can't swim in the sea with the rest of us, that's a political sign," Dewburry ponders.

At the risk of increasing the intensity of annoyance amongst the group, Jonathan returns to the development issues, "Why isn't Britain helping with the infrastructure? There's lots of development going on all round the island."

"Exactly. Thank you; and from a white man no less." Pippa claps her hands together.

Again, Mr. Cork, Head of the Montserrat Chamber of Commerce, gains our attention and informs the group: "He does six laps every morning. That's what our Governor from the Foreign & Commonwealth Office does." We all start to imagine those slow, painful strokes. "Here's what happens on Montserrat, Jonathan: ..."

"Listen to this, put it in your book," interrupts Pippa.

"Here's what happens on Montserrat, Jonathan: because Montserrat is a British colony it has a parliamentary system modelled upon the motherland's House of 'Commoners'. You know all this: about Fergus, the Speaker; the five politicians and the constitution we just had imposed upon us by a Governor who then had to leave. Well, not only is this model of democracy ridiculous, but it doesn't work: the population's too small to have all these little political parties aligning and realigning according to family, business, and colour – pigmentocracy! It doesn't work because there are no salaries, 'so only the wealthy need apply'. And then, the Governor is like the Queen of England, he vets everything and is above the law. This system needs to change. But more importantly, WE need to effect the changes, not the Foreign & Commonwealth Office with their seminar trips all around the world for the loyal and dutiful."

"Fergus is going to Namibia to teach them parliamentary democracy," chips in Mary. She's greeted with shushes.

"Now, Britain says it will neither push us towards independence, nor will it stop us. If we want independence, we need a two-thirds majority on the island."

"You mean like devolution in Scotland?" compares Jonathan.

"Yes, sort of, but England doesn't want to lose Scotland and Britain doesn't want to lose her colonies, they're too important loop holes for banking and trade outside Europe. So, Britain doesn't encourage any move to independence but shows the people how much they rely upon England, how much better they are being a dependent territory ..."

"Even though we can't go and live in the UK and they turn us away because we're black." Mary is angry with these recent changes which Thatcher imposed so that all colonial-born people are a part of the British Dependent Territories with no right of abode in Britain. "Except for the Falklands' people. They can go. 'They're our kin' Thatcher said. They're white. This is racist." Pippa joins in with Mary.

"If you look at the levels of aid and development which come to this island, it's on the level of hundreds of millions of dollars. But what do you see for all of it with such a small population? Very little local development."

Dewburry mutters: "Everything went with Hugo, everything. But Montserratians rebuilt with money sent back from families abroad. This has always happened and when a British worker arrives, they can't believe the lifestyles that 'the natives' lead compared with their own dreary commuting job from Milton Keynes. They don't like us blacks better off than them. We know all that. But they don't know about the separated families; the children who never even met their fathers or brothers ..."

"This aid is all bilateral;" Ed ignores Dewburry. "Give with one hand and take with the other! The money goes from Barclays Bank in London to Barclays Bank on Montserrat to pay the expat salaries who take the money back to Barclays Bank in England when they leave. None of it stays here. So with less money than you think, Britain ensures that Montserrat remains dependent."

"A British Dependency, that's 'the hidden agenda'," Mary concludes.

"Arr. Now I see. But what can be done about it?" asks Jonathan, the sceptical anthropologist.

"Education. Education. Education. Educate the young to stand on their own two feet, break the colonial mentality. But the challenge is, independence first to unleash the creative forces of our abilities, self-confidence, resilience, self-sufficiency, or should those come first, then independence? That, my friend, is our scary choice. The young want the first, the old consider the second but doubt the viability of both. Look at the other independent islands, independent to beg to anyone: as a colony, at least we have stability and the assurance of assistance from Britain in the case of a natural disaster like Hurricane Hugo."

Faces are radiating earnest inspiration for the long challenge ahead of them. Jonathan realises that each person is a piece on a huge checker board like the one the taxi drivers play on when they wait for customers: the dimensions are twenty spaces by twenty, and there are teams of counters opposing each other; once the Montserrat team can reach the other side, without giving away too many positions and pieces, then they are 'crowned' and their abilities magnified. In their way are the TCO pieces played by the Crown.

The plates are cleared and stacked but conversation continues unabated; dessert waits.

Dewburry joins in: "That was a colourful meal, Pippa. Delicious. And speaking of colour, what do you think of that new building for the Government, eh?"

"Pink! Pink! What do they think it is, an iced-cake Government from a fairy tale?" interrupts Mary.

"Shocking. They built it in an old-fashioned colonial style and paint it pink just to remind us who we are and where we are," continues Dewburry.

"That's for tourism too. It's all heritage tourism for the Americans."

"Damn them." Pippa's annoyed. "We've got no middle class because of them. Instead of growing as a group we competed to be on their invitation lists they drew up when they arrived on island. Now they feel comfortable, they don't invite us and we've no middle class that they have in Antigua and St. Kitts."

"WE are the middle class," adds Mary.

Cork continues to criticise the new Government Headquarters with Ubike and Dewburry whilst Dr. Zambiqué, Pippa and Mary consider the new hospital he has to work in. Jonathan bends an ear to each conversation floating around him; Sally dozes.

"I hear that the air conditioning is the latest technology again."

"Silly. We could have done that ourselves. There's a few qualified at that."

"Of course. Nothing but the best for Montserrat."

"So how's it going to be repaired. They going to fly down an American each time it breaks down?"

"You mean there's no air conditioning at all. Crazy!"

"Oh, you mean every room in the building has air conditioning. Why?"

"Their experts are *their* experts and aren't experts here."

"Yes, and if one person decides to stay at work for one hour then the entire building has to be on. And if there's a failure then no one can go to work at all."

"But that's ridiculous. Why don't they ask any Montserratians about it?"

"Once I had to pull an appendix. Sweat was everywhere. The spare fan didn't work in the power cut, nor the backup generator. Luckily we were able to smash a hole in a boarded up window, sterilise everything and finish the op. outside. The patient never knew a thing of course!"

"That sounds more like it with the civil service."

"But this is the tropics. How could they do such a thing?"

"We should have been involved in the planning."

The fragmented conversations unite with Ed Cork's comment which becomes a conclusion: "THIS IS A FIRST WORLD SOLUTION TO A THIRD WORLD PROBLEM."

Jonathan takes the leftovers of the pig back into the kitchen. The dog howls outside, so when Jonathan returns he asks Pippa, "Do you want me to give the pig's head to the dog?" The conversation stops suddenly.

Pippa repeats Jonathan's request, this time to the guests. "Did you all hear what Jonathan asked me? He wanted to know if he should give the pig's head to the dog!" She bends double as if in pain; she surfaces with tears on her face. She howls, holds her belly, and suddenly everyone's laughing hysterically at Jonathan – Pippa putting her arm around Jonathan whilst wiping the tears from her face. "Ooh. Ooh. Jonathan. I swear, you're always doing this to me. The head's the delicacy! Ooh dear. Let me sit down. You just bring in the fruit cocktail and the vodka sauce."

Jonathan never saw anyone ever eat the head of a pig, but thereafter, he never asked if it was a delicacy or not.

COMMENTARY

Lee, the student medical worker is on Montserrat because he lost his job in England, his talking-point is that Montserrat is *"a nightmare"* to work on. Frank, His Excellency The Governor and senior TCO, equates development with tourism: for him, Montserrat is a tourist development site. For many other TCOs Montserrat means a comfortable and high standard of living, if not a trouble-free working environment; Montserrat is only *"a fucking artificial cesspit"* for Euan. Terry is the only expat who exhibits qualities of altruism, but these are dampened by his patronising attitude to the indigenous West Indians – for whom slavery was an apparent benefit. Can such altruism be attributed to the Overseas Development Agency (1994: 1) which defines its purpose as "promoting the development or maintaining the economy of a country or territory outside the United Kingdom, or the welfare of its people"? Cynics like Hobart (1993: 2) may note that without underdevelopment "the West could not represent itself as developed", and furthermore, that without the public knowledge that Britain is aiding other countries Britain would lose her status in the international community. Nor should we not forget that development projects on Montserrat are useful for the incumbent Montserratian Government who can use the projects in their appeals to the public to be re-elected.

Though not representative of Montserratian reactions, both Mary and Dewburry hold sentiments and outlooks which are shared to a certain degree. Whereas Lee considers development to be a series of stages on an evolutionary scale for a progressing society tested by the presence and absence of the U.S. Peace Corps and U.K. Voluntary Service Overseas workers, Mary has the perspective that development is synonymous with dominance and dependency. In fact, Mary suspects that the development projects on Montserrat are part of Britain's 'hidden agenda' to maintain control of the colony with high standards of care at the hospital, but a poor infrastructure around the island. Here, I deliberately give space to I.M. Lewis's (1988: 378) warning to other anthropologists: "we should guard against becoming involved in the professional legitimation of projects (with or without 'hidden agendas') which seem more for the benefit of the developers than for the 'underdeveloped' clients."

Mr. Cork has the impression that development workers are arrogant and prejudiced, impressions substantiated by Euan's diatribe. Terry's view combines development experience in Africa with an inability to empathise with a West Indian, 'black' world-view. How aware are TCOs of Montserratian perspectives and responses to the projects, responses which consider the context of the project as well as its shortcomings? Dewburry makes sense of the projects out of his ambivalent point of view towards (neo-) colonialism and dependency theory: *"the TCO grouping is an elite within the island population which perpetuates relationships of dependency with Britain; Montserrat is an underdeveloped product of capitalist expansion and dominance."*

Development work on Montserrat is different to development work found in many other parts of the world. Developing hospitals, runway extensions, Government buildings, is very different to the agricultural famine relief work of Paul Richards and other development workers which can have immediate, life-saving results. Nevertheless, Richards's (1985: 116; see also Escobar 1991) assessment of food production in West Africa criticises Western development for similar reasons, for ignoring the local world-views of participants, just as I would argue for the inclusion of local world-views – world-views which "belong" – in the development of Montserrat. Yet, when Brokensha and Warren and Werner (1980: 4) argue that indigenous knowledge should be included when development is considered, is the anthropologist truly redressing the imbalance – confronting the rhetoric with the reality of the situation (Hirabayashi & Warren & Owen 1980: 354)? As a solution, many applied anthropologists simply incorporate the native point of view within the constructed scientific label "ethnoscience". This, Warren and Meehan (1980: 318) claim, is the dialogic solution to development problems, seeing "peasant's problems 'through their eyes'". Although this ethnoscience – local science – approach contrasts with the global, "world-ordering" knowledge Hobart criticises at the start of this chapter, it does not often range further than a brief incorporation or consideration of indigenous knowledge or local perspectives.

According to David Fetterman (1987: 344), ethnography is the continual assessment of contrasting world-views. What this chapter has attempted to show, by juxtaposing development worker and Montserratian conversation-narratives, are some of the contrasting occupations and outlooks from people such as Jonathan the anthropologist, Francis the UNDP worker, Pippa the retired civil servant: Jonathan introducing himself and memorising the gist of conversations as a practising anthropologist; Francis hungry for samozzas and other development projects; and Pippa, the entertainer, who rates herself and her fellow islanders according to the quality and class of the British working on their colony Montserrat (*"They don't send us the ones that they used to"*). For this chapter I abandoned the tape recorder in favour of field notes. This is because a tape recorder would not have been appropriate at either dinner party, and I am sure that the development workers would not have been so candid, critical or revealing in their conversations had a microphone swayed in front of them from time to time. Furthermore, I do not believe that a tape recorder or a video camera can capture fully or represent accurately the conversations – let alone the heterogeneous events of the evenings – in this chapter or in the calypso scenes in Doc's den in the next chapter. To rely upon them and to use them in transcription would result in what Paul Atkinson (1995: 13) refers to as an "illusory fidelity" of unreadable and over-detailed, meaningless textual representations. I do not view this as a sacrifice or a compromise to the situation in which I found myself. In other situations I do make use of the tape recorder, but less than I expected because a tape recorder stultifies fieldwork records and numbs fieldwork interactions; nor can the bland transcription of a taped conversation give an impression in the writing of, say, my unstated feelings – "Jonathan's" empathy with the Montserratians at Pippa's dinner party, or "the anthropologist's" estrangement from the TCOs.

The development workers form a diverse and experienced constellation with much experience in West Africa and South Africa, and more first-hand knowledge of Africa than the Montserratians who sometimes label themselves "African". As the crowned whites on the island's checkerboard, they have a range of opinions and perspectives about Montserrat – that small island with a tiny population favoured by more development money than any British town back home. So too, their opponents on the same board "perspect" differently, with different world-views (Rapport), but sharing their diverse realities (Skinner): Montserrat – where money flows in and out of Barclays Bank without settling; Montserrat – dependent home desperately seeking education to break into the United Nations. This difference between the two constellations – the kernels of their overlapping realities "underlying" their opinions and perspectives – is partly to do with the members' place of origin, their colour, but also, in my view, their temporal commitment to Montserrat and her people: short-term and impersonal for the development workers, long-term and partisan for those at Pippa's who would not hesitate to refer to themselves as "Mons'rat neaga", though they might use less colloquial language. Such constellations, to reiterate, are fleeting mutual realities which derive from our inability to divide and distinguish between fact and opinion, world-view and world-reality.

On Montserrat, and elsewhere, development work is still being practised without reflexive consideration of indigenous knowledge, perceptions and world-views. This chapter poses the adoption and extension of Rapport's approach to Hobart's problem. This part-solution, part-resolution, of development problems has also shown that different inter-subjective constellations should be recorded in anthropological accounts. No matter how distinct or diffuse they may be, these constellations are temporary, partial and inconstant; hence the need to situate them and privilege them according to Tyler's (1986: 127) "perspectival relativity". Let me end this chapter, then, by recalling the indeterminate anthropological discipline I mentioned in the Academic Preface, so that I might add some more lessons given to us, respectively, by Lucy Mair (1957: 7) and Raymond Firth (1981: 193):

> [s]ometimes the anthropologist can do a simple job of interpretation to people who just do not know what the life of the people whom they are seeking to improve is like.

> [A]n important part of the anthropologist's job is to expose the difficulties, the contradictions, the conflicts of interest in a situation in order that false hopes of easy solutions should not mislead.

This is the challenge to the anthropologist, but the final words and comments must come from the eloquent natives; in this case, from the Montserratians themselves:

"What do you think of that new building for the Government, eh? Pink! Pink! What do they think it is, an iced-cake Government from a fairy tale? They built it in an old-fashioned colonial style and paint it pink just to remind us who we are and where we are. That's for tourism too. It's all heritage tourism for the Americans. I hear that the air-conditioning is the latest technology again."

"Of course. Nothing but the best for Montserrat."

"Every room in the building has air-conditioning. Why? Do you know how expensive that is or how we can repair the latest technology? They going to fly down an American each time it breaks down? And what if one person decides to stay at work for one hour then the

entire building has to be on? And if there's a failure then no one can go to work at all?"

"But that's ridiculous, this is the tropics. Why don't they ask any Montserratians about it? That's not what we want. We should have been involved in the planning. We have qualified people who can do that."

"THIS IS A FIRST WORLD SOLUTION TO A THIRD WORLD PROBLEM."

Student recalls volcano island ordeal

A St. Andrews University post-graduate student yesterday gave an account of his last few days on the Caribbean island of Montserrat, which for some time has been under threat from a volcanic eruption – and, more recently, from a hurricane.

Jonathan Skinner (25) described his ordeal as "pretty frightening."

He is now back in St. Andrews, where he is completing his studies in social anthropology.

Jonathan, from Bristol, had been on the island since October as part of his studies.

He had been due to return to Scotland later this month but the increasing fears that the volcano could erupt at any time prompted him to shorten his trip.

The Chances Peak volcano has been spewing dust and debris for more than six weeks, forcing many inhabitants to move to other areas away from the immediate danger.

Jonathan said yesterday, "the first indication that there was a problem came in July, with a strong smell of sulphur. Over the ensuing days there were loud rumblings and they were followed by earthquakes. Smoke could clearly be seen coming from the mountain. The series of earthquakes got worse and several buildings developed cracks. It was very worrying to be walking along a supermarket aisle and then suddenly see the shelves start to sway back and forward. Ash was falling continually and everything was coated."

Jonathan's rented apartment was at the foot of the peak and he had a perfect view of the activity, with smoke belching from the top continually.

"Initially we were told we would be given a 24 to 36-hour warning if the volcano was about to erupt. However, that time-scale was reduced to only six hours. I eventually couldn't sleep or eat and the situation became unbearable. I decided then to leave," he said.

He brought back only a few belongings, leaving money in the bank there and also most of his clothes.

Although glad to be away from the island, he is keen to return once the crisis is over. He said, "I was very warmly accepted by the local people and made a lot of friends."

Jonathan graduated from St. Andrews in 1993.

His studies on the island involved interviewing inhabitants and asking how they perceived their own nationality.

(Anon., *The Courier and Advertiser*, 6 September 1995: 4, no other references available)

"RUM & COKE" AND CALYPSO:

EXPLICIT COMMENTARY IN PRIVATE AND PUBLIC

SPACES

Indignant, he replies, "Boy! Boy! Me caan believe me ears! A wha' you mean by dis – 'So Mr. Greenaway, what is calypso?' Calypso. Calypso! Calypso is social commentary ya know. What else it be?"

I try another tack: "So you singin' 'bout the island den, Mr. Greenaway?"

"Dat's right, dat's right. But listen, look at me shop, what me call it?"

"Top Secret's," I answer.

"Dat's right, dat's right. Nobody call me Mr. Greenaway – me gotta name 'aven't I? Top Secret's me name. Dat's wha' me always bin called. Only de Government calls me Mr. Greenaway."

It's in the middle of the night, but only now do Mr. Greenaway's shades come off. Top Secret leaves his fedora hat perched upon his Afro. I've asked another dumb tourist question, but now I've caught his interest. He tucks his thumbs into his braces so I volunteer more ignorance: "Why 'Top Secret' den? How you get dat name?"

Top Secret replies with a knowledgeable "Arrr."

He pulls his braces, composing himself for his story.

"Arrr, well. Me build during de day, someone else have fu look after de store during de day – ¿hola, qué pasa amigo?"

An old Spanish speaker from Puerto Rico, a man in a hair net, wanders by and takes a seat outside the store. He is oblivious to Top Secret's greeting.

We both shrug at each other.

"Where was we now? Arrr, yes, dat's right, me name. Right, well, me drivin' taxis 'fore de business, an' you know, some people dey waan fu keep t'ings secret like ..."

My thoughts turn to contraband, smuggling, boot-legging?

"... Yeah, dat's right," Top Secret continues. "Me pick dem up and take dem to places to meet others."

"Rendezvous?" I volunteer.

"Yeah, dat's it, like. You know de kinda t'ing: a man an' a woman, gettin' togeder widout others in de know. Yes man, dey waan t'ings Top Secret."

"Arrr, right. I get it." I accidentally repeat Top Secret's style of speech.

"Dis is me firs' time calypsonian. Me wrote de lyrics by de till, an' some o' de boys, we jam de tune togeder real nice. Somet'ing for de kids to sing to, dat's right. Come an' listen to dis."

I venture an intelligent guess: "'Tropical Gal'?"

"Dat's right ... ." Top Secret leads us into a corner of his store where a cassette player rests. He plays "Tropical Gal" for me:

Tropical gal – where you come from
You look so neat
Dress so sweet
Tantalising man
Always in de latest fashion
Yet still you work for no one
Like you have a plan
To rob down every man[1]

Inside de store, Top Secret sings along to dis firs' verse he has on tape. He then explains this tale of rampant women roaming the streets with sexually transmitted diseases: a man sets up a date; the woman Elsa's always late; they meet in the quiet south of the island. I get to join Top Secret with the chorus – catchy and colloquial:

You're a jig-saw
Or a power – saw
A – trick saw
You gal Elsa
If you want me money – wuk fu um
I must take de honey – wuk fu um
You sexy – wuk fu um
You think you've fool me – wuk fu um
You can't even wine
You can't even grine – gal
You can't even wine

You can't even grine – gal
You can't even grine – gal
Come better than dat
Come better than dat[2]

A chorus-line gal must use her body to best effect: if she expects to get paid then she has to work for it; to try better, to do better. "*Tropical Gal*" is a calypso song which many consider to be about the sexual dynamics of male–female relations from a male perspective. Top Secret also has another calypso, "*Don't Rock The Boat Dada*". This, he explained to me, is a more focused commentary upon recent political developments on Montserrat concerning Neville Tuitt, commonly known as "Dada", who holds one of the crucial opposition votes in the House of Parliament. When fellow member for the Government in opposition, Ruby Wade, introduced a motion for the opposition, Dada compromised his critical stance towards Chief Minister Reuben Meade. Dada was conscripted to the Government side and was told by Justin "Hero" Cassell – noted calypsonian and Government Public Relations Officer – to continue to toe the line, for it was in both of their interests for him to do so. The second verse and the chorus run:

Hero in the front seat driving
Dada in the back seat hiding
Yes they compromising
And this what they were saying

Don't rock the boat – Dada
Don't rock the boat – Dada[3]

CALYPSO AS SOCIAL COMMENTARY

In conversation, Top Secret makes it clear that his understanding of calypso it that it is a form of "social commentary", an expression or definition shared by many other calypsonians I spoke with on Montserrat. His two songs are similar to those by Trinidadian Mighty Sparrow (1992[b]; see also 1992[a]), international King of Calypso, such as "*Sell de Pussy*" and "*Wood in the Fire*", bawdy tales, carnal cultural commentaries, lyrical parables of prostitution and sexual and political abandon which rely and play upon locally-known words, dialects and knowledge. Like the barbarian poetry by Sir Fergus, leader of the Montserrat Writers' Maroon, calypso on Montserrat is a creative medium and mode of social expression, of social situations, social issues, ills and opinions. Calypso is explicitly a form of social commentary, and calypso as social commentary can be very explicit in its content as calypsonians sing their salty realities. This chapter examines calypso on Montserrat by presenting examples of its use in both private and public realms – during Carnival, on the Festival stage, in the local newspapers and in the neighbour's den. The multiple facets of calypso require a range of techniques of representation to convince you, the reader, that calypso evokes Montserrat place and Mons'rat neaga. Above, I referred to the calypsonians' general understanding of calypso as social commentary, and I gave just one local reading of some calypso messages – Top Secret's. Below, I show how this "music of the masses" (Rohlehr 1970: 87) is understood according to several Montserratian calypsonians, songwriters and journalists. I note with caution that these interpretations of calypso are partial and variable: they depend upon the context and background of the listeners who are being influenced by the performer/writer – whether tourist first setting foot on the island, long-established belonger on the island, or fellow Montserratian calypsonian. I have thus, where possible, sought out the calypsonian's own personal understandings of their work, calypso's social, political and carnal nature. Here, I am attracted to *their* "message" which they seek to take to the listeners, judges, dancers and curious tourists, rather than how the message is received.

Popular history on Montserrat supports the idea that calypso originated on Trinidad and spread throughout the English-speaking Caribbean in the twentieth century, becoming a part of the local culture on many of the islands. "Calypso verses are witty and humorous and mirror popular social attitudes on personal, social, economic and political problems, or philosophise, teach and appeal to the social conscience" (Lewin 1980: 634; see also Hebdige 1987: 41). Indeed, the academic historian Olive Lewin goes on to note that in the nineteenth century all Trinidad songs making pointed social commentaries ended with the words *sans humanité* to absolve the singer from responsibility for their risqué remarks; such was the candour of the calypsonian. Whereas pre-Glasnost Russians circulated social opinions and commentaries on home-printed *samizdat* sheets, pre-independence Trinidadians criticised colonialism and local Government from the calypso stage. With impunity, Sparrow taunted American GIs brought to Trinidad during her oil boom, celebrating their departure with lyrics – "[i]t's the glamour boys again / [w]e're going to rule Port of Spain".[4]

With their distinctive calypso titles, singers can assume another personality from themselves. The names which they are given, or create for themselves, often suit aspects of their personality. They are more than stage names because they become nicknames and are associated only with a particular calypsonian. Whereas a writer might use a *nom de plume* in the newspapers to write with impunity as an unknown person, a calypsonian has a calypso name which is used both on and off the stage. Though the calypsonian is clearly identifiable, the calypso name – a projection of his or her persona – allows the calypsonian to absorb criticism as a singer without it affecting their character, absolving them from punishment by those targets of their satirical gibes. Furthermore, the timing of the subversion is significant: a calypso competition on Montserrat is held at Carnival time (Christmas on Montserrat, Easter on Trinidad). This is a time when disorder – anti-structure – is permitted in the volatile and lyrical recapitulation of the year. To use Victor Turner's (1996) symbolic terminology, this is an example of "social drama" taking place at a symbolically liminal time between one year and another which brings about a sense of *communitas* amongst the participants (the calypsonians and spectators).

As social commentaries, the calypsos consider all manner of social, sexual, and political topics. Drawing upon calypso's non-liable dispensation, calypso's lyrical licence, Herman Francis, a school teacher on Montserrat and a popular calypsonian known as "Cupid" or "Q-pid", is well known for political calypsos such as "*What's Inside de Box*" (1987). Q-pid's song criticised the failure to reopen ballot boxes following an allegation of fraud in the 1987 General Election.[5] It caused such embarrassment to the Montserrat Government that they banned it from airplay on the Government radio station.[6] Another well-known calypsonian, Pat "Belonger" Ryan, writes and sings her calypsos throughout the year. Belonger works with the social memories available on Montserrat: a native of Trinidad who became a legal "belonger" (a resident with the right to vote) by marrying a Montserratian on the island, Belonger has been working with her impressions of Montserrat since she migrated there after teaching French in Britain for several years. Well placed at third position in the 1988–

1989 Calypso Competition,[7] one of the many calypsos Belonger
wrote that year, one which took her to the finals, was *"Bring Dem
Back"*. This calypso was a complaint about the recent loss of island-
known cultural practices and characters such as John Bull and
Miss Goosie – both popular mummers, a bull dressed in sackcloth
wearing horns and carrying the devil's forked stick, and a very
tall wooden puppet manipulated by a masked person on foot
(reintroduced by Josh Irish in the 1995–1996 Carnival). Her
concluding lines in the calypso make reference to other masked
masquerade dancers on the streets who come out in troupes at
celebrations; for her, they should be the celebrated:

> Culture shouldn't be a mask
> That we wear on Festival day
> Take it to the classroom
> Parade it in every way
> Let's be proud and glad
> Of a heritage that's our own
> Foreign culture bang water come here
> Is here we tradition born[8]

Ironically, Belonger "bang water coom ya" herself. Yet she is now
as attached to her calypso name, which she adopted in 1988,
as she is to her new island which adopted her in 1981.

"Calypso, the commonest song-form of the Caribbean," so local
cultural artist Ann Marie Dewar (1977: 75, 76) states:

> is one of the most communicative forms of music, enabling the composer
> to comment on any situation with a freedom of expression and language.
> [...] Calypsos as sung by local calypsonians are now locally composed,
> and while some simply invite listeners to join in the Christmas merriment,
> to 'jam' and 'shake up you' wais'', most are true commentaries on local
> and regional topics.

Calypso song topics generally attempt to subvert dominant forces.
Even the chosen linguistic form of expression within the calypso
contributes to this activity. Dewar draws attention to the freedom
of the calypsonians' use of language, their freedom of expression,
and to the question of 'nation language' (a *Monglish* creole language)
versus non-standard/sub-standard pidgin or dialect. Discussing
"nation language" in the use of dub performance poetry (music
tracks which the poet improvises to), anthropologist Michael
Angrosino (1993: 74) points out that since the 1970s West Indians
have denounced their forced adoption of a standard language
such as English as a damaging form of imperialism: "'[n]ation

language' has thus become 'a potent symbol of a nascent consciousness of an identity separate from that of the old colonial 'metropole.'" The international calypsonian Alphonsus "Arrow" Cassell promotes the validity of the nation language of his native Montserrat in his calypso *"Montserrat English"*,[9] perhaps a response to attitudes such as those expressed in the following delightfully written letter to *The Montserrat Mirror* in 1967 which, unfortunately (grammatically speaking), tries to complain about both the teachers and the teaching of English at primary school level on Montserrat:

> [w]hy cannot these primary school teach English? Because they do not speak English themselves. They speak Montserratian, which is a garbled patois completely divorced from – or unaware of – the basic rules of English grammar. Granted that most of their pupils use this patois, and that the teachers themselves were brought up in it – but what are they being paid to teach – patois of the Queen's English? To teach proper English, as spoken and written by educated English people, the teachers themselves must know, and be at home in, the English language.[10]

Dewar (1977: 78) explains that *"Montserrat English"* is a rebuttal against such sentiments, "to all who think that Standard English is the only 'correct language' and who scold and scorn those who speak dialect." In his calypso, Arrow deliberately oscillates between Standard and Dialect English, explaining to his listeners his pride in Montserrat English which is a part of his pride in Montserrat and her culture. His calypso begins:

> People think that it's wrong
> To talk real Montserratian
> They say it ain't right – grammatically
> Day can't find them words in no dictionary
> Call it bad language
> Despising we heritage
> But don't care if dey call we foolish
> Dis is Montserrat English[11]

After beginning in Standard English, the verse continues in dialect whilst the chorus skilfully emphasises the argument for a Montserratian nation language by exemplifying some common Montserratian expressions:

> Gee me lee – wha you ah yete dey *[Give me a little of what you are eating there]*
> Dat ah wa we just say   *[That is how we say it]*
> Pick um up – han um gee me   *[Pick it up and give/hand it to me]*
> Dats de Montserratian way   *[That's the Montserratian way]*

Com – ma sisah – fetch me de poh *[Come here my sister, fetch me the potty]*

Wan pain na me belly yah so so   *[I have a pain in my belly right here]*

Dis is Montserrat culture
We'll be proud of it forever
Dis is Montserrat culture
We'll be proud of it forever[12]

In Fergus's (1994: 252; see also Arrow 1971; 1994) mind, Arrow and his popular calypsos are a part of the Mons'rat national conscience: "warning against profligate squandering of the landed patrimony in '*Hold on to Your Property*', the upholder of creole language in '*Dis is Awe Culture*', the celebrator of national resilience in the face of vicious adversity in '*Man Mus' Live*'." In Montserratian dialect, "um" stands for "it" – an important difference with Standard English for the proud dialect speakers on Montserrat who can thus use dialect as a distinctive and exclusive feature of their identity, one which they know that visitors and tourists have difficulty in fathoming (many have to read aloud the local newspaper gossip columns with a nation language dictionary beside them [see Irish 1985]). Elsewhere in the English-speaking Caribbean, Chris Searle (1984) and Gail Pool (1994) have examined the role of calypso in the Grenada Revolution (1979-1983) showing that language is an important aspect of the revolutionary culture, making calypso a technique for mass mobilisation and a way of expressing the cultural power of the people. In other words, calypsos can be powerful mobilising social commentaries.

CALYPSO AS CARNIVAL PERFORMANCE

Like reggae songs – with their disclosure and affirmation of ghetto values, concerns and discontentment in Jamaica – calypso songs are concerned with resistance and the subordination of domination. Whilst on Montserrat, I attended Sir Fergus's West Indian history classes where we learned that this musical genre and cultural tradition originated on Trinidad and Tobago in the eighteenth and nineteenth centuries as Carnival became indigenised (Myers 1980), a history which is not known to many Montserratians, belongers or tourists – with the exception of Belonger, school children and mature students at the Adult Education Centre. Following the emancipation of slavery (1834), slaves in Trinidad's capital, Port of Spain, came to dominate and overturn the white minority's Catholic celebration of Lent. The former slaves brought African songs, dances, instruments and customs to a more 'sedate' religious holiday. They introduced night-time processions through the streets featuring stick fighters (*batoniers*) accompanied by *kalindas* – men who sang obscene songs to encourage their favourite fighters. Kalindas were expected to rally crowds to the side of their batonier, and to improvise insults against his opponents. They were the early calypsonians which the white ruling classes were unable to suppress. In 1884, the Peace Preservation Act was passed in an attempt to suppress the regular street fights, many between blacks and whites; part of this Act forbade the public use of African drums.

The ban failed as processionists/percussionists improvised a beat by striking bamboo tubes, blocks of wood, strips of metal or the ground ahead instead of the emotive African drum. The carnivalesque festival of disorder remained an annual event and by 1900 it had turned into a masquerade event of "bands" of Port of Spain neighbourhoods dressed up in various costumes and disguises. Calypso continued to develop in this fashion – as a means of social protest and class and ethnic struggle (Campbell 1988). Individuals took to satirising society by releasing topical songs through the year, popularising them for the Carnival when they competed against each other in calypso tents. Both calypso and Carnival now attract tourists to Trinidad, but calypso still maintains a key vocal position in "Trini" society with calypso commentaries still facilitating social protests and unrest such as the 1990 attempted coup (Birth 1994).

Calypso – *capoeira* with the kick in the song rather than the foot – and Carnival were exported and diffused throughout the English-speaking Caribbean, each island adopting and adapting a distinctive hybrid as their "symbol of national culture" (Miller 1994: 109). The English-speaking island of Nevis, for example, has celebrated Culturama week at the end of July and the beginning of August since 1974, whereas Montserrat holds Festival over Christmas and the beginning of the New Year.[13] Both islands, however, do have a similar programme of events: calypso competitions and morning J'Ouvert Jump Up dancing in the streets from sunrise to sunset, cultural pageants, street fairs and performances, and a Miss Culture Talent show or Festival Queen

Show, respectively. On Montserrat, the calypso competition often has several heats, giving a long lead-in to the Festival: in 1994 the calypso eliminations opened the Festival season on 2 December, the semi-finals were held a fortnight later on 16 December, and the finals occurred another fortnight later on 30 December. One band, composed of bass and acoustic guitars, drums, synthesiser and a section of trombones and trumpets, plays for all the calypsonians. Each of the thirty or so "eliminees" have two songs for two rounds of singing and performing to a listening and dancing audience. Half that number will go on to the semi-finals, and the numbers will be whittled down again to approximately ten calypsonians for the finals.

In the second round of the calypso competitions on Montserrat, the calypsonian is allowed to enter an alternative song to their original selection – as with all the songs, they cannot have been sung in any previous year, yet they can have been released on the radio during the year. In practice, calypsonians will try to keep exciting the crowds by improvising some of their lyrics, by dressing in glittering costumes, or by acting out the storyline of the calypso in the finals. Only the king or queen of the previous year's Festival is exempt from competition. He or she alone enters the competition, to defend their crown, in the finals. The more popular the calypsonian is, and the more well known their calypso, the greater the support at the competition and thus the greater the chance of their winning of the competition. In the 1994–1995 Calypso Competition, the judge (Abdul Weekes, English teacher and Maroon poet) was allocating marks for Lyrics (0–35), Melody (0–20), Rendition (0–25), Presentation (0–5), Performance (0–15);[14] and the organisers were offering a pair of holiday flight tickets to another island, a trophy, EC$5000 (£1500) and the opportunity to represent Montserrat at the Inter-island Calypso Competitions to the winner. All the other competitors would receive financial prizes ranging from EC$150 at the eliminations, to EC$400 at the semi-finals, and EC$1000–1600 at the finals. Though not necessarily the winning song, the most popular calypso to dance and sing to is voted the Road March Song and is played throughout the streets – Glanville "Spoiler" Roach's "Wet me down" in 1994–1995 (with its chorus: "t'row water pon me / look how happy me be", and catchy expressions about being drenched – "Oh Lord / wet me down / sappin'").[15]

Though Culturama on Nevis is only 20 years old, the Montserrat Festival has been running since 1962 when Justin "Hero" Cassell won the first of his thirteen crowns. His brother Alphonsus "Arrow" Cassell competed from 1968–1974 before going to Trinidad to make his fortune as "Soca Ambassador to the World" (*soul*/*calypso*) with his 1994 album "*Hot Hot Hot*". Both calypsonians practised in the junior high-school competitions and promoted calypso on an island whilst it was being deluged by Beatles producer George Martin's business associates: at his AIR Studios, Stevie Wonder cut a version of "Ebony and Ivory", Duran Duran recorded "Rio", Elton John recorded "Jump-up" and Boy George, Paul McCartney, Sting and the Rolling Stones all wrote and recorded songs.[16]

Music has always been important on Montserrat, be it "Fife and Drum" for the Masquerade dancers, "Soca and Dance Hall" for the all-night jump-ups, "Reggae and Ragga" for the Rastas, "Hip-hop and Techno" for the AUC students, "Gangster Rap" for the street corner posse or "pop music" for the tourists. Yet calypso maintains its own special place on the island, not least at Festival time. It does not matter that some of the calypsonians' subtle and not so subtle meanings are lost on the audience. Apart from "Bob Marley-like" reggae, calypso is the only musical form with which a wide spectrum of Montserratians share and identify. Calypso is highly egalitarian in the sense that any person – of any age, colour, gender or level of literacy – can enter the eliminations with a song written by themselves or someone else. Calypso is traditional in the sense that it has a history which most will be intimately aware of, a history created by friends and colleagues who chronicle the social history of the island. And calypso is also contemporary in the sense that each performance "lyricalises" the present social and political concerns. Finally, along with Festival, calypso is "bacchanal", a period of confusion, disorder and scandal when the facade of public life is collapsed by the sexual earthiness and realism of calypso commentaries (Miller 1994: 245–255).

CALYPSO AS EXPRESSIVE PERFORMANCE

Fergus (1994: 253–254) mentions that Carnival was proposed on Montserrat in 1958, but was postponed for four years as powerful individuals resisted the introduction of "calypso and cutlass" from cosmopolitan Trinidad to the placid Emerald Isle. According to *his* history of Montserrat, the island was already undergoing irreversible change with the success of the struggle to achieve adult suffrage in 1952, and the rise in strength of the unions who worked against the centuries-old stranglehold of the plantocracy landowners. Many of the calypsonians consider themselves to be drawn from this new "working class" on the island – taxi drivers, airport luggage handlers, Cable & Wireless employees, the Seamen's Union port workers, farmers and traders. No doubt, Fergus would argue that calypso has entered the collective memory and conscience of these islanders as phrases, tunes and songlines can be found in constant use in conversation and local interaction: Top Secret's "come better dan dat" is a well-worn put-down; "Mons'rat neaga" (Montserratian folk) from Teknikal's "A News Dem A Look"[17] is an all-inclusive reference similar to "all-a-we" (all of us), one which plays upon the slave legacy and present colonial condition.

Calypso is a performance art form which places calypsonians into the category of cultural artists and heritage brokers who highlight each year and each decade, starting – historically – with the trade union dances (with the only sound systems on the island) and the 1962 Christmas Festival Show.[18] Nearly every year, from the 1960s to the present, there have been scandals turned into calypsos, and calypsos causing scandals. The performance or presentation of the calypso – "[t]he ability of the contestant either through movement, attire, stage presence, audience communication, etc., to dramatise the theme/message of his/her calypso" – has remained a key element of the Calypso Competition, making up 15 percent of the marks in 1994–1995 and 10 percent at other times.[19] The unknown quantity, then, lies with the performance of the calypso in front of a vocal crowd of familiar faces. This also means that one of the calypsonians' fears is to have to sing a relatively unknown song to a potentially hostile audience; the Government sanction against Q-Pid's "*What's Inside de Box*"[20] could thus be viewed to have been a severe blow to his competition chances, unless he was able to capitalise upon the controversy of the ban by publicising the notoriety of the song.

The calypsonian, described by Patton (1994: 60) as "a voice for pent-up feelings, frustrations, and attitudes of the people affected by social and economic problems", produces calypsos which are social and symbolic actions. In the moment of performance, when performer is accountable to audience, the calypso articulates and symbolises the thoughts and values of the audience, and "becomes the means for defining and redefining issues of central importance to the shared cultural world of performer and audience" (Patton 1994: 55). It is whilst on the stage that the calypso's verbal performance becomes "*constitutive* of the domain of verbal art as spoken communication" (Bauman 1984: 11, author's emphasis). In the calypso contests, the audience and judges need to identify with the calypso performance (lyrics, rendition, and all). The calypso and calypsonian fail if the audience does not feel that the calypso is "speaking" to them. In 1987 and 1990 the calypsonians Mighty Trini and Denyse Plummer, respectively, were jeered and bombarded with rolls of toilet paper and orange skins by unruly crowds attending the preliminary rounds of the Trinidad Calypso Monarch Competition. Keith Warner (1993: 275) explains these reactions to calypsonians because of "the feeling that calypso is the exclusive province of the black section of the population" and the fact that Mighty Trini was from a Syrian family, and Denyse Plummer was a white woman born on Trinidad, both of them were, essentially, "venturing into what is virtually a black man's territory". In these two situations, the predominantly "black" audience did not identify with the calypsonians' ethnicity. These situations are rare; for Patton (1994: 61) – who treats public discourse as a rhetorical text – the usual "shared meaning" fails due to a breakdown in the rhetorical signature between "rhetor – text – audience".

During the Montserrat calypso competitions there do not appear to be significant instances of sexual discrimination against the female calypsonians (Calypso Bee, Rachael Collis, Singing Maro and Belonger are all well-respected calypsonians), nor is there discrimination against the ethnicity of entrants – though reigning monarch Cecil "Cepeke" Lake's unsuccessful 1992 song "*White Man's World*" was an "uncomfortable" entry by a "black" Montserratian with a "white" father from England (Peter Lake, a part-time poet and writer for *The Pan-Afrikan Liberator*). One awkward calypso performance, however, was made by Hero in the 1986–1987 calypso finals when he acted out a version of his song "*Body-to-Body*", wining – in a skin-tight costume – with a much younger woman. Hero won the competition, his sixteenth crown, but was criticised in the press for appearing "paunchy-paunchy" rather than the "sexy-sexy" which he used as a self-description in his song.[21] After an exchange in *The Montserrat Reporter*, Edgecombe explained why, in his opinion, Hero was out-performed in the finals by Hustler and Q-Pid but still managed to win the competition on aggregate: that year performance counted for only 10 points whilst "lyrics and melody combined commanded a whopping 65 points."[22] The most consternation caused by calypso on Montserrat, however, occurred at the 1988–1989 finals when the audience disagreed with the judges' decision to crown Earl "Hustler" Browne, place Drago second and Belonger third, thereby unseating Monarch Cepeke to fourth place. Bottles and stones were thrown onto the stage in anger at what many considered to be a bad decision, namely, either omitting Cepeke from the top three,[23] or misplacing first and fourth place.[24]

So far, I have broadly focused upon calypso's identity and history, and shown how calypso is a form of expression – social, sexual, political commentary, controversial and communicative, understood and received diversely by different audiences (Government, calypsonian peers, journalists, judges and local competition audience). One of the calypsonians, Teknikal, was particularly concerned about the uncertain performative aspect of being a calypsonian. Prior to the 1994–1995 heats and finals he tried to familiarise all his friends, and as many people liming on the streets as possible, with his songs, greeting everyone with one of his chorus-line phrases, checking that they would be at Festival City – the stage area with several dozen temporary bars alongside, all built for the occasion in a car park in Plymouth.

Many of the topical lines in Teknikal's work are well-understood by his audience who have recently experienced the problems outlined in his calypso presented below. Despite the indeterminacy of writing and listening to calypso, and the various diverse internalisations of the verses, for many there is a successful shared local understanding as to the meaning of Teknikal's lines. One of his calypsos for the competition, *"A News Dem A Look"*, is a commentary upon the back-biting gossip which is the preoccupation of small-island communities. Less sure than most Montserratians and belongers about the background to the calypso, I spoke with Teknikal about his reality – his impressions of Montserrat – which he was expressing. Its message, so he explained

it to me, was that the people of Montserrat are more concerned
with other people's comings-and-goings than doing their own
business: life for Montserratian folk becomes a tabloid newspaper
such as the local *Montserrat Reporter*. Verse one of *"A News Dem
A Look"* begins:

> I wonder what happen to Mons'rat neaga
> Dis woman askin' she neighbour
> Some of dem was starin' de Mons'rat Reporter
> You business is deir business, yes me sister
> But if your [Pfc?], dem a come
> You better pick it up, put it in your pocket an' try to run[25]

The chorus picks up on the addictive desire for gossip and
information about the neighbours – advice for the idle to go and
buy a newspaper and to stop wasting people's time and energy.
"It's news you're looking for". Desperate for news, the scene –
carried to the extreme – results in neighbourly visits to examine
the condition of the neighbour's house, and the condition of the
neighbour's body:

> Come in den
> Come by you house, an' dey come a visit you
> A news dem a look
> Dey want to see if you house clean or if it dirty, a true
> A news dem a look
> Watch dat one dere, wasn't she a pea
> A news dem a look
> Dey want to open you mout' see if you carry false teet'
> A news dem a look
>
> A news
> A news
> A news dem a look
> A news
> A news
> A news dem a look
> But ohhh, oh me neighbour
> Who a look news, tell dem to go an' buy newspaper[26]

The second part of the chorus is the popular calypso jingle with
a catchy ring to it. It is also Teknikal's solution to the problem
with the neighbours; all other sections in the song present a narrative story. Teknikal uses his calypso to recommend that neighbours
buy their news rather than create it. Generally, if there is no gossip
to be found, or no gossip is forthcoming from neighbours, then
it will be made-up. Characteristically, this destructive gossip often

embroils inhabitants of the street, the village, the island – from
Wapping, to Plymouth, to the House of Parliament. Verse two
goes on to describe Shirley's unfortunate fate:

> And if you no tell dem you business
> Believe it, dem tell you any means
> Them make up them own story 'pon you
> And on the Bible, swear it is true
> Five-o-dem sit down attack Shirley
> An' as one-o-dem left
> The other four turn an' talkin' 'bout she[27]

Criticism feeds upon criticism in a cycle of self-destruction:
Montserrat – where liming takes precedence – eventually comes
to a standstill.

> Dat's why dis country nat movin'
> Because it's people business we mindin'
> Long Town Patsy say Montserrat so hard
> But 'pon she phone an' send news abroad
> Mons'rat dis country take dem no care
> We beg all-o-them apply fu work wid de CIA[28]

The only job opportunity left for spying and snooping neighbours
is for them to apply for work with the CIA!

I would argue, here, that calypso is much more than public
tune, public expression, end-of-the-year phenomenon. Calypso
maintains both public and private spheres: calypso narratives
are internal and external, both inner and outer. Lines from calypsos
which capture the public's attention are internalised and surface
as personal commentaries, reappearing in Wapping, Plymouth;
in Chapter 1 in this book; or *Miguel Street*, Port of Spain (Trinidad),
in one of V.S. Naipaul's (1971: 98) novels. In this way calypso
is – and can become – mother wit, social counsellor, whereby
the lyrics internalised over the years come out at opportune
moments to guide and assist with the present situation: calypso
expression of public values is turned into calypso expression of
private situations. Pithy, apt and quotable lyrics make a song
memorable, popular and useful. Like Top Secret's line "come better
dan dat", [29] Teknikal's calypso line "a news dem a look" stood
the test of time far into the New Year of 1995. Like art, calypso
reflects life and life reflects calypso.

There are private, public, playful, parodying dimensions
associated with calypso. It is more than just a constellation of
individual calypsonians presenting their perspectives of Montserrat,

perspectives with which the audience only sometimes identify. Calypso is as much public social commentary as it is private inner commentary – for the singer as much as for the listener. My postmodern partial commentary about calypso social commentary thus continues in the next section where I consider a private calypso occasion in Wapping, where people were repeating calypso to each other, playing and parodying the songs, and generally making sense of their lives by recourse to calypso. It is not possible to get "closer" to the private situation than by recourse to a personal, private, heterogeneity of events shared between several people. This is, however, "closer" to the internal thoughts and feelings people have than the public interview with Top Secret at the beginning of this chapter. Thus, here, I go on to present some scenes from an evening of calypso and "rum & coke" at Doc's on 3 December, the day after Teknikal and his song, "A News Dem A Look", passed through to the calypso semi-finals. All the contributors to the evening, bar myself, are Government-employed firemen, a close hard working group. The sections, with interspersed comments, are my impressions of the evening which do not privilege my "original" tape recording.

CALYPSO AS IMPROMPTU PERFORMANCE

CHARACTERS

DOCTOR – senior fireman and poet in his thirties, known also as 'Doc'
TEKNIKAL – fireman, calypsonian in his thirties
DJ – fireman in his late twenties
FAB – fireman and occasional tour guide
ANGEL – fireman in his early twenties
JONO – anthropologist from Scotland in his mid-twenties, Doc's neighbour

The following dialogue is at pace, an interspersed dub sung whilst one of Teknikal's instrumental calypso tapes plays in the background. Speech follows the speaker's colon: the "left column" – (DOC: OK, a'right). Improvised dub calypso – social commentary made up on the spot and set to the calypso beat on the dub side of the tape – appears in the middle column which begins with a hyphen (-Music, music, music). The calypso lyrics sung to the music are found in the right hand column which begins with a pointer (>A news dem a look). The chorus refers to both the calypso chorus and when all the characters make noise together. Below is an example of Doc talking to the group, followed by Teknikal singing his calypso song, and Angel with some improvised dub calypso.

DOC: OK, a'right, let's sing dis song

TEKNIKAL: >A news dem a look

                >ba-ba-ba-bam-ba-day-do-da-day-do-die-day-die

ANGEL: -heeiiiiiiii

        -Music, music, music

One night after the island calypso eliminations. Six men sitting in a circle with three bottles of Mount Gay rum, and calypso tunes in the background. Singing along to Teknikal's instrumental calypso tape, they have been trying to make as much noise as possible all evening – a traffic jam is forming outside as people stop their cars to listen to familiar calypso lyrics.

Doc – broad, bald and very muscular – is swaying his head to the music, sitting cross-legged on the floor to the right of Jono, like Marlon Brando in Apocalypse Now. *The only whiteman, JONO, is fiddling with his tape recorder. Angel is in front of Jono on a couch: the youngest fireman, he is wearing a Chicago Bulls singlet and has just had an angel sign shaved into his hair. Fab is sitting quietly on Angel's left. He's next to the door. On the other side of the door DJ is slumped on another couch. Teknikal is on his left leaning forward close to Doc. He has his trademark red felt cap on. There has been a lull in the evening's activities as the dub side of Teknikal's calypso tape rewinds to the beginning again.*

SCENE I – CALYPSO IN THE DEN

DOC: (*addressing everyone*) Yes

ANGEL: (*quoting a Road March lyric in reply*) Oh Lord

DJ: Yes, yes

DOC: Let's sing dis song

FAB: (*languidly*) Yes

DOC: By de –

(*Doc takes a mouthful of rum & coke and is interrupted by Teknikal singing, shouting and then screaming to the rhythm of his calypso song which is about to be played again*)

TEKNIKAL: -Music, music, music

DOC: Let's, hello, hello

TEKNIKAL: -Music, music, music, music

DJ: (*joining Doc against Teknikal*) A'right, a'right

DOC: Hello, hello

TEKNIKAL: -Music, music

(*Angel and Jono watch Teknikal ignoring Doc and Fab. DJ takes up Teknikal's rhythm*)

DJ: -A'right, a'right

DOC: OK, OK

TEKNIKAL: -Music

DOC: OK, OK

(*Teknikal looks like he's finished his outburst, DJ continues, Angel appears to be about to join in*)

FAB: Sssshhh, sssshhhhh, sssssshhhh

DJ: -Music, music, music

TEKNIKAL: A'right

FAB: (*calming DJ*) OK, OK

DOC: (*growing angry*) DJ, Angel, shu-shu-shu-shut-shut-shut you flap

DJ: -Where's de music?

TEKNIKAL: -Music - music - music

DJ: Arrrrgggghhhh

TEKNIKAL: Where's de fuckin' music?

DOC: DJ, DJ, DJ, shut you churc—you turret

TEKNIKAL: -Music

(*Angel joins DJ and Teknikal with guttural ragga lines to the imagined beat of* 'A News Dem A Look')

ANGEL: -You ask for it, you get it

DJ: -Music, music

ANGEL: -You ask for it, you get it

DJ: -Music, music, music

ANGEL: -You ask for it, you get it

                        -You ask for it, you get it

TEKNIKAL: -Definit-el-y

DJ: -Music

ANGEL: -Wet me down den, wet me down (*changing to another calypso*)

TEKNIKAL: Come again

ANGEL: Me warm

DJ: (*to the calypso beat*) -Huhuhuh

ANGEL: Me warm now

FAB: Well warm

DOC: (*deferring*) Angel you sound good y'know

ANGEL: Me rub up

TEKNIKAL: (*agitating Doc*) Yeahesssssss

ANGEL: Me rub right up

DOC: But de song sound bad wid dat

TEKNIKAL: -Re-remix, re-remix, re-remix

The fire-fighters and the anthropologist have already belted out "*A News Dem A Look*" several times. Everyone is thoroughly familiar with the song and can take Teknikal's place as the lead singer. It is Teknikal's song, however, so he leads most of the singing. The dub side of Teknikal's calypso tape is rewinding on Doc's stereo, Doc trying – but failing – to control the evening. The evening is loud and local, a deliberate attempt to arouse the interests of meddlesome neighbours. It is part celebration of Teknikal's success last night in the public calypso eliminations, and part private gathering of friends. It is a success in that the singing had enticed the anthropologist to join in, and later it attracted the attentions of bar staff at The Green Flash, and the Chef at The Emerald Cafe.

Though the Chef and bar staff are friends with Doc, the firefighters and Jono, the singers in Doc's house have created their own privately shared *communitas*. All six in the room sing and participate in the calypsos; those entering the room can only spectate. Fortunately for Doc, Vicki and Lou-Ann cannot complain about the commotion. They are away in America visiting relatives. Pippa, however, is at her window further down Wapping, listening to the noise coming from The Flash and looking at the disturbance at Doc's. Passing her house is Saltfish tapping away complex rhythms on the walls of the buildings he passes with his drumsticks: another calypsonian – Saltfish is his nickname derived from his favourite food – Archibald "Lord Alfredo" Mills has been singing calypso since 1972. Alfredo is a simple man: a part-time construction worker who helps unload ships when they arrive, and plays in a steel band for tourists on Wednesday nights. His *"Socialism Jam"* won the 1980 Road March Competition and is now marketed as *"Push To The Rear"* in a tourist souvenir cassette, *Emeral City Festival Volume 1.*[30] The tourists are unaware – as were many of the locals, at first – that the song's catchy chorus:

> Ah say a jam to the left
> Wail to the right
> A make a wine to the centre
> Push back to the rear[31]

evoke poignant memories of his rapist's instructions to him (move to the left, to the right, wine and push back). Such local contextual knowledge forces a response from the listener who is at first unaware of the personal dimension, the painful significance, of the dance lyrics. I can think of no stronger case for the argument that calypso is explicit commentary, personal expression as well as public performance; and that calypso can be interpreted variously and partially.

Once the tape has rewound and the dub side is in play again, the spontaneous dub calypso singing restarts.

SCENE II – *DUBBIN' IN DE DEN*

TEKNIKAL:　　　>A news dem a look

　　　　　　　　>ba-ba-ba-bam-ba-day-do-da-day-do-die-day-die

JONO: (*joining in*) -heeeiiiiiiiiii

(*Fab slaps his thighs to the beat*)

ANGEL:　　　　-hound de ray die slip me be be

DJ: Oh Lord, warm

Chorus:　　　　>A news dem a look

　　　　　　　　>But ohhhhhhhh

　　　　　　　　>Ohhh me neighbour

　　　　　　　　>Who a look news

　　　　　　　　>Tell em to go an' buy newspaper

TEKNIKAL: >Here dis

                   >I wonder what happen to Mons'rat neaga

(ANGEL spills his rum & coke on the carpet whilst Teknikal continues singing the entire song)

ANGEL: Sorry 'bout dat

DOC: Yeah mon no problem

TEKNIKAL: >... Dis woman asking de neighbour

ANGEL: Me don't see 'bout dat

TEKNIKAL: >... *Mons'rat Reporter*

DOC: Wotcha

ANGEL: See 'bout dat rum & coke

DOC: Yeah

ANGEL: Sorry sorry

TEKNIKAL: >... me sister

DJ: (*to Doc and Jono*) Wha' 'bout dis place getting crazy doin' dis

ANGEL: (*hysterical*) hahahahhahah

TEKNIKAL: >... system a come

                   >He na want um

                   >He said you pick it up

                   >And put it in your pocket ⅃nd try to run

(Fab starts clapping, Jono pours some rum, Teknikal loses place in his calypso song and Angel takes over - improvising about those in the room, backed up by DJ)

DJ: (*pointing to Jono, addressing everyone*) He a want um

ANGEL: >A news dem a look

DJ: -But wotcha

ANGEL: -But watch DJ isn't he a pea

                   >A news dem a look

                   -Dey want to look down your clothes

                   -To see what boots you got in ... a puss

DJ: -But wotcha

Chorus: -Aaaheeyyy

Chorus: >A news

                   >A news

                   >A news dem a look

>A news

>A news

>A news dem a look

Chorus: -Ahhhhhhhh

Chorus: >But ohh

>Oh me neighbour

>Who a look news

>Tell dem to go an' buy a newspaper

>Watch me now

ANGEL: -ooooouuuuu

DJ: Doc

ANGEL: -Me tie de guttie and be bestest in a world

-Me tie de guttie and be bestest in de hi hi

-Me tie de guttie and be bestest in a world

-He say a look news

-Me tie de guttie and be bestest —

DJ: - — News

ANGEL: -But me gat a tiny girl, she a look news too

-Me gat American, she a look news too

-Me kinda gat a neaga, he a look news too

-Jonathan matters, he a look news too

-Dey want to feed your belly, who a look news too

-Dey want to know what time to a go poo poo

Chorus: -Oohhh-ooohoohhh-aaaiiiiiii

ANGEL: >A news dem a look

FAB: Stars

Chorus: >But ooh

>Oh me neighbour

>Who a look news

>Tell dem to go an' buy newspaper

(Doc claps Angel, everyone slumps back laughing hard, Angel wants Jono to take over for the next verse)

Chorus: -Aahahahahaha

ANGEL: -Go Jono

(Jono gets ready, DJ breaks Angel's rhythm)

DJ:	-Heh
ANGEL:	-Go Jono
DJ:	-Heh
ANGEL:	-Go Jono
DJ:	-Heh

In this spontaneous dub calypso scene, the ludic, playful and disorderly nature of calypso is made manifest. In-between chorus-lines which everyone sings, and Teknikal's lead singing of his calypso, the others hold conversations and join in with their own versions of the lyrics – screaming, tapping the floor and thighs, clapping and making other noises to the dub rhythm of "*A News Dem A Look*". Angel, in particular, *ad libs* his own lines about the people in the room. He plays with his "neighbours" in the room, letting DJ into his version with key words and phrases. There is even a joke about neighbours meddling in the midden, trying to find out what time they "poo poo" (release their bowels). In this instance, Angel lyricalises the present, using the calypso medium which acts as a fragment of national culture on each Caribbean island, appropriating the calypsonian heritage broker's expressive and evocative tools.

Angel, with his guttural rendition of a muted commentary, and his friendly interjections with DJ, plays a significant part in this private calypso performance. A release valve in public, calypso can also be a release valve in private. Given more time, Angel may have worked and played with some more of the firefighters' collective knowledge, their work jokes, island memories, and sexual slogans (*"We find t'ings hot an' we leave dem wet"*). Unlike Teknikal and Doc, who grew up in neighbouring villages on Montserrat, Angel came to Montserrat from Dominica when he was very young. Perhaps this affects his dub calypso, forcing him to use only his impressions of Montserrat gleaned from his time as a firefighter? Not to be curtailed or misunderstood in his contribution to the evening's private calypso performance, Angel resorts to imitating a well-known rasping gangsta-rap delivery, whilst the others take over his well-timed rival calypso interjections. Jono is included in the proceedings, though no one is really quite sure of how much he really understands and follows, and how well he will perform.

Scene III – CALYPSO FINALE

DOC: (*Doc speaks into the tape recorder, quoting from the rival calypso before waving it around*) Oh Lord

ANGEL: (*speaking to the tape recorder, pointing at himself*) Dis is Angel

DOC: Wha' you have fu decide, after dis song, after dis song, after dis song

TEKNIKAL: -Le' we go Tyrone, le' we go Tyrone, le' we go Tyrone, le' we go Tyrone, le' we go Tyrone

DOC: (*to Teknikal, annoyed with disruptions*) Eh

TEKNIKAL: -Le' we go Tyrone, le' we go Tyrone

DOC: Eh, wha' de fuck, me got fu have a' interview wid Angel

DJ: Wooaaah

ANGEL: -Angel an' Teknikal

TEKNIKAL: -Le' de song play, le' de song play

ANGEL: (*to Doc, wanting Jono to sing solo*) Jonathan

TEKNIKAL: -Le' de song play

DJ: -Rubber

TEKNIKAL: (*joking with Jono*) When, when your girl come here she gonna enjoy herself

Chorus: (*laughter and shrieks as the same music starts up again*) - OOOOOOOOO AAAAAAAA HHHHHHHHHH WWWW WWOOOO

TEKNIKAL: -AAARRRIIBBBBBAAAA

ANGEL: -Yeeeeaaaahhh, pump it up, pump it up, pump it up, pump it up, pump it up, pump it up

DJ: -Pump it up

(*Fab starts tapping the beat on the couch. All the firemen note Jono at last joining in with all the words; the rhythmic repartee echoes the calypso beat*)

ANGEL: -'E a want um, 'e get um

JONO: (*to Angel with mock innocence*) Excuse me

ANGEL: (*to the others in the group*) Excuse mind me now

JONO: (*to the group, replying to Angel*) -News

DOC: Yea right, a news dem a look

TEKNIKAL: For real?

DOC: (*offering rum to Jono*) Yeah, you na want um?

(*Angel and Teknikal play to the others with their exchange*)

TEKNIKAL: -Indeed

ANGEL: -Induce

TEKNIKAL: >A news dem a look

DJ: (*shouting into the tape recorder back in the middle of the room*) Doc

TEKNIKAL: (*to Angel about Jono*) Boy, 'e rub right up

ANGEL: 'E warm

TEKNIKAL: Jonathan warm, aarrgghh

FAB: Jonathan warm, boy

DJ: (*shouting into the tape recorder again*) Boy

(*Doc takes the tape recorder to use just by himself*)

FAB: Wassie Jono

TEKNIKAL: A'right, Jonathan

DOC: (*Doc paces the room lecturing bibacious wisdom into the tape recorder*) Respect, respect, respect, you know what I mean

JONO: A'right

DOC: Pure respect, dat's wat Jah say, you know what I mean, yeah mon, Doctor Doc Productions, ... le' we go de song right ...

Finally, the dub calypso party disintegrates. My tape recorder in the centre of the room becomes the centre of attention. Imitating the inquisitive anthropologist, Doc tries to interview Angel, but Angel and Teknikal are more interested in hearing my version of '*A News Dem A Look*'. Here, they too are involved in the topic of the song: at the end of the evening they act out the role of the neighbours in the song, and they make me the subject of their speculation and gossip. Angel and Teknikal still rebound phrases off each other, invoking the form of the calypso, and the licence to engage in sexual innuendo (*"pump it up, pump it up, pump it up"*; *"E a want um, 'e get um"*). The teasing wordplay continues after the calypso with these rejoinders, all framed within the context of the phrase 'a news dem a look'. By the end of the evening, we are all illustrating the content of the calypso in our conversations – juxtaposing private chit-chat in-between the lines of the public calypso which essentially reviles and criticises such private gossip-mongering.

As a postscript, at the end of the 1994–1995 Calypso Competition, the Crown went to Roland "Kenzie" Johnson despite a successful final performance of "*A News Dem A Look*" by Teknikal. At the calypso finals, Teknikal sang his calypsos wearing his red felt cap and dressed in a sparkling gold jacket. He waved a rolled-up copy of a Montserrat newspaper from his fist and, because everyone already knew and understood the chorus, the crowds sang along with him. No doubt, if the calypso commentator David Edgecombe had been on Montserrat during the competition, he would have reiterated his comments from a few years back when he paraphrased Arrow's winning chorus-line in *The Reporter*:

Calypso a ah we culture
[w]e'll be proud o' um forever.[32]

NOTES

1. 'Tropical Gal" (Top Secret 1994: l.1–8).
2. 'Tropical Gal" (Top Secret 1994: l.25–36, chorus).
3. 'Don't Rock The Boat Dada" (Top Secret 1994: l.5–8, 9–10, chorus).
4. 'Jean and Dinah" (Sparrow 1992[a]: l.30–31).
5. Staff Reporter, *Montserrat Times*, 23 December 1987, no other references available.
6. See Edgecombe, *Montserrat Reporter*, 23 October 1987: 4; Edgecombe, *Montserrat Reporter*, 18 December 1987: 1; Edgecombe, *Montserrat Reporter*, 18 December 1987: 4).
7. Edgecombe & Burns, *Montserrat Reporter*, 13 January 1989: 6.
8. 'Bring Dem Back" (Belonger 1988: l.48–55).
9. 'Montserrat English", winning song for Calypso King The Mighty Arrow 1974–75. See 'Ole Time Calypso Medley" (Arrow 1994; see also Edgecombe, *Montserrat Mirror*, 10 January 1975: 2).
10. G.S.C., *Montserrat Mirror*, 29 April 1967: 1, continued on 4, *sic*). A patois is 'the dialect of the common people in a region, differing fundamentally from the literary language" (Thompson 1995: 1001).
11. This non-standard transcription was given to me by Arrow. An older version of this medley contains a verse beginning 'English grammar you cyan' neglect / But hold on to we dialect" (Dewar 1977: 78).
12. Arrow 1994: l.13–22, first chorus.
13. Presumably this is to coincide with 1st August Caribbean Emancipation Celebrations (Nevis Culturama Committee 1994: 55).
14. Lewis, *Montserrat Reporter*, 2 December 1994: back cover.
15. 'Wet me down" (Spoiler 1994: no other references available).
16. Hanley, *Sunday Cape Cod Times*, 5 August 1984: 48.
17. 'A New Dem A Look" (Teknikal 1994).
18. Flasher undated; see also Dewar 1977: 75–80. In a more lengthy account, the following calypsonians and calypsos would be covered: 'Determination" (Collis 1992); 'Save This Country" (The Patriot 1982); 'Montserrat is for Montserratians" (Rockamaya 1993); 'Lift This Nation" (Cutter 1994); 'Iraq's Invasion" (Accident 1990).
19. 'Calypso Workshop – Criteria for Judging", undated, anonymous handout from the Division of Culture (Anon. [b]: no other references available).
20. 'What's Inside de Box" (Q-Pid 1987).

21. Edgecombe, *Montserrat Reporter*, 16 January 1987: no other references available.
22. Edgecombe, *Montserrat Reporter*, 30 January 1987: no other references available; see also Anon., *Montserrat Reporter*, 23 January 1987: 4, no other references available.
23. Edgecombe & Burns, *Montserrat Reporter*, 13 January 1989: 6.
24. Galloway, *Montserrat Reporter*, 13 January 1989: 5.
25. "A News Dem A Look" (Teknikal 1994: l.1−6, first verse), unknown reference in the penultimate line.
26. "A News Dem A Look" (Teknikal 1994: chorus, no other references available).
27. "A News Dem A Look" (Teknikal 1994: chorus, no other references available).
28. "A News Dem A Look" (Teknikal 1994: chorus, no other references available).
29. "Tropical Gal" (Top Secret 1994: l.35).
30. "Push to the Rear" (Lord Alfredo 1980) in *Emeral City Festival Volume 1* compilation of festival hit songs arranged by Eddie Duberry (no other references available). The title deliberately omits the "d" in Emerald.
31. "Push to the Rear" (Lord Alfredo 1980: chorus, no other references available).
32. Edgecombe, *Montserrat Mirror*, 10 January 1975: 2.

Business as Usual for the Tourism Industry

The Montserrat Tourist Board wants to ensure that potential investors and visitors to Montserrat know that it's business as usual once again. Tourism Director Leona Midgette says they've now embarked on an extensive information distribution campaign to its representatives in the United States, United Kingdom, Canada and Europe. She says they'll also be targeting the international and regional media, cruise lines, international travel publications and magazines.

The information package includes updated information on the island's tourism industry, in light of the volcanic activity and then two recent hurricanes. She also notes that they want to emphasise that the disasters did not significantly cripple the island's tourism infrastructure.

She says tourist operators here have confirmed that they'll be offering complete services to visitors including sight seeing attractions. Mrs. Midgette acknowledges that they're now seizing the opportunity to give a big boost to the tourism sector, now that most of the mainland tourist attraction islands have been ravaged by the hurricanes.

(Anon., *The Montserrat Reporter*, 22 September 1995: 2, no other references available)

"BLACK BUT NOT IRISH":

CHEDMOND BROWNE'S TEACHING THE PAST,

PROTESTING THE PRESENT, ALTERING THE FUTURE

The purpose of this chapter is to add some more diverse and debated impressions to the few individual and inter-subjective impressions of Montserrat which I have chosen to articulate in previous chapters. From an individual's poetic set of impressions in Chapter 2, I went on to show how realities can converge into constellations in Chapter 3 – expats versus locals on the topic of development work on Montserrat. I then returned to the individual's creative impressions of Montserrat in Chapter 4 where I considered the work of the calypsonians on Montserrat. In this chapter I consider one Montserratian man's particular reality, namely, the reality of Chedmond Browne, a West Indian, a Vietnam veteran, a Pan-Africanist, a politician and General Secretary of the Montserrat Seamen and Waterfront Workers' Union (MSWWU). Like Pippa, Mr. Cork and Mary – whom we heard from in Chapter 3 – Cheddy is firmly opposed to an increasing dependence of the island upon British aid and British and North American tourism. Cheddy's impressions of Montserrat are similar to those of Sir Fergus, but he also has his own extreme position that I believe it is very important to articulate. Cheddy's own particular stance calls for an aggressive Pan-Africanism on Montserrat, one underpinned by an education in independence. As such, the ideas and themes contained in this chapter converge and diverge with previous chapters. The chapter begins by linking with Chapter 1 where I introduced Cheddy. Its content links with Chapter 2 where historian, poet commentator and social agitator Sir Fergus advocated education on Montserrat as a crucial developmental platform for equality and independence, topics which also featured in Chapter 3. Cheddy's local and impressionistic "historical" reality contrasts so markedly with other histories that it shows the relativity of historical trajectories, but also the significance of ideological convictions which shape such trajectories.

In the last chapter I presented examples of calypsonians singing social commentaries, evoking their Montserrat, expressing themselves. Only the most risqué of calypsos were censored from the public with the refusal of radio airplay. This, I mentioned, happened to Q-pid with his calypso "What's In De Box?". Unlike the poets of the Writers' Maroon, or the calypsonians, Cheddy does not seek to express his impressions of Montserrat, or to evoke support for his ideas by singing songs, writing poetry or attending dinner parties. He does not enjoy such poetic and calypso licence. Cheddy has been banned from the radio by the island's Executive Council which is led by His Excellency The Governor, and is prevented from teaching history in all of Montserrat's schools. Cheddy is forced into preaching his "independence for Montserrat" protest on the streets: an ostracised intellectual, he mobilises support through the sale of his newsletter *The Pan-Afrikan Liberator*, a newsletter which he created and edits with the deliberately provocative spelling of "Afrika", and an equally provocative re-writing of "Britain" which rejects her capitalised status.

Here, I offer a detailed account of the life and work of a man who is harassed by the British for proposing an alternative future, for protesting the present colonial condition and for teaching a blackened history of the island's colonial past. In articulating Cheddy's realities, I incorporate interview material and quotations from his newsletter. Though Cheddy roots his "extremist" arguments and opinions in a history of Africa, the West Indies and Montserrat which he has read about and experienced, I insist upon treating them as but "one" set of impressions of Montserrat which he espouses; but "one" native reality, one which I hope to show is also at odds with many other native realities and ideologies. I begin with a personal narrative of my meeting with Chedmond Browne. This initial meeting gradually develops into an account of his beliefs and realities which he outlined, for me, at great length and with great conviction. Then, the chapter goes on to consider some conflicts which arose from holding such ideologies – in the politics of the island, on the island radio and in the island port. I have made use of tape transcripts in this chapter, along with newspaper snippets, because Cheddy was always very precise, consistent and repetitive in his choice of words, and because Cheddy was just as articulate with or without the tape recorder in front of him. With my use of transcripts in this chapter, however, I do not assume that I have captured "the" reality – a better, truer or more authentic version – of the conversations; this is simply another way of representing impressions of Montserrat. The words are but verbal notes from our meaningful meetings and need a great deal of context and interpretation to them.

MEETING THE TASK MASTER

My daily tour of the town sometimes saw Cheddy at the Evergreen Roundabout in Plymouth, talking to men sitting with their backs against Miss Josie's bar, Heinekens lying at their feet in similar disarray. Once, he was forcibly ejected from the bar and the police were called to what was considered to have been an affray. On a small island, the police station is always just down the road, and people with such personalities and public profiles as Cheddy are always easily recognised and easily detained. His workmates had hurried him out of the bar after two American tourists had attacked him. He'd joined their conversation about Columbus's discovery and naming of Montserrat: Columbus had sailed past the island and thought it reminded him of a monastery he had once known in Spain and, well, the Spanish were paying his bills. And so the island was named.

The Americans had not appreciated Cheddy's historical commentary that had begun with the Amerindian landing long before any European Renaissance. They didn't like his comments or his disrespectful, offhand way of speaking to them. The Americans were on holiday, and this wasn't a part of their pre-paid package at the Vue Pointe Hotel. Who was this man who was telling them about Alliouagana – Amerindian land of the prickly bush (see Fergus 1992: 6)? The Royal Montserrat Police sent him home for disturbance of the tourists' peace, one of the worst crimes imaginable on an Eastern Caribbean British Dependent Territory dependent upon the predilections of one-time visitors.

One afternoon, I saw Cheddy was in the Memorial Square, downtown sleepy Plymouth. He was still carrying his rolled wad of newsletters, and he was animatedly slapping them into his other hand; one workman's boot was up on the memorial balustrade, as though he were cutting off his colleagues' escape route. This time his audience shared his views, many of which he articulated for them. They were fellow port workers, old men without pensions, Seafront Union members who relied upon Chedmond Browne's leadership to retain an income at the port. Without him, they would have no income: without him, there would be nobody to represent them; nobody to make sense of all the letters they were receiving from the Government and Port Authority.

I wanted to make contact with him, this intriguing figure in local politics; a man who lectured in workboots and a shirt hanging around his bare torso; a light-skinned black man of mixed African–European descent; a man with a long, grey and wispy beard that shook with every angry gesture or comment he made. There was a lull in the conversation during which I moved through the circle of black figures surrounding Mr. Browne.

"... jackasses. We na waan alla dis crap ya," finished Cheddy when he saw me in front of him. In retrospect I was sold a copy of his newsletter by surprise rather than by reason. He later told me that he never sold to expatriates or white people. There was just no point.

I left him to his heated exchanges for a few months. All I did each time I saw him about Plymouth – accosting limers and arguing – was to buy his $2.00 newsletters for myself and my landlady. I knew that Cheddy knew and admired my landlady, Pippa, and that they sometimes exchanged phone calls and support for each other. He respected Pippa for the way that she had battled her employers in the civil service. She must have mentioned me and my work on the island and how, despite my colour, I had a sympathetic ear to local causes. The fourth time that I bought his newsletter, he accepted my request to talk to him. All other times he'd looked through me and my greetings.

"Could I get two copies please ... Er, Mr. Browne, I'm looking at the literature on the island, and, and I wondered, um, if I could talk to you about it – sometime?"

"A'right, anytime. Everybody knows where I live."

And for him I wasn't there anymore.

This was the first recognition and acceptance I'd had from him. It was hardly a confirmed meeting, and I'd have to find out from Pippa where he lived. I followed up his invitation the next evening. I found that he lived in a long, low concrete bungalow with open glass-slats. The house was guarded by dogs and was surrounded by long grass which was continually cropped by goats. He was out.

Two evenings later I saw Cheddy through the slats. I called. "Yo, who's dere?" he replied. I lifted the rusty levers on the gate and brushed past a goat, two inquisitive dogs and a cat feeding her kittens on the porch – a ground-floor balcony which served as the entrance. I passed through the back door into the kitchen. The main room was a dining room-study-lounge which led off into several smaller bedrooms. Cheddy was sitting wearing just shorts, reminding me of images of Gandhi. He was setting up a computer board for a game of chess:

"Do you play? I haven't been able to teach anyone on the island."

We play three games on the dinner table. The window slats are open for ventilation and moths dart between us, kittens play with my out-of-place socks, and we have to brush a colony of ants from the table – they've become dependent upon the food scraps occasionally spilled on the table. The television stays on and my eyes flicker from the board game to a Benny Hill Show on satellite. Behind Cheddy are pictures of his family and a poster of Christ in his "true" black colour with the messages – "I am black and comely [...] look not upon me because I am black [...]"; "Christ has hair like pure wool"; "his feet were like fine brass burnt in a furnace". Opposite, behind me, is a bookshelf stuffed full of black histories and biographies of Marcus Garvey, Martin Luther King and Malcolm X. All of the works had to have been imported onto the island at great cost, and a few are in plastic wrappers to protect them from the humidity, cockroaches and woodslaves which can also live off them. Beneath some books about Black Athena, African Civilisation, Muslim philosophies and Islamic dietary manuals, are rows of science fiction books ranging from early Isaac Asimov to late Robert Heinlein and Arthur C. Clarke. All of the books are well-thumbed, worn and yellowed copies.

Cheddy recognises a retiring mind and we put away the board. "I try to play at least six or more games each night. It trains the mind. It increases my concentration, you know."

"So, how are the Montserrat newsletter, er, I mean, newspaper sales going?" I inquire, nervously correcting myself and taking the opportunity to look around the room again.

"I caan be seen talking wid you out on the streets. That's why I ignore you. It's nothing personal, it's white people. I can't let people see me with them. So that's it, OK. You understand.

"Er, I, I think so. So why see me now?"

"I would have done the same as you. You know, try a different approach, keep buying the newsletter and asking. I like that. That's sincerity. Dere's no point selling the edition to alla the white people on the island, not that they'd buy it or anything like that, or, or come up to me and ask for a copy, no." All this is said with a bitterness directed not at me, but at those with the colour of my skin. I feel even more colour conscious then usual. I'm a white token again.

The TV turns to basketball, and Cheddy churns out his doctrines and orders two of his children to bed. He does this as his wife comes in and chastises him for letting them stay up late, and me for not leaving my shoes at the back door. Her son is as black as she is, but her daughter is light-skinned, taking after Cheddy. This observation becomes relevant to Cheddy's doctrines which he reiterates with each visit at the end of our chess games. In my formal interview with Cheddy at the end of my stay on Montserrat, he tells me that he is deliberately attempting to change the colour of his family and his descendants, to blacken them with a strong African gene pool, thus reversing the trend followed by his mother when she married a white man. The following is in his own words, unfiltered:

> I am reintegrating my gene pool into what I know is the original gene pool of my mother, my grandmother, a'right.
>
> *Uhuh*
>
> And to, into the gene pool of the people who accepted me as a human being.
>
> *Uhuh*
>
> A'right. This is the reality for me. I've lived in England, I know what racism is. I've lived in America, I know what racism is. The European man doesn't accept me as a human being.
>
> *Uhuh*
>
> He doesn't look at me as a person. African peoples accept me as a human being, but beyond that part of my genetigene pool is an African um, genetigene pool.
>
> [EDIT]
>
> The, the reason that I am the way I am is because my mother perceived that power lay in this direction. So my mother determined

that it would have been better for me to exist in this society having the physical features that I have. So she pursued a male or a man that would produce within, or help her produce somebody that has the physical features that I have, because she perceived that was a means of success in the society. I've grown up and I perceive it differently. I am just reversing some of the things that were put into her mentality because she made an assessment based upon the conditions under which she lived.

> *Uhuh*

I've made the same assessments and I've determined that the direction that she had set up is not the right direction, and I have no desire to continue in that direction.

> *But, I, I would have thought that was more of an unconscious –*

Well, it's not.[1]

I am reminded of psychological theories of colonisation – that historically the black woman's child had a better chance in life if it had a white father, whether legitimate or not (see Lazarus-Black 1994; Fanon 1986; Mannoni 1990).

Once, I held Cheddy to a draw at chess when he was testing my defences. This was during my second evening visit which followed a shared nod during the day as we passed each other on the streets. Each successive visit over my ten-month stay on the island followed the same format: a concealed greeting, a curt nod or upward flick of the wrist in the streets, an evening call, a chess match and discussion. If we'd had used a chess clock for the monologues I received, then the dial would average – Chedmond Browne 3 hours 47minutes : Jonathan Skinner 16 minutes.

CHEDMOND BROWNE – PAN-AFRIKAN LIBERATOR AND HIS
LIBERATION IDEOLOGY

In-between interviewing Cheddy, I researched his position on the island, read some of his black histories, built up a collection of his newsletters, and followed the events on the island with which he involved himself. In this way, I was able to elicit public reactions to his actions and reactions. Here, I would like to convey a sense of Cheddy's beliefs, his sympathies and antipathies with Fergus, and his ideology of liberation which is clearly outlined in his newsletter, *The Pan-Afrikan Liberator*. My choice of presentation and narration here is as evocative as my impressions of the man himself discussed above. After Nash (1994: back cover), I use storytelling – the use of a narrative discourse "which dominates the way we relate to each other and to the world" – to give voice to my thoughts and experiences.

In the back of the public library's reference section there are files and shelves filled with hundreds of Government pamphlets, local poetry publications, newspapers and reference copies of *The Pan-Afrikan Liberator*. Cheddy leaves copies of his newsletter in the library so that, over the years, they will develop into an educational and inspirational resource base. With a print run of several hundred, the rest of the copies are either mailed overseas or sold on the streets by Cheddy himself. Number 1 of Volume 1 dates back to August 1992. Its size is almost that of an A3 sheet folded in half to give four pages with three columns to a page. The format is to have a headline on the front page underneath several slogans and the Montserrat newsletter title (itself sandwiched between outline sketches of Montserrat and Africa). Under the title, the slogans read:

> **Agitate** until we create a stable society that benefits all our people.
> **Instigate** the nation until we remedy the injustices of society.
> **Motivate** our people to set a meaningful path for the coming generations.
> **Educate** our people to free our minds and develop an Africentric consciousness.[2]

The initial August edition was timed to appear when the nations and colonies of the West Indies were celebrating 1st August Emancipation Day – and August Monday, international holidays and commemorations of 1st August 1833 when the Emancipation Proclamation came into effect. The leading article in this edition describes how the Proclamation compensated owners for the loss of their slave property.[3] Two of the central arguments in the article are that slavery was a European invention, and that it was continually resisted by Africans, in other words, that there was no passive acceptance of slavery. For example, the article notes that "[t]he Empire of Great Britain lost two hundred thousand soldiers and over twenty million pounds in their attempt to take Hispaniola by defeating the Afrikan army". It continues by making the points that "[t]hroughout the entire region the greatest fear of the would-be master was what his slave would do to him"; and that "[o]ur ForeMothers and ForeFathers paid the price in blood for our physical freedom".[4] Browne, the presumed author of the article, then concludes with the following comment:

[o]ur Fore-Mothers and Fathers destroyed forever the shackles of physical
slavery. The task now left to us is to continue the battle to remove forever
from our minds and the minds of our children the shackles of MENTAL
SLAVERY that have us bound to our former would-be masters even tighter
than the chains that once held us.[5]

Mr. Browne is aware that his present reality is conditioned
by historical events, actions and reactions. In this way, Browne
shares a sense of history with Sir Fergus, Deputy Governor of
Montserrat. Unlike Mr. Browne – Union leader and political activist
– however, Sir Fergus is more cautious and tentative in his
proposals for individual and national independence in thought
and deed. If Fergus is the Du Bois of the island, then Cheddy is
the modern-day Garvey of Montserrat, another latter-day Moses
(cf. Cronon 1969: 4). No doubt the differences in their individual
realities, actions and convictions all stem from their different
personalities, personal experiences, skin colour, upbringing and
positions on the island. When Vincent Thompson (1969: 42–43)
accounts for the personal differences between Du Bois and Garvey
(who controlled the Pan-African Movement outside of Africa), he
may just as well have been describing the differences between
Sir Fergus and Cheddy when he wrote the following:

[t]he one was a scholar and university don, the other a mass leader,
largely self-taught; the one a retiring figure, the other a showman and
great orator; the one a diplomat in his approach to his people's problems,
the other a vociferous and daring character. [...] So far as Garvey was
concerned Du Bois was a 'traitor to the race', and 'White Man's nigger',
while to Du Bois, Garvey was 'insane'.

Both Cheddy and Sir Fergus consider themselves to be historians,
though their historical activities and regard for each other varies
immensely. Sir Fergus holds a PhD in education, teaches history
at his University Centre for Adult Education, has published a
history of Montserrat through Macmillan, and he also reads
snippets of slave history on the radio. For Cheddy, Sir Fergus holds
a PhD certificate which is the result of funding opportunities to
which he does not have access. Again, for Cheddy, Sir Fergus is
in the ideal position to campaign, lobby and agitate for
independence – which Sir Fergus also desires. Yet his quiet, slow
and diplomatic policies and advances are too slow, quiet and
diplomatic for Cheddy, and Sir Fergus's positions as Speaker and
Deputy Governor are more signs of his complicity with the *status
quo* than his advocacy against it. For Sir Fergus, Cheddy is a

dangerous voice on the island: he is an agitator, an extremist with a vision of Montserrat as a socialist, black island with an independent agricultural economy – features which will scare off the staid and conservative nationalists on the island to whom Sir Fergus is trying to appeal.

Cheddy shares with Sir Fergus the same formative colonial education that they received at Montserrat's primary and secondary schools. However, when Cheddy finished off his secondary education in Britain, he went to the United States and volunteered to fight in The Vietnam War. Fergus, in the meantime, remained on Montserrat before studying at Bristol University and then Manchester University. It was, thus, as a combat soldier and not as an academic student that Cheddy experienced first hand the competing global ideologies of capitalism, socialism and Marxism, their institutions and propaganda mechanisms. For Cheddy, capitalism became a force synonymous with a firefight with an invisible foe:

> *In, in, in what way were, were, the sort of, the American Government, confusing, what, or, propagandising*
> Well, basically, in, in, in the way they reported what was happening.
> *Uhuh*
> A'right. We, we would go, we would get into a firefight as they sometimes call it, which sometimes was a pitched battle. We would be, be totally destroyed, maybe, maybe out of sixty – seventy men out of a company, at the end of that firefight, or that battle, six or seven of us would be walking; the rest of us would either be dead or wounded.
> *Uhuh*
> We would not have seen any enemy. We would not know how we got killed or destroyed. We would not have seen one dead body. We would not have seen one person shot that was supposed to be an enemy.
> *Uhuh*
> Right. We, we went through the area. We would not have picked up anything recogn – looking like a dead human being and you would read a report a few days or weeks later, whenever you got caught up with a newspaper that reported that same particular incident and you will see little or no American casualties and hundreds of dead enemy casualties, OK.[6]

For Cheddy, a seasoned veteran of physical, mental and ideological struggles, his repeated calls for independence for Montserrat are but more calls to arms in the generations-long battle for self-determination and decolonization. These battles for the minds and the energies of the labouring forces of the world's population are fought on island land, in the Caribbean sea and in the polluted air. Geographically, Cheddy points out that Montserrat is one of two bizarre locations in the world where a radio signal can be received at any point in the globe (the Cable & Wireless mast atop Chances Peak, and a mountaintop in Peru). Ideologies have embraced technologies and have changed life on Montserrat, whether or not people subscribe to any: on Montserrat, Radio Antilles, for example, used to broadcast from Montserrat throughout the Caribbean, North America, South America, Europe and Eastern Europe – articulating political philosophies, glossing capitalism and propounding democratic virtues:

> Radio Antilles was the reason for um, bringing down the Berlin wall, for breaking up Eastern Europe, OK. Radio Antilles was a subsidiary of Deutsche Welle.
>
> *Uhuh*
>
> And Deutsche Welle subsidised Radio Antilles for 25 years and Radio Antilles broadcasted 24 hours a day on a short-wave station for 25 years in six different languages non-stop, OK.
>
> *Uhuh*
>
> The day the Berlin wall came down, Radio Deutsche Welle cut off its subsidy to Radio Antilles. Radio Antilles ceased to operate the same point in time and day that the Berlin wall came down. So the whole objective for Deutsche Welle and Radio Antilles and the German Government was to propagandise Eastern Europe, to destroy the communist empire – the Russian Empire, and to reunite Germany. Major, their major priority was the reunification of Germany. Everything else was secondary. But they got all of it in one bag anyway, because a few years after the reunified Germany, the Russian Empire fell apart. And the main reason for the Russian Empire falling apart was the huge amounts of propaganda that they were able to pump into Eastern Europe, attempting to convince the Eastern European population that all they had to do was to turn over their governments from a communist government to a capitalist government, and the western hemisphere would funnel all the money in the world into their industries to help them to um, become western capitalist, um, free-enterprise systems.[7]

All that remains of Radio Antilles, according to Cheddy, is when the BBC, Voice of America and Deutsche Welle hire use of the short-wave radio station to present their world news hours – a succession of international communities presenting their linguistic, cultural, political and economic ideological perspectives. All of these organisations purvey ideological goods. They are the "means" with a neo-colonial capitalist "end" which Cheddy abhors – an ideology inherently flawed, an ideological snowball of ever-increasing destruction, in his opinion:

> Now, the United States currently boasts itself as the only superpower left in the world. That means that the United States assumes that the whole globe now is its world market, not only for economic influence, but for political control and military control, OK.
>
> *Uhuh*
>
> Which means that for it to maintain a hold on that empire, it and Europe, when it and Europe ever comes together and starts to see eye to eye, are going to have to hold politically, economically and militarily that empire together, and they're gonna have to use their resources to do that. They also gonna have to use their resources to look after their people at home. Now, the two, the two are contradictions, OK. They can't do both.
>
> *Uhuh*
>
> A'right. And this is where they goin'; this is where they are on the verge of collapse; this is where they gonna continue to collapse because they going – capitalism, by itself, demands expansion, capitalism by itself, demands military intervention and, and, and a military type of economy.
>
> *Uhuh*
>
> They have to: they have to continue to ferment wars; they have to continue to expand; and they gonna over-reach – they nat going to be able to hold onto the vast global empire that they, that they perceive. They're extremely greedy people, and the greed is gonna blind them to the other realities that are in front of them, and they are gonna collapse, they just gonna reach out too far. They nat gonna have the pillars necessary to hold it up and they gonna collapse from the inside.
>
> *And, and you say that, what will, you say that something else will*
>
> I say that a window of opportunity will open, for the oppressed peoples in the world who want to get out from under that oppression.[8]

DEPENDENCY, CONSPIRACY AND *THE PAL*

Though Sir Fergus and Cheddy both pursue an independent Montserrat, they both work differently, speak differently and have completely different backgrounds, interests and acquaintances on Montserrat. Both are involved in the education of the Montserrat populace, but in different ways: Fergus through adult education classes in Caribbean history for example, his public poetry and championing of national figures and national pride; Cheddy through the rhetoric of revolution on the streets, agitation through his newsletters and education in independence and black power his study groups at home (despite being an experienced college lecturer in history in the United States, Cheddy is not able to enter Montserrat's secondary schools). Cheddy is brash and forthright, using these personality traits to foster a viable system for civilisation, one that is humancentric and not egocentric, creative and not self-destructive in its appropriation and maintenance of the environment. Consequently, the intentions and objectives of Cheddy's newsletters are explicit and direct. They have to be in a society, a British colony, where secondary school education was traditionally only an option for the children of the merchant and planter households, and it was only after 1972 that junior secondary school education was available for those who failed the British eleven-plus exams. It is not surprising, then, that Cheddy's "Message from the Publisher" reads as follows:

> [t]he objective of this publication is to counteract the mental slavery and genocide being perpetrated on Afrikans through the creation of an Africentric mindset.
>
> By an Africentric mindset we mean a consciousness that recognises the legitimacy and validity of our interests, goals, objectives, values, history and culture and develop a world view that utilises the research of our scholars to organise our frame of reference.[9]

Cheddy is countering two activities which have been institutionalised by Europe: first, white racism, the superiority of the white race based solely on the lack of pigmentation (melanin) in the skin; and second, the invention of Greek and Roman histories and traditions at the expense of African civilisations. Cheddy counters these activities by promoting Pan-African philosophies and ideologies in his *The Pan-Afrikan Liberator*. His newsletter is a Pan-African nationalist outlet which aims to unite black people of the Diaspora and black Africa. It does so as the "Monthly Newsletter of KiMit", one of the newsletter's subtitles which refers to a Montserratian historical society named after the ancient name for Egypt. Through this KiMit outlet, Cheddy is reiterating Garvey's "Back to Africa" message. Even the bold slogans at the end of pages – "KNOWLEDGE IS POWER", "KNOW YOUR HISTORY"[10] – are part of this black-consciousness-raising-independent-self-determination-for-Montserrat voice. These intentions are vocalised in the interview:

> *So, so, it's, it's like, um, working towards a sort of nationalism?*

Well, that's what it is. That is the whole objective. That is the objective of Pan-Afrikanism. The mere fact that the papers' name is *The Pan-Afrikan Liberator*

Uhuh

means that the prime motive of it is, number one, to become your own, your, to have control of your own um, national territory.

OK.

[EDIT]

But you cannot, you cannot unite with someone until you are free to unite with that someone. So the first prerequisite for us is to get free so that we have the freedom to make the choice of who we want to attach ourselves to – if we have to attach ourselves to somebody. Or who we want to make our economic links with, or who we want to make our cultural links with, or who we want – ya understand?

Yeah

But, but we don't have that initial freedom.

And, and, and the choice of Africa is because obviously, historical

Yes, 98 percent of the population on Montserrat is of pure African ethnicity regardless of what they gonna tell you at the Tourist Department, and regardless of what they tell the Irish people.[11]

This political and ethnic position is reflected in every edition of *The Liberator* and is discussed in more detail in the next chapter. Though the newsletter has a limited print run of some 350 copies, *The Liberator* does make a calculated impact in Montserrat as well as overseas. For example, late 1994, when the National Youth Council organised a debate in the Montserrat Allied Workers' Union (MAWU) building opposite the University Centre in Plymouth – "An Independent Montserrat in the Twenty-First Century?" – involving Sir Fergus of the University Centre, amongst others, the following was reported in a local newspaper:

Speaking first, Fergus set the historical context and emphasised the conservative nature of Montserratians as far as sovereignty is concerned. Among other things, he pointed out that no island newspaper except Chedmond Browne's *Pan African Liberator* has seriously canvassed the independence cause and that in 1967 Montserrat chose colonial status instead of statehood in association with Britain, a semi-independent position, with the option of full independence later.[12]

The newsletter is recognised for its impact by influential inhabitants of Montserrat, and the newsletter is bought in secret by the British Government and sent back to the Foreign & Commonwealth Office in London where it is scrutinised and digested as a reflection of Montserratian feelings, or so Cheddy alleges. In some cases, then, the articles are written to be read by the coloniser through the sale of the newsletter to the colonised.

Cheddy is not the only writer in his newsletter. In *The Pan-Afrikan Liberator* there are contributions from a wide range of "conscious" individuals: articles by Rastafarians about Garvey and Afrika the mother of civilisation; interviews with the Governor and current affairs pieces by the calypsonian and government employee "Hero";[13] speeches by politicians on Montserrat, other West Indian British Dependent Territories and Pan-Afrikanists such as Garvey; book reviews; poems by Rastafarians such as Ras Atiba,[14] and the sympathetic British expatriate/belonger, Peter Lake.[15] There are also highly informed articles by Cheddy writing under his "Christian" name, Chedmond Browne, or under adopted "African" names such as Mwongozi Shujaa C. Browne or Cudjoe Kwame Browne. These are useful, critical and personal "voices" which Cheddy brings to the colony, not in an attempt to gain the calypsonians' impunity which they get through using their calypso names, but because African names show the colonials that there are other perspectives, cultures and ways of living. Finally, at the end of the newsletter, there is a section devoted to news of events from the African continent.

As Cheddy noted in the above interview, a free Montserrat would allow Montserratians to ally themselves with other nations of their choice, perhaps even countries in Africa. Strictly speaking, this type of African nationalism is slightly different to Garveyism. Cheddy agrees with Garvey's belief in self-determination for all peoples. Cheddy advocates a racial nationalism, a *lebensraum* for black people, to cover the continent of Africa as well as regions such as the West Indies. But, Cheddy is not seeking to repatriate his black colleagues from Montserrat to the African continent, something which Garvey attempted to do with his establishment of the fated Black Star Line in 1919. Cheddy often cites Garvey, particularly Garvey's speech when he visited Montserrat in 1936,[16] but this is as a part of his attempt to break the dependency cycle – "the beggar mentality"[17] – which Britain fosters with her political and economic stranglehold over the colony.

In "Breaking The Dependency Cycle", the main article in Number 10 of Volume 1 of *The Pan-Afrikan Liberator*, Peter White outlines the Montserratians' colonial condition. To counteract their colonised status, he calls for an independent government which is "responsible to the people and responsive to their needs and aspirations", one which is underpinned by a strong infrastructure and embedded in the 'sacred' notion of self-determination – a principle which the British have accepted as a right for all people throughout the world.18 The problem on Montserrat is that Britain's foreign policy neither encourages nor discourages self-determination. Furthermore, for self-determination and independence to be granted, a two-thirds majority of the Montserratian electorate need to vote for it. This means that there needs to be an island-wide self-confidence and pragmatic optimism for this motion to be first called and then carried. Montserratian critics, however, argue that Britain embarks upon aid projects such as building hospitals and government buildings and promoting the tourist industry, but Britain does not really assist with the educational emancipation of the Mons'rat people, and Britain does not develop a basic local industrial or economic infrastructure which can be maintained by a devolved and independent civil service.

Both White and Browne agree that Britain is not breaking Montserrat's dependency upon Britain, that Britain is not establishing "an economy with the potential for internal regeneration".[19] In fact, both White and Browne believe, along with many other Montserratians, that Britain is pursuing her own hidden agenda. With the – then – anticipated loss of Hong Kong, Britain needs, more than ever, to keep her remaining Dependent Territories to continue to use as the offshore banking arms of her Empire. Britain has already firmly established the expatriate multinational corporation Cable & Wireless on the island, and broken the local Cable & Wireless Union so that there is a cheap and plentiful labour force to maintain the sophisticated telecommunications business. So, Montserrat has become an island ripe for mercantile expansion of the virtual money variety, particularly so what with the Governor's personal control of offshore financial developments. In effect, Montserrat is set to become a haven for British money-brokering, an offshore loophole for money-laundering. According to Cheddy, this will all be at Montserratian expense:

> We are still a colony. And we're still being run and controlled as a colony, even more so now because it is more important for the British to maintain and hold onto the rest of its remaining colonies.

Why is that?

Because of what is going to happen in 1997. Because Hong Kong is going to go back to China in 1997 and Hong Kong is the most important colony for Britain right now. In its financial, in its financial offshore industry, Hong Kong plays a key hub. In that industry for Britain, Hong Kong plays a key hub period in the British financial empire in the shifting of money out of the Eastern hemisphere into Britain. When that, when that infrastructure is going to be impinged upon by Chinese, by Chinese legal laws, they cannot operate in the same manner as they used to operate when they only had to deal with a Governor. The entire, the entire financial structure of Hong Kong can only function under an atmosphere where a Governor is the sole head and control of the colony. So the whole entire financial infrastructure of Hong Kong has to be shifted, and the only place it can be shifted is to places where there are remaining colonies – and for this reason, and for no other reason, for the most overriding reason, Britain cannot afford to release any more of its colonies no matter what the Governor says, no matter what Britain pushes out diplomatically. Britain has all the intentions of holding onto those remaining colonies because it is integral to its financial Empire that it maintains them.[20]

As evinced above, Chedmond Browne's written work carries the same rhetoric as his speech whether it is an interview for tape, a conversation or a union meeting. His body of literature is, so I suggest, closer to that of Leopold Senghor, Kwame Nkrumah and Marcus Garvey than D.E.B. Du Bois or Howard Fergus. It is an articulation of oppression. His is the voice of the reluctantly colonised, and his impressionistic voice is gathering a tide set to remove the colonial footprints on Montserrat.

LIBERATION IDEOLOGY IN CONFLICT

Finally, let me end this chapter with three short ethnographic examples of conflict between Cheddy's liberation ideology and ideologies held by others on Montserrat. My intention is to show his public strategies to disseminate his reality, and to reinforce the serious nature of – and serious struggle for – alternative realities on Montserrat. Although he is an experienced union leader, Cheddy's own personal economic base has been removed with the "illegal" termination of his Montserrat Seamen and Waterfront Workers' Union by the Montserrat Port Authority in early 1995. In response to this "government/governor-sponsored" action, Mr. Browne filed suits against the Government of Montserrat on behalf of the union. The governor expected these actions and tried to immobilise Mr. Browne's campaigning; *"[t]his should put an end to his childish little rag. If they're going to behave like children, then they should be treated like children"*, to paraphrase one of the governor's uncalled for comments to me during an evening drinks party at Government House. At the same time as this conflict was taking place, Mr. Browne stage-managed a "coup" against the governor and British authorities by organising an illegal visit to the island by Marcus Garvey's disciple, fellow revolutionary to Malcolm X, Honorary Prime Minister of the Black Panther Party, Kwame Ture – previously known as Stokely Carmichael, Chairman of the All-African People's Revolutionary Party. Although banned from setting foot on British soil, and hence technically banned from visiting a British Dependent Territory such as Montserrat, Ture was able to visit and preach to Montserratians, as Garvey did before him, by claiming a social call upon his mother who lives in the north of the island. The visit to Montserrat by an eminent Pan-Africanist was well-publicised by all local newspapers including *The Pan-Afrikan Liberator*, as well as cable TV and the local radio where Cheddy and his views are banned. Interestingly, the meeting was opened by Sir Fergus and closed by Mr. Browne. At this unusual occasion, the two individuals were noticeably visible, whilst the Governor, the British representatives and all the expatriates living on Montserrat were noticeably absent. I turn, first, to this political rally before considering Cheddy's ban on the radio and the trouble at Plymouth Port.

THE POLITICAL RALLY

The rally was held at the University Centre on 23rd March 1995. The meeting was organised by Mr. Browne, opened by Sir Fergus, and attended by approximately two hundred "concerned" Montserratians. It was a public success and coup for Cheddy and his KiMit. Presumably Stokely Carmichael changed – de-Westernised – his name to Kwame Ture when he was brought up on Trinidad. It is made up from the first name of the founder of the All African People's Revolutionary Party (A-APRP), the late Prime Minister of Ghana and co-president of Guinea, Kwame Nkrumah (for whom he worked as political secretary), and a version of the last name of the deceased President of Guinea, Ahmed Sekou Toure (where Ture lives). Ture, Fergus, Abdul Weekes (calypso judge and member of the Writers' Maroon) and many others were dressed in white African clothing for the evening of political preaching. For several hours, Ture preached his views and answered questions. Throughout the next day, snippets of the talk were broadcast on the island radio station, interspersing Ture's rhetoric with "socially conscious" music. Several of the DJs had been in the audience the night before and had been swept up in the support for Ture such that they were willing to risk their jobs disseminating his message to Montserratians.

Ture's talk stressed the importance of independence, echoing Cheddy's work and liberation ideology. Ture criticised the mental, political and economic control of the Afrikan in America; the religious conspiracy that promotes the belief that Christianity is not African when, in fact, Jesus was black; the educational system on Montserrat which fosters a mental colonial dependency; and the vices of an individualistic capitalism in favour of a collective and supportive socialism. His talk concluded with the following summary of A-APRP ideology which is extracted from a special edition of *The Pan-Afrikan Liberator*:

> [t]he A-APRP is an Independent, Socialist, Mass, Revolutionary political party, working to organise the masses of African People scattered all over the world. Our objective is Pan-Africanism, the total liberation and unificatio.1 of Africa. Our ideology is Nkrumaism.
>
> Nkrumaism is an ideology which has developed through centuries of struggle by African people to free ourselves from brutal, racist oppression of our nation and class exploitation. It is scientific. It is revolutionary. The A-APRP is a small but growing party with members and supporters throughout the world – Africa, Europe, South America, The Caribbean, North America, and all places where our people have been scattered. Its members and supporters are struggling and working hard to educate and organise our people into a unified, strong, and revolutionary political force to liberate our land, Africa and our people, Africans.[21]

At the end of the evening talk, Cheddy, who had been listening from outside the converted classroom, was given a standing ovation for organising the event. And Fergus, who had been sitting in the front of the room, concluded the proceedings by plugging sales of his book about Montserrat, his history of a Caribbean colony.

THE RADIO

Though Cheddy has been banned from the radio, he was able to get "his voice" heard through Ture's public address. Both Cheddy and Ture gained a lot of support and publicity from both the radio "ban" and its indirect breach. It was the British Governor of Montserrat who, acting as Leader of the Executive Council, had cancelled Browne's weekly "Conscious Connection" radio programme until further notice in a letter to the Director of Radio Montserrat.[22] The programme was popular on Montserrat and other neighbouring islands and had needed rescheduling from Fridays to Wednesdays to meet its growing audience; its ban gave Cheddy a great deal of free publicity. The editor of *The Montserrat Reporter* describes the programme as follows:

> [t]hrough the medium of conscious reggae music interspersed with discussion, Cheddy had been exploring themes such as African History, Colonialism and the re-interpretation of Black West Indian history. Similar material is echoed in his newsletter *The Pan-Afrikan Liberator*.[23]

The purpose of "The Conscious Connection" was, in Cheddy's words, "to raise the level of the awareness of our people. We attempted to make people realise that we too have a right to determine our own destiny."[24] Though many Montserratians did not necessarily agree with Cheddy, complaints were directed at the restriction placed upon his freedom of expression rather than at the 'offensive' nature of the material he broadcast. An extract from Hilton Samuel's letter to the editor of *The Montserrat Reporter* is a good example of this:

> [t]here is a deliberate and calculating effort by a certain 'few' to stifle and stamp out from among us freedom of expression. The Executive Council appears to have started to blaze a trail of intimidation on anyone who has the guts to express his true inner feelings.[25]

These letters to the editor, the editorial and article about the cancellation of the radio programme all appeared in *The Montserrat Reporter* at the same time that Sir Fergus (1993[a]) was releasing his fifth volume of poetry, *Calabash of Gold*. Certainly, Cheddy has his detractors, but many who dislike his opinions, and his aggressive dissemination of them, still have great respect for him. Even the editor of *The Montserrat Reporter* recognises Cheddy's rights on Montserrat, rights which should not be overlooked or overruled:

> Montserrat is small enough for Mr. Browne to be viewed as an extremist and probably a bit of a crank to certain segments of the population. It is safe to say that he has some strong support and some mild support; there are those who oppose everything he represents and those who ignore him and wish he would go away.

It is safe to conclude that someone in Montserrat who has a lot of power or influence, does not like something Cheddy has said. [...] It should be pointed out that the actions like this do not go unnoticed by our neighbours. They make us look parochial, petty and COLONIAL. It's time we started having some dignity in the way we conduct our affairs.

Cheddy describes a conversation on the street with the Chief Minister's Permanent Secretary. In answer to his query, he is told that he has not been put off the air, but that the program is merely 'suspended' while the 'constitutionality' of the programme such as his and what they are permitted to say is investigated.

Utter baloney. If this is how our Government thinks and operates, we should focus on praying for a new one next week.[26]

THE PORT

My last example shows how Chedmond Browne was able to combine his Pan-African ideals and media outlets with his leadership of the Montserrat Seamen and Waterfront Workers' Union, much to the consternation of the British Government and Government of Montserrat. Cheddy was able to devote the majority of his January/February 1995 edition of *The Pan-Afrikan Liberator* to protesting against the Machiavellian destruction of his Union. Under the headline "Seamen Union Smashed With A Whimper – Continuing Saga of Britain's Agenda for Montserrat Played Out", Cheddy explains that organised labour was the only means for Montserratians to secure an independent and prosperous economy and that when the Cable & Wireless Union was destroyed, the MSWWU became the new number one target for the "Colonial Controllers".[27] He goes on to give a post-mortem record of union events from Tuesday 17 January 1995 when all 100 of his men were summarily dismissed by the Montserrat Port Authority (MPA). The next day the men marched on the chief minister at the new government headquarters, and the governor at Government House. The following day, the port manager advertised to rehire – on new non-union low wage contracts – the first 28 of the workers who came back to the port. They also ran a mass propaganda campaign on behalf of local businesses, accusing the union of forcing their demise by holding onto their old-fashioned stranglehold on moving all imported and exported goods on and off the island. Cheddy countered such ads in the same papers as well as his *PAL* – often writing in nation-language to reinforce the indigenous/foreigner divide running through the dispute –

arguing that the high duties on goods moving through the port were the result of the mismanagement of a port development loan, and that the lack of overt government support was because the chief minister had signed an illegal labour agreement with an offshore rice milling industry which guaranteed cheap handling rates.[28] Here is an example of solidarity for his cause written in nation-language by a sympathiser:

> [d]em min ha fu do something, cause when de rice business come on stream dem couldn't ease up de man from St. Vincent, and cripple a-we, if dem min a go charge he $5, and want to charge a-we $37, you see de big drop? Somet'ing really wrong, t'ink about it.[29]

During this conflict, the newspaper media, especially *The Pan-Afrikan Liberator*, became an important outlet where Cheddy could express himself and get his reality or world-view into the public domain.[30]

For Cheddy, the destruction of his union was not an individual event but part of a callous policy which began with the destruction of the Cable & Wireless Union, and will continue until there are no forms of collective labour representation left standing on Montserrat. For him, the chief minister and the governor colluded to destroy all forms of organised labour because it does not fit with their vision for Montserrat as a country where multi-national and international corporations are welcome to set up and make use of the labouring black man. To date, Cheddy's men were coerced into breaking rank, and he lost the propaganda war played out in the Montserrat newspapers: some 68 men eventually crossed the picket line, but only 28 were given new jobs at the port. Whilst this took place, Sir Fergus attended "parliamentary democracy" seminars in Botswana (convened by the Commonwealth Parliamentary Association) and in Washington (a Partners of the Americas International Fellowship Seminar).[31]

Though weakened by all the defections, Cheddy maintained the integrity of his union, supporting his men and their families who had been hounded by the government and MPA, and assisting them when their terminal benefits failed to materialise in full. Throughout his negotiations with the MPA, Cheddy faced another military man, Port Manager Roosevelt Jemmotte, who was reputed to bring a sidearm to work. Matters came to a head, again, in April when Jemmotte put four female workers in the Port Office on "forced" leave. The Montserrat Allied Workers' Union (MAWU), the umbrella union organisation on Montserrat, immediately went on the offensive, forcing the port to reinstate the women. David Brandt, Windward region representative on the Legislative Council, was so appalled at this "cannibalistic treatment" of the four workers that he spoke out, echoing some of Cheddy's usual rhetoric:

> as the children of former slaves and field workers, we should not try to progress by destroying our brothers and sisters. Progress can only be achieved if we have concern and sympathy for one another. When one person is deprived of her rights, we should all resist it and unite to fight against it.[32]

Cheddy's response, however, was more of a reaction to Brandt and MAWU's sudden action in defence of the office workers at the port – actions which had not been forthcoming for his labourers at the port. As General Secretary of the Montserrat Seamen and Waterfront Workers' Union (MSWWU), Cheddy responded to the Montserrat Trade Union Congress with the following comment, "[i]t hurts me deeply to see the response our sisters and brothers make for four workers. What has happened here is that a hundred labouring men do not add up to the same thing as four clerical workers."[33]

For Cheddy, the future is fast becoming the past. These political, ideological and port conflicts are signs that the days of slavery are still present on the island, and that history continues to repeat itself. Montserratian society, allegedly working class due to an ancestral slave descendancy, is shown to still be riddled with class, colour and ideological divisions. When an office worker feels that they are better than a dock labourer, and they obtain better treatment, then Cheddy sees this insidious class system copying an older and more horrific slave management system which once existed on the plantations. When four port staff workers are dismissed, there is more public protest, sympathy and empathy than when one hundred dockers are dismissed. Again, I cite Cheddy's own analytical words, a sociology of a present-day plantation society, to explain the situation:

> Everything of benefit to everybody in this country has come from the labouring man's sacrifice, through the Labour Union, through the activities of the Labour Union, and through the activities of the old Labour party, and the first Chief Minister of this country, W.H. Bramble.
>
> *Uhuh*
>
> But the people now, the young people, the second generation who now occupy these positions are not aware of the fact – or choose to

ignore the fact – that they occupy their, those positions based on the sacrifices of their own foreparents, recent foreparents. We're not even going back into our slave past now. We're going back as far back as their own mothers and fathers and grandmothers.

Wait. Could, could you draw, like, a bizarre parallel to a slave past where you had – the slaves working in the fields, and then you had the domestic servants, and um, you had the, sort of, the slave overseer

Uhmm

and, and, and then, sort of the expat?

Well, it's not bizarre! What you saying again is exactly correct. What, what is happened again here is this, um, we have a certain a level, a certain class of people now who have now found a niche in the society that satisfies them and that niche means to a great extent that they have to deny the true realities of who they are, and where they came from, in order to satisfy someone else and something else, so they can be – continue to be – upwardly mobile. It is a, it is not bizarre, it is a classic example of how slave societies and systems exist and how they operate. It doesn't matter what you call it now because the overall impact of the system has not changed, OK. So changing the names and the terminologies and putting on better clothes and driving in a vehicle and alla those things does not change the reality of the dynamics of the system. And it does not change the reality how, how people interact within that system. When we had slaves and we had slaves who worked in the field and slaves who worked in the houses, it was a clear definition. Well, it's the same thing now: you have labourers who still labour and you have clerks who work in better clothes.[34]

By interview, newspaper dialogue, anthropological narrative and case study of island politics, we build up an understanding of Cheddy's bleak present-day reality, one of propaganda, competing ideologies and political protest. From this commentary upon "modern" Montserrat, it is apparent that, for Cheddy, an alternative future to colonial and commercial exploitation is required, one which necessitates a popular protest base to break out of a mercantile cycle which has continued to abuse a group of Africans brought to the island as slaves in the seventeenth century, emancipated in the nineteenth century, and given the right to vote in the twentieth century. But can this be achieved by a group of "Afrikans" impressed upon by a colonial ("Afrikaner") mentality, blackened with a colonial history, isolated from mainland representative democracy, confused by ideological propaganda, and sold out by their government majority? A king cannot castle out of check. There are few options available to Cheddy with his mission to persuade other Montserratians to see Montserrat the way that he does.

In sum, as an anti-colonial historian, Cheddy is a worthy opponent of the likes of Thesiger. Furthermore, Cheddy's more circumscribed, Waugh-like prose distinguishes him from Fergus's equivocal poetry. Unlike Sir Fergus, Cheddy has made few political allies during his teaching of a blackened history of the island's colonial past, his opposition to the island's colonial present, and his writing back to Africa through the British Empire to alter the future. The organisation KiMit may be a part of the wider Pan-Afrikan Movement, but the only avenue that KiMit and Cheddy have through which to express their philosophies – which is necessary to build a popular protest base to achieve what they see as a predetermined and inevitable future – is to sell *The Pan-Afrikan Liberator* up and down the streets of Montserrat; to talk, argue and harangue: to agitate, instigate, motivate and educate the Montserratian public. *The Liberator* continues to be published and the KiMit organisation continues to clamour for independence from Britain – Chedmond Browne was the political candidate for Plymouth in the local elections during the volcano's first eruptions. As for the last labouring Union on Montserrat, the Montserrat Seamen and Waterfront Workers' Union now only exists in the courtroom.

NOTES

1. Transcript of an interview between Chedmond Browne and Jonathan Skinner (10 July 1995).
2. Slogans which appear under the title of each edition of *The Pan-Afrikan Liberator* (Monthly Newsletter of KiMit, published by Chedmond Browne, P.O. Box 197, Plymouth, Montserrat).
3. Probably by Chedmond Browne (Anon., *Pan-Afrikan Liberator*, August 1992: 1, no other references available).
4. Anon., *Pan-Afrikan Liberator*, August 1992: 3, no other references available.
5. Anon., *Pan-Afrikan Liberator*, August 1992: 3, no other references available.
6. Transcript of an interview between Chedmond Browne and Jonathan Skinner (10 July 1995).
7. Transcript of an interview between Chedmond Browne and Jonathan Skinner (10 July 1995).
8. Transcript of an interview between Chedmond Browne and Jonathan Skinner (10 July 1995).
9. Browne, *Pan-Afrikan Liberator*, August 1992: 2.
10. Anon., *Pan-Afrikan Liberator*, August 1992: 4, 2, no other references available.

11. Transcript of an interview between Chedmond Browne and Jonathan Skinner (10 July 1995).
12. Anon., *Montserrat News*, 2 December 1994: 15, no other references available.
13. Cassell, *Pan-Afrikan Liberator*, October 1993: 1–4.
14. Ras Atiba, *Pan-Afrikan Liberator*, August 1992: 4.
15. Lake, *Pan-Afrikan Liberator*, October 1992: 3.
16. Garvey, *Pan-Afrikan Liberator*, August 1993: 1–4, entire edition.
17. White, *Pan-Afrikan Liberator*, May 1993: 1.
18. White, *Pan-Afrikan Liberator*, May 1993: 1.
19. White, *Pan-Afrikan Liberator*, May 1993: 3.
20. Transcript of an interview between Chedmond Browne and Jonathan Skinner (10 July 1995).
21. Anon., *Pan-Afrikan Liberator*, April/May 1995: 8, no other references available.
22. Fenton, *Montserrat Reporter*, 22 October 1993: 14, back page; see also Anon., *Pan-Afrikan Liberator*, October 1993: 5, no other references available.
23. Anon., *Montserrat Reporter*, 29 October 1993: 4, no other references available). The show was also hosted by the Montserratian radio DJ Owen Roach who went on to sing calypso for the first time in the 1994–1995 Calypso King Competition as Owen 'Stud' Roach.
24. Fenton, *Montserrat Reporter*, 22 October 1993: 14.
25. Samuel, *Montserrat Reporter*, 5 November 1993: 6.
26. Edgecombe, *Montserrat Reporter*, 29 October 1993: 4, author's emphasis.
27. Browne, *Pan-Afrikan Liberator*, January/February 1995: 1–5.
28. See Browne, *Montserrat News*, 13 January 1995: 12–13; Browne, *Montserrat Reporter*, 13 January 1995: 7.
29. Anon., *Montserrat News*, 20 January 1995: 24, back cover, no other references available.
30. Browne, *Pan-Afrikan Liberator*, January/February 1995: 1–5.
31. Anon., *Montserrat Reporter*, 5 May 1995: 10, no other references available.
32. Anon., *Montserrat News*, Port Extra, 2 May 1995: 9, no other references available.
33. Anon., *Montserrat Reporter*, 5 May 1995: 1, headline article, no other references available.
34. Transcript of an interview between Chedmond Browne and Jonathan Skinner (10 July 1995).

Emerald Isle Taken By Storm

Montserrat makes much of its Irish heritage. But *Lucretia Stewart* found the similarities nowadays limited to insouciance when the volcano rumbles.

THE DAY before I left Montserrat, the Chief Minister, the Honourable Reuben Meade, declared a state of emergency and ordered a phased evacuation of the capital. The volcano had been acting up for months, since July 1995, and Plymouth, the island's toy-town capital, and the surrounding villages had already been evacuated more than once. When the news broke on the radio I was at the other end of the island in the far north at Carr's Bay. I had gone there to see the oldest burial ground in Montserrat – Theodore, my guide from the tourist board, used that term rather than "cemetery". No sooner had the Chief Minister finished speaking than Theodore was on the telephone to the mother of his children telling her to pack; we cut short our tour and drove back towards the capital.

A low cloud of black smoke lay over the Soufriere Hills and the roads were choked with cars and trucks taking people and possessions to the safe north. On the way into Plymouth, we passed a street preacher bellowing, "The wrath of God shall fall upon the island". Theodore dropped me at the Montserrat National Trust where you could get a T-shirt bearing the words "Now she puffs / But will she Blow / Trust In the Lord / And Pray it's No". I bought the local paper, *The Montserrat Herald*. The leader writers were having a field day:

"Fire in the mountain
Run Montserratians, run!
The brave ones shall sound the alarm
At the sound of the alarm, the faint-hearted will run
Fire in the mountain
Run! Run, Montserratians, run!"

People were already queuing in the banks and supermarkets; from the next day, everything would close down for four weeks.

The taxi driver who took me to my hotel had gone to Antigua for a month when the volcano first started acting-up three months earlier. Now he was staying put, perhaps in response to the example set by Arrow, the local calypso star, who had just released a song called "Ah Just Can't Run Away" from an album chirpily entitled "Arrow Phat".

Montserrat, one of Britain's six remaining Caribbean colonies (now known as Dependent Territories), has the distinction of being the Caribbean's only "Irish" island; the Tourist Board makes much play of the Irish connection, distributing leaflets revealing that Montserrat, the self-styled "Emerald Isle of the West", is 3,000 miles west of Ireland and lists some 73 Irish surnames to be found on the island: Fagan, Farrell, Maloney, O'Brien, O'Donoghue, Reilly, Ryan and so on. Catholicism is the main religion. "Present-day natives of Montserrat have retained many Irish customs and beliefs," continues the shamrock-festooned pamphlet. "A popular folk dance, the 'heel and toe', has been attributed to Irish customs as well as the national dish, goatwater, which is believed to be a popular Irish stew." The island's crest depicts Erin with her harp; as you come through immigration, your passport is stamped with a shamrock, and 17th March, St. Patrick's Day, is a public holiday.

There are many apparent similarities between Ireland and the Caribbean: both share a casual, anything-goes, what-the-hell attitude to life; they have in common an enthusiasm for religion and a passion for music and poetry, for debate and rhetoric, and for drinking and dancing. West Indians, like Irishmen, are big talkers and full of charm. But is there any more to Montserrat's Irishness?

In the 17th century Montserrat became a sanctuary for victims of religious persecution. Protestant intolerance in St. Kitts caused the first wave of Irish Catholic settlers and Catholics from Virginia made up the second. "Montserrat was unique among the Caribbean English colonies in having freedom of religion as a dominant motive for its establishment," wrote Dr. Howard Fergus, the island's Deputy Governor, in his *History of Montserrat*. Cromwell dispatched more Irish Catholics to Montserrat as political prisoners, following his victory at Drogheda in 1649.

Dr. Fergus is Senior Lecturer in Caribbean history and education at the University of the West Indies and the author of an essay entitled *"Montserrat 'Colony of Ireland': The Myth and the Reality"*. He was less than enthusiastic about the Irish connection when I went to see him on the island one afternoon.

"It is now used as a means of attracting tourists," he said. "We get a number of Irish people making enquiries about their roots, some from North America, some from Ireland. Montserratian leaders have gone to Ireland to cement the relationship. I am one of the few people who try to play down the Irishness of Montserrat. The Irish did not influence greatly the life and culture of Montserrat — they themselves were discriminated against. Their main legacy is Catholicism. The Irish came here seeking freedom of worship, but during the heyday of plantation life in Montserrat, most were only a few removes from slavery." And the 17th March celebration in Montserrat has nothing to do with the Irish saint; it commemorates the nine leaders of a slave rebellion executed in 1768.

I had asked if there were any Irish Montserratians for me to talk to and, somewhat to my surprise, one was found. Miss Teresa Sweeney lives out in the countryside in St. Peter's parish (where no Roman Catholic church has ever been built; if the ancestors of the people there were Irish, the landlords were Protestant). The day was overcast, presaging rain; we drove through villages with curious names: Weekes and Salem and Frith. The island was all velvety hills and valleys scattered with ruined houses of dark volcanic stone.

Miss Sweeney was a light-skinned women with "soft" hair (as opposed to African hair, which is called "hard"), but she seemed about as Irish as reggae music or rum punch. Had she perhaps answered as advertisement in *The Montserrat Herald* for an Irish person? Did she perhaps think that all light-skinned people qualified as Irish? She told me that her maternal grandparents were from Ireland, that they were white overseers. She said her mother was "like" a white woman and that her father was a "brown-skin man" from Montserrat. One uncle had been married to an Irishwoman in the United States. She tried to be helpful but knew little of her forebears. I thanked her for her time and took her photograph.

The Montserrat Tourist Board also claims that the island is "The Way The Caribbean Used To Be". This seems to have about as much basis in reality as the Irish connection, though Montserratians have a reputation for friendliness. The island, however, is pretty sophisticated. I was staying at the Isles Bay Plantation, a lavish development of houses each with a 40-ft swimming pool, overlooking a golf course. There is no shortage of luxury villas for rent or sale in Montserrat; the most torpid island in the Eastern Caribbean with a population of only 11,000, it is also remarkably free of the shanty-town appearance that characterises much of the region. There are only two hotels; most of the tourism is in villas. Rock stars such as Sting appreciate the island's tranquillity; George Martin has a house here. It is a favourite retirement spot and the streets of Plymouth are littered with elderly white men in shorts and socks. Many of them have built beautiful houses on Montserrat's emerald slopes. Other islands have cricket; Montserrat has golf.

But Montserrat's placid exterior can be deceptive; the volcano has been providing excitement for months now and the first time I went there, in 1993, I was bitten by a dog and attacked – well, accosted anyway – by a man with a machete. All in the space of two days.

The dog bite happened as I was concluding an almost certainly illegal transaction to hire a car from a friend of the hotel barman; it was Sunday and more conventional outlets were closed. The dog had been barking hysterically at the end of a chain throughout the negotiations and finally managed to bite me on the calf. I insisted on going to the hospital where a nurse glanced at my bruised and swollen leg, said that there was nothing they could do for me, but not to worry, there was no rabies on Montserrat.

The encounter with the machete-wielding maniac occurred when I went to photograph the Philatelic Bureau, whose roof had been blown off by Hurricane Hugo in 1989. Montserrat was badly hit by Hugo, which rendered more than 2,500 people homeless. No part of the island was untouched by the storm. In the harbour at Plymouth, the 180-ft quay completely disappeared.

As I aimed my camera at the decapitated building, a man waving a cutlass lurched towards me, shouting and screaming. I tried to explain that I was photographing the building, not him, but he could not or would not hear. He came so close that I could feel his spittle on my face and brandished the machete under my nose. Two school-girls walking by came to my rescue. "Leave de white woman alone, man," they said, and he went away.

Carved round the doorway at Andy's Village Place in Salem were the words *Céad Mile Fáilte*, "One Hundred Thousand Welcomes" in Gaelic. But inside was the Caribbean at its most laid-back. Andy, muttering darkly about "woman-mongering", was planning a special menu to lure people to "safe-zone Salem". Despite the government newsletter headline "Montserrat Volcano Crisis Unfolds", nobody seemed too bothered. As a friend back in Antigua put it: "That volcano bin jerkin' off for years and he ain't ever come yet."

TRAVEL NOTES

GETTING THERE: Transatlantic Wings (0171 602 4021) has flights to Antigua from Gatwick with Caledonian Airways. Prices start from £330 and go up to £540 depending on travel dates. From Antigua return flights with Liat cost $144 (£95) to St. Martin and $68 (£45) to Montserrat. Other companies that arrange holidays and flights to the area include Caribbean Gold (0181 742 8491) and Carib-tours (0171 581 3517). Harlequin Worldwide (01708 852 780) organises tailor-made luxury holidays to 59 Caribbean islands. Prices, including flights, start at £880 for a week in Montserrat or £1,200 for a week in a deluxe garden room in St. Martin. Harlequin can also arrange bookings at Isles Bay Plantation.

GETTING AROUND: Various Liat Air Passes are available through Transatlantic Wings (0171 602 4021). For $199 (£130) the Liat Explorer, valid for 21 days, offers three stopovers from a selection of 23 islands (including St. Martin and Montserrat). The pass must be purchased outside the Caribbean. Carib Express (0171 730 2214) operates a limited service between islands and also offers a Caribbean pass. The minimum of two island hops costs $98 (£65) and the maximum costs $392 (£260). All Caribbean airports have a charter company on call. Montserrat Airways (001 809 491 6494) offers sightseeing tours, day trips and shopping excursions.

MONTSERRAT HOUSES: To buy or build, contact Isles Bay Plantation (0171 482 1418), 12 Stucley Place, London NW1 8NS.

FURTHER INFORMATION: Montserrat Tourist Office (0171 242 3131), Suite 433, 52-54 High Holborn, London WC1V 6RB. French Government Tourist Office (0171 629 2869), 178 Piccadilly, London W1V 0AL. Caribbean

Tourism Organisation (0171 233 8382), Vigilant House, 120 Wilton Road, London SW1V 1JZ.
FURTHER READING: *The Weather Prophet: A Caribbean Journey* by Lucretia Stewart (Vintage) will be published in paperback in March.

(Stewart, *The Independent on Sunday*, 4 February 1996: 51–52)

"The Way The Caribbean Used To Be":

the "Black Irish" and the celebration or

commemoration of St. Patrick's Day on the

'other' Emerald Isle

A tourist reading about Caribbean islands may peruse the many
travel brochures, trying to distinguish the differences between
the many islands. Because each island shares the same sun, sea
and sand with the others; because so many of the beaches are
indistinguishable from each other; and because, for the
undiscerning tourist, all the indigenous West Indians look the
same – tourist promotion in the Caribbean has sought to facilitate
the tourist's choice, helping the tourist to distinguish one island
from another. Tourist Boards' distinctions have, thus, become the
tourist's expectations. And, in turn, a great deal of the tourist
literature has been internalised by the inhabitants of the islands.
This chapter is a case study of these shifting local and foreign
realities, of marketing by dissimilarity. A visit to the island of
Montserrat is advertised as a visit to both a little sparkling version
of Ireland – "The Emerald Isle of the Caribbean" (Fergus 1992),
and a colonial haven – "The Way The Caribbean Used To Be"
(Montserrat Dept. of Tourism 1993). In this way, Montserrat is
being marketed to appeal to a range of different tourists, from
British monarchists to American republicans. This "colonial" and
"Irish" characterisation of the island is in contrast with Antigua
– the island of 365 beaches, Trinidad – home of Carnival, or
Jamaica – land of reggae and Rastas.

All the Caribbean islands are dependent upon the fluctuations
of their fair-weather visitors. Sometimes they work together to
attract tourists to the Caribbean Basin, and sometimes they work
separately, competing amongst each other for foreign currency
revenue. A small island such as Montserrat receives a small share

of the tourists to the Caribbean, approximately 30,301 in 1993, barely 2 percent of Jamaica's number of visitors.[1] In competition with the larger islands, Montserrat is forced to promote herself, "bigging up" her assets: a volcanic island with black sand beaches, a soufriere, a bird sanctuary, the "Great Alps" waterfall, a bamboo forest at the top of Chances Peak, several sugar plantation ruins (Galway's, Waterwork's, Trant's Estates), and her friendly people with their unusual connection with Ireland. This chapter undermines some of the more blatant tourist propaganda projections by examining in detail the consensus and variety – "the congeries of meanings" as Fernandez (1965: 908) would say, the heterogeneity of historical events for me – given by academics, tourists and residents of Montserrat, to the past, present and future celebration or commemoration of St. Patrick's Day (17 March) on Montserrat.

Tranquil, colonial, up-market and exclusive resort island, Montserrat is not a package holiday site or backpacker destination. Indeed, according to West Indies Real Estate, Montserrat is "The Best Place on Planet Earth" – "What you dreamed a CARIBBEAN ISLAND would be".[2] Such adverts attract "white" British, Canadian and North American long- and short-term tourists, as well as some American medical students needing to improve their grades. For all these visitors, Montserrat would appear to be the ideal Caribbean vacation and study location: "English-speaking", "mild" in climate and with "political stability" as a British colony.[3] Almost every tourist piece promoting the island, the people, their history and culture also plays upon the connections between Montserrat (the Emerald Isle of the Caribbean) and Ireland (The Emerald Isle). For example, during the winter season, the Montserrat Springs Hotel offers a two bedroom suite for "the Quiet escape". For US$335, a couple can share a ladle full of a unique island which is simultaneously a replica of Ireland, a Caribbean original and an authentic Imperial outpost:

> Montserrat's Irish heritage comes alive with a shamrock stamped in your passport, places with names like Fogarty Hill and Kinsale, rolling green hills and valleys that rival those of the original "Emerald Isle," and warm friendly people.
>
> But our Emerald Isle has a distinctively Caribbean flavour, with beaches ranging from golden to shimmering black, bubbling sulphur springs and spectacular waterfalls, and landscapes dotted with centuries-old sugar mills and cannons.[4]

But there is more to Montserrat's Irish connection than a marooned shamrock stamped in the tourist's passport, or the tourist emblem of an emerald shamrock inset with a Caribbean palm tree.

Many of the tourists coming to Montserrat are Irish-Americans attracted to an island that is four thousand miles south-west of Cork; they come because their impression of Montserrat is that it is an anachronistic part of *their* "old sod" diasporic empire (see Akenson 1997), a place settled by Irish refugees in the seventeenth century when their ancestors were also settling in North America. These tourists thus come to Montserrat with the expectation that they will find a sense of "belonging". In 1994, travel writer Brian McGinn (1994: 20) sought to explore Montserrat's curious status with the article "How Irish is Montserrat?" in the magazine journal *Irish Roots*:

> [i]t is a British Crown Colony that calls itself the Emerald Isle of the Caribbean. A carved green shamrock adorns the centre gable of Government House, overlooking the Union Jack that flutters from a nearby flagpole. It observes St. Patrick's Day with one public holiday, and three months later the Queen's Birthday is another.

He was following in the footsteps of Sir Fergus's (1993[b]: 2) attention to the Irish legacy which was summarised in the 1993/ 4 Tourist Board brochure:

> [t]he Irish legacy lives on in goat water, a national stew, in music, an Irish drum, the bodhran, and in names of people and places such as Farrells, Cork Hill, Kinsale, O'Garro, Galway, Blake's, Rileys, O'Brien and St. Patrick's; and Erin of Irish legend still poses on the national crest and flag.

But Fergus – along with Cheddy – is unhappy with this "Irishness of Montserrat", in particular the Tourist Board's "staged [Irish] authenticity" (*cf.* MacCannell 1989: 98–99) with their cultivation of Irish symbols and emblems on Montserrat, and their increasing involvement in *his* St. Patrick's Day national holiday.

Significantly, Sir Fergus (1992: 43) notes that it was not until 1971 that "local scholars rediscovered the day", referring to his historical research and highlighting of 17 March 1768 on Montserrat, St. Patrick's Day. Ever since 1971, Sir Fergus, himself, has campaigned relentlessly in his poetry and newspaper articles for St. Patrick's Day to become a national holiday on Montserrat – *not as a celebration* of Montserrat's Irish connection, *but as a commemoration* of one St. Patrick's Day celebration (1768) when the slaves on Montserrat attempted to overthrow their Irish and

British masters.[5] Fergus's (1994: 266) efforts culminated in the establishment of a St. Patrick's Day national holiday in 1985, an achievement recorded in the final paragraph of his *Montserrat – History of a Caribbean Colony*, "[t]he decision in 1985 to make St. Patrick's Day a national holiday and to celebrate Montserratian heroes past and present with activities rooted in creole culture, is contributing to the development of a national and cultural identity."

Ideally, for Fergus, the 17 March would be known as Heroes Day on Montserrat, an occasion commemorating those who died in the failed slave insurrection – a psychological statement for present-day Montserratians that their ancestors were noble and dedicated in their resistance to slavery. However, the Government is considering establishing an August national holiday called Montserratian Achievers Day to combine with emancipation celebrations (1 August is Emancipation Day throughout the Caribbean, and August Monday is a national holiday on Montserrat). This would reserve for Montserratians the August celebrations of Montserratians past and present, thereby "freeing up" St. Patrick's Day, leaving it as a national holiday to attract tourists interested in the Irish connection during the tourist season. Naturally, the August event would emphasise present successes on a modern colony, rather than dwell upon the colony's oppressive past which the authorities would prefer to remain buried.

Speaking in the same interview which featured in the last chapter, Cheddy points out the errors and problem with blurring the commemoration of the St. Patrick's Day rebellion with a new Montserratian Achievers celebration:

> The Governor has the whole thing backwards and I don't know who explained it to him, OK. But there's two clear and distinct dates. Emancipation Day in Montserrat, was, has always been, from the year 1834 to the present, the first of August, and not just in Montserrat. In the entire English-speaking Caribbean the 1st August 1834, the Emancipation Act – I can show you a copy if you want –
> *Aha, I've seen it*
> declared all former slaves to be no longer named slaves. It was a trick in legislative writing but the reality is, the way we have interpreted it that we were no longer slaves, we were set free on that day. That has been a traditional holiday in the entire Caribbean since the year 1834. Don't confuse the issue whatsoever. The 17th March in Montserrat in the year 1768, on the 17th March – there was a plan by the slaves

of Montserrat to destroy the colonial masters because they celebrated, a Irish holiday of St. Patrick's Day, OK. And they planned, the slaves planned to kill all the white people in Montserrat because they know that they would meet at Government House on that day and they would drink and be drunk and they would be celebrating and they would catch them in a position where they could destroy all of them. So the 17th March to us – which is St. Patrick's Day to the Irish around the world – is a day where we celebrate our capacity to rebel against oppression. A'right. That, again, was confused again by the Tourist Department and the British Government to be turned into a traditional St. Patrick's Holiday to lure Irish tourists back into this country on that day. We did not create it for that day. We have been demanding the change of the name of that day from St. Patrick's Day in Montserrat to Heroes Day or Slave Rebellions Day or some Day that allows us to understand why we rebelled under the conditions that we lived under. But there's two distinct things altogether. No, they're mixing it up. They're going to confuse the issue by putting an Emancipation Day – another holiday called Montserratian Achievement Day – you understand, which is then going to totally remove from the minds of the younger generations the implications and the huge impact of Emancipation Day and the contributions that our forefathers made over two hundred and fifty years to make that their reality.[6]

Cheddy's cynical impressions about the management of Montserrat's national holiday on March 17th converge with those of Sir Fergus, but diverge with those of others. In this way, this chapter is where some of the individual and group voices and identity debates featured in previous chapters start to come together. This chapter goes on to unravel the complexity of this St. Patrick's Day battle by first presenting an ethnographic narrative of St. Patrick's Day 1995, sketched from my fieldnotes and the local media (local radio and press). The synchonicity of this lived-through experience turns, first, to a stream of consciousness account. Then, second, it turns to a selection of diverse impressions of St. Patrick's Day itself – to understandings of St. Patrick's Day other than my own, though still predominantly academic. Here, I show that my postmodern anthropological position – though relativistic – does allow for academic criticism and comment. And finally, the third part of this chapter links the various competing histories and impressions of Montserrat to the various economic, political and media interest groups which will continue to agitate for control of St. Patrick's Day.

CELEBRATING OR COMMEMORATING ST. PATRICK'S DAY, 1995?

"When it comes to news, information and entertainment, there's simply one place to turn, ZJB Radio, 885AM, 92.5FM. We are 10,000 watts of pure and living energy. Get to know us and you'll know why!"[7]

Morning, afternoon and evening, the island is tuned to the local radio, one of the key media elements for preparing Montserratians and tourists for St. Patrick's Day.

MID-FEBRUARY

A schoolchild reads over the radio a series of short information bulletins throughout the day:

"[...] many years ago. It is observed here more in the context of bringing home to us the significance of St. Patrick's Day in our history, our culture and our evolution from bondsmen to people who are truly free. Modern celebrations of St. Patrick's Day actually began in the 1970s. At that time most of the activities centred around the University Centre with lectures on aspects of Montserrat's history and a display of the creative arts with the Emerald Community Singers singing patriotic – and slave – songs. [...] More recently, however, activities became focused in St. Patrick's village in the south of the island. Keep listening for more on St. Patrick's Day – another important aspect of our cultural heritage."

EARLY MARCH

Prior to St. Patrick's Day, the radio bulletins gain in length and detail. The listening public are geared up for the 17 March St. Patrick's Day week of social and cultural activities, just one of eleven official holidays on Montserrat which occur every year. Just before the St. Patrick's Day "week", The *Official St. Patrick's Day Programme 1995* (James 1995) is marketed in the streets by news vendors. Emerald green, it is headed with the outline of a palm inset within a shamrock on the side of an emerald silhouette of the Emerald Isle. In-between lists of Irish names and adverts from local businesses, tour operators (Emerald Tours) and even the Tourist Board (an Irish pub crawl, there is a message from H.E. The Governor F.J. Savage (1995: 4) who stresses the "re-emergence of cultural ties with Ireland": Savage has forged close ties between Ireland and Montserrat, arranging for the twinning of Kinsale (Montserrat) with Kinsale (Ireland) to help business links,[8] and for the Chief Minister to meet Irish Ministers in the British Embassy in Dublin. The Vue Pointe Hotel, for example, has an advert describing its traditional menus of goatwater and mountain chicken with the addition of corned beef and cabbage, and a barbecue accompanied by *"Danny Boy"* on the steel pans.[9] There is also a message from Chief Minister Meade (1995: 6, my emphasis) which draws attention to the small St. Patrick's community in the south of the island, and their contribution to the annual celebration. The message ends with the following comment:

"[i]t is our hope that all our visitors will have an enjoyable stay. We hope that they will share our sense of history and appreciate that this occasion signifies a rich cultural tradition of which we are proud."

The final message in the programme is a "Celebration of Achievement" by Sir Howard Fergus which discusses how he successfully pressured the Government into changing the name of the airport from Blackburne Airport to W.H. Bramble Airport – a campaign which he had begun in the early 1980s (see Chapter 2). He notes that the re-naming of the airport will take place in August when the Caribbean is commemorating Emancipation Day (August Monday), soon to be known as Achiever's Day on Montserrat. Sir Fergus (1995[b]: 7) also makes the important point of returning to the original reason for the St. Patrick's Day celebration:

we must never lose sight of those martyrs of freedom, those who dared to take up arms, such as they had, against the perpetrators of slavery and oppression, on March 17, 1768. Their achievement (it was certainly a great triumph of the human spirit) will shine better in an environment in which our heroes are no longer imported and look a little more like ourselves. [...]

While it is politically safe to do so, let me congratulate Chief Minister Reuben T. Meade for his wise decision. My preference was for linking the honour with St. Patrick's Day, which I unofficially christened Heroes Day, but this is not the issue. Our people participated in their own emancipation in the nineteenth century and making Emancipation Day Achiever's Day will hopefully re-capture lost meaning for the anniversary of emancipation and re-invigorate our August festivities.

The radio completes the St. Patrick's Day build up with more limited information about the ("sense of") history of the occasion which has recently become a national holiday. Dramatic messages are broadcast over the airwaves to promote public awareness of St. Patrick's Day, and support for the Government's tourism and national identity initiatives:

"St. Patrick's Day: although it's a public holiday on Montserrat, its observance here is tied in with our historical past. It was on this day, March 17th 1768, that

the slaves on Montserrat revolted and planned the seeds for war by attacking Government House while their colonial masters fêted at that seat of power. In order to fully understand the slaves' decision to do this, we must first know something of the conditions under which the slaves on Montserrat had to live. For instance, any black person or slave found stealing cattle or carrying away stock would suffer death. That was the law. Under that same law, slaves found guilty of stealing provisions worth twelve pence could receive a severe beating or have both ears cut off if this was a first offence. If a slave was found guilty of the same offence a second time, he would be put to death in such as manner prescribed by the Governor and Council in power. But we will tell you more of your cultural heritage another time, here, on your community radio station, ZJB."

By 10 March, the build-up to St. Patrick's Day celebrations is complete – the Montserratian and British Government departments (Meade and Savage), the island academics (Fergus and Cheddy), the local businesses (such as Cork mentioned in Chapter 3), the Montserrat Tourist Board, and the individual operators (street vendors, guides, taximen) have all been acknowledged and prepared for the occasion – the seven-day event begins.

SATURDAY, 11 MARCH

The week incorporating 17 March carries a series of traditional events which begin with a "Roman Catholic Dinner" held in the Catholic Church's St. Joseph's Hall. For EC$25 "guests" receive a meal of West Indian cuisine and are serenaded with Irish songs.

SUNDAY, 12 MARCH

The St. Patrick's Community Centre hosts an impromptu "Cultural Concert", a local event of skits and verse by members of the community about other members of the community, much of which is lost on myself and the two Irish-American tourists.

TUESDAY, 14 MARCH

The annual St. Patrick's Lecture, scheduled to be given by Sir Fergus, is cancelled without notice.

WEDNESDAY, 15 MARCH

Whilst members of the expatriate and tourist public go on an island-wide pub crawl, a local Cultural Concert is held in the University Centre for EC$5. A family show is held which includes performances by a children's steel band; school story tellers; the Nubian Dancers (a chorus line girls dance troupe organised by an expatriate former dancer); the Emerald Community Singers (an adult singing troupe singing West Indian songs); and calypsonians such as Belonger singing Irish orientated calypsos, and Sean "Teknikal" Martin singing "A News Dem A Look" and a song about the slave rebellion.

THURSDAY, 16 MARCH

There is a street fair of stalls on the bay front of the capital, next to Plymouth Port. Belonger sings and sells her calypsos; others sell home-made Montserrat trinkets, cake desserts, local drinks and barbecued chicken. A group of calypsonians liming on the Harbour wall invite me to an unofficial calypsonians' St. Patrick's Day celebration at the Inn on Sugar Bay in the evening.

EARLY THURSDAY EVENING

ZJB Radio news introduces the events for the following day. Political activist Chedmond Browne is interviewed about St. Patrick's Day on Montserrat. His interview contrasts with tourist-slanted broadcasts because he speaks to Montserrat and excludes tourists and off-islanders in his comments:

Newscaster: "[...] historian and social commentator Chedmond Browne says that March 17 should not be just a public holiday for Montserratians. Browne says that March 17 is an extremely significant day for people of African descent who now occupy the island called Montserrat or Alliouagana. On March 17, 1768, slaves on Montserrat staged an uprising, but the slave revolt was put down by their colonial masters after an informant leaked details of the plan."

Cheddy: "The significance of this, this, particular rebellion is that at the same point in time, throughout the entire Caribbean region, throughout the Americas, anywhere the African man was held in physical slavery, he rebelled. Now, our history books would want us to believe that, that we sat through – we went through – slavery in a complacent manner and that our slave masters, our colonial masters, treated us benevolently. That is the whitemans' history. That is the Europeans' version of the history. The reality of the history is that we were brutally treated, we were dehumanised and in each and every instance that the Africans' people got an opportunity to rebel against this type of treatment, they rebelled."

Newscaster: "Browne, Dr. Howard Fergus, Clarice – Clarice Barnes and other like-minded Montserratians have been calling for St. Patrick's Day to be renamed Heroes Day in commemoration of the slaves who lost their lives in the struggle for freedom."[10]

Over dinner, Pippa complains about this news broadcast. She explains to me that no West Indians from other islands are likely

to visit Montserrat to celebrate the honours of contemporary
Montserratians, whereas they might be attracted to the island
by Montserrat's exotic Irish connection whether or not they
empathise with the slave insurrection of 1768. These are the same
comments she is reported to have made to McGinn (1994: 22)
when he interviewed her for his article.

Late Thursday evening

At the Inn there are no tourists, but anyone buying more than
three drinks is given a free St. Patrick's Day beaker which changes
colour to emerald green when cold. Whilst the Inn is set up for
a night of calypso, drunken expatriates and tourists wearing
shamrock T-shirts, "Kiss me – I'm Irish" badges and "I love Ireland"
caps arrive. They are escorted by members of the Montserrat Tourist
Board who do not drink with them and apologise for their
behaviour when they move on to the next bar. Several
calypsonians such as Top Secret sing their songs for three quarters
of an hour before the show suddenly stops.

Friday, 17 March

The Montserrat News rather gauchely notes that "the triple heritage
of Montserrat – Africa, Irish, and Caribbean", the cultural trinity
of St. Patrick's Day activities, is the subject of an Afro-American
magazine, Afrique News.[11] *The Montserrat Reporter*, in contrast,
reports on Her Majesty the Queen's Commonwealth Day Message,[12]
and features Fergus's satirical poem, "When Justice Came to Church"
(see Chapter 2).[13] It also runs an editorial on "Good Manners"
which is about respect for elders and courtesy to visitors to help
build a "meaningful tourism trade". The article concludes by
imploring the younger members on the island to exercise maturity
and restraint in their celebration of St. Patrick's Day.[14]

Again, ZJB Radio promote and celebrate St. Patrick's Day,
starting with Claude Hogan's summary of the Chief Minister's St.
Patrick's Day message:

Newscaster: *"This is ZJB Reports: the national vision is to transform Montserrat's
St. Patrick's Day celebrations into a major tourist attraction. Chief Minister, The
Honourable Reuben Meade, has registered this hope. This year a number of journalists
are on island to film and write about St. Patrick's Day. The Chief Minister believes
this will increase interest in Montserrat's Irish heritage in other countries."*

Chief Minister: *"Greetings my Brothers and Sisters. Montserrat is the only island in the Caribbean to celebrate St. Patrick's Day as a public holiday. We continue to place emphasis on St. Patrick's Day as we remember the first European settlers who lived in Montserrat were Irish. St. Patrick, as you know, is the Patron Saint of Ireland. Most importantly however, St. Patrick's Day celebrations mark a March 17 slave revolt by our forefathers. It is a significant day because it underlines our struggle for freedom. [...] Today it is realised that St. Patrick's Day celebrations must assume national attention and priority as we strive to build a nation called Montserrat."*[15]

Most of the message is broadcast over local radio, and presumably over Cable TV. Hogan continues:

Newscaster: *"The significance of St. Patrick's Day to Montserratians should be two-fold – that's the view of historian Dr. Howard Fergus. Dr. Fergus says the day should bring to mind the historical links between Montserrat and Ireland. Dr. Fergus says, in addition, Montserratians should remember what was done on St. Patrick's Day in 1768."*

Sir Fergus: *"We, as a people, um, recognise those, er, those planners as freedom fighters. We salute them and we think that this is a good day to celebrate, um, what they did. And to use it, not just to vilify anybody, not just to talk about our, our oppressors, but to use it positively, to display our art and our culture – which is not just Irish certainly, but African, and, and creole, the whole mixture, the whole amalgam of Europe and Africa coming together. And I think, in essence, this is the reason why we celebrate it."*

Newscaster: *"Historian Dr. Fergus on St. Patrick's Day March 1768. A planned slave revolt against the Irish was put down. This after an informant leaked the plan.*

Three Montserratians have been formally invested with Royal and National Honours. Commander of the Order of the British Empire, the CBE medal has gone to Dr. Howard Fergus. Member of the Most Excellent Order of the British Empire, the MBE, has gone to Mrs. Rosanna Dyer Ennis. And the Montserrat Medal and Certificate of Honour to legendary sportsman Sir Fred Davis. His Excellency The Governor Frank Savage presided over last evening's investiture ceremony at Government House. [...]

And to round off now: hundreds of residents are converging in the south of Montserrat. That's the news tonight as Montserrat celebrates history and pride in the island's oldest fight for freedom."

FRIDAY AFTERNOON

St. Patrick's village is perched up on exposed, dry, rocky hills with cliffs overlooking the southern shore of the island. There are old plantation windmill remains on the cliff tops which the single road to the village winds around; goats scrape for food in the dust and rubble; and huts, shacks and houses line the road through the village. A huge "Welcome to St. Patrick's" sign is suspended from telegraph poles on the final ascent into St. Patrick's village (300+ inhabitants).

The St. Patrick's Day schedule of festivities lists a morning Freedom Run from Plymouth around to St. Patrick's in blistering heat, followed by a local cricket match, a noonday slave feast of local foods, and cultural entertainment running on into the evening. Throughout the day, guided hikes (EC$45) are organised by the Tourist Board for tourists to visit the ruins of Galway's Estate nearby, a soufriere just above the village, the Great Alps Waterfall to the south of the village, and the bamboo forest at the top of Mount Chance which overlooks the village and the rest of the island.

At noon, St. Patrick's is quiet. The Freedom Run is over and only a dozen North Americans, dressed in Irish Shamrock caps and T-shirts, are left to either pan video cameras across the streets or practise the intricacies of the "black" handshakes that they've learned. Some chairs are set out in the shade of the Protestant church. Several St. Patrick's women are cooking up goatwater, barbecued fish and chicken by the side of the road. Rumour has it that the Slave Feast will be held near the Catholic church in the village. But there is no sign of any activity. The main preoccupation is the cricket match on the side of the hill. A few locals sit in the bars or in their porches. One bar on the corner of a bend in the road, where the two sides of the valley intersect, plays music from stacked speakers – the start of a Jump Up party in the road. Less than half a dozen dancers, with Carib and Heineken beers, are there enjoying the liming-light.

After returning to a deserted Plymouth, I hang around Wapping. There, Vicki tells me that because her skin is light, she must be Irish. Doc, with a surname coming from one of the estates in the south of the island, also professes his own – more than nominal – connection with the south of the island.

FRIDAY NIGHT

Back in St. Patrick's and Missie O'Garro, Pippa's cleaning lady, tells me that St. Patrick's Day is celebrated because, during the slave rebellion, a slave called Patrick helped free the other slaves and the Irish on the island. The Montserrat String Band is playing under a tent to the bystanders, a few self-conscious Irish and

North American tourists sitting on chairs provided for the performance. For a half-mile along the St. Patrick's village road, Montserratians are crowded together greeting each other, drinking, dancing by the various music centres, or simply following or joining the masquerade dancers – themselves either clearing a path for cars or blocking cars, depending on whether or not the drivers have thrown them some change. Everyone seems to be in St. Patrick's: villagers from the north, south, east, and west of the island; AUC students; development workers (several from Ireland trying not to get roped into performing jigs); and expats and tourists. Suddenly, everybody is plunged into a dark mass of moving bodies as the extra street-lighting fails, leaving the music centres, with their own generators, to pump music to the St. Patrick's Day pilgrims.

Saturday 18 March

Only six people turn up to the Fourth Annual St. Patrick's Day Bike Race: the owner of Island Bikes, his two mechanics, an AUC student, and two British development workers. The meet is cancelled.

Diverse impressions of St. Patrick's Day

St. Patrick's Day is the recent product of a cultural elite, what Eric Hobsbawm (1992: 1) would refer to as an "invented tradition" – a constructed and formally instituted set of practices claiming a link with an immemorial past. For me, this recent tradition is diverse and multiple, but this is not necessarily the case for other academics both on and off Montserrat. Here I present three varied impressions of St. Patrick's Day: first, Montserrat 1995 – both lay (celebrators of St. Patrick's Day) and academic (commemorators of St. Patrick's Day); second, new work revealed by the black American anthropologist and historian Michael Mullin; and third, the work of white American anthropologist John Messenger who has worked in Nigeria and Ireland as well as Montserrat. I then go on to consider the future of St. Patrick's Day and Messenger's "Black Irish", an analysis which leads into this book's Conclusion – a closing discussion about anthropology, Montserrat and the nature of meaning.

St. Patrick's Day 1995, Montserrat

There would appear to be a variety of local and non-local understandings of St. Patrick's Day, different realities held by a range of different people. No doubt, this is the case even amongst the tourists enticed to Montserrat by Government and Tourist Board adverts to visit this Caribbean island and to celebrate vacation time or St. Patrick's Day alongside Irish-Africans – a quirky, quaint, inter-racial brotherhood of former fellow slaves equally mistreated by the English. Many islanders understand that the island is depen–dent upon the tourist industry and that they need these tourists for their economy. They are happy to celebrate alongside these tourists, treating the St. Patrick's Day celebrations as simply another opportunity to "jump up" and party in the streets of another village; several of the other villages already have a day in the year to celebrate their community – there is a St. John's Day for the village of St. John's, so it is inevitable that the village of St. Patrick's should celebrate a St. Patrick's Day. In other words, the contest to command the national holiday between the Montserrat Government and the Montserrat Tourist Board on the one side, and the cultural and intellectual elite on the other, rages whilst most are happy for an excuse to party. In their contest for the heart and soul of Montserrat, neither side has been able to completely control the diversity of world views and understandings of St. Patrick's Day.

St. Patrick's Day on Montserrat touches the lives of all Montserratians across the island, no matter how the "event" is regarded. For Missie O'Garro, the cleaning lady, St. Patrick's Day celebrates a slave's victory in the 1768 revolt. For Doc, St. Patrick's Day is a time for additional airport work during the day and partying during the night. For Teknikal, St. Patrick's Day is a party and a calypso topic. For Belonger, St. Patrick's Day is a chance to perform for a good cause. For Vicki, St. Patrick's Day allows her to account for her skin colour and ancestry. For the Irish-American tourists visiting Montserrat, St. Patrick's Day can at last be celebrated in a hot and sunny climate. For the Irish development workers, St. Patrick's Day is to be avoided with an inter-island break. For the AUC students, St. Patrick's Day is a party and a cycle race. For me, St. Patrick's Day is a diverse and fiercely contested heterogeneous and partial historical "event". For Pippa, St. Patrick's Day is a black celebration which attracts tourists to Montserrat. For the Montserrat Tourist Board and the Governor of Montserrat,

St. Patrick's Day is a tourism marketing opportunity. For the Montserrat Government, St. Patrick's Day is a trade opportunity combined with a community and national celebration. For Cheddy and Sir Fergus, St. Patrick's Day is failing to retain its national significance as a reminder to Montserratians of how "the Caribbean used to be", instead, it is becoming a holiday for North Americans to lose their worries by getting drunk on green beer on an island idyll; and, more importantly, it is a time when the historical suffering of the Afrikan slave is diluted by equating it with the suffering of Irish indentured workers, slave owners on a par with the English colonists in their eyes. For Claude Hogan, the newscaster, St. Patrick's Day is a social movement and a news report. And for the journalists visiting Montserrat, St. Patrick's Day is just another exotic story.

So, St. Patrick's Day means different things to different people. Indeed, I would go so far as to state that St. Patrick's Day has a different reality for different people. Much like the expat and Montserratian constellations mentioned in Chapter 3, people generally subscribe to an inter-subjective understanding of St. Patrick's Day: it can be a commemoration deriving from the 1768 uprising "event", a celebration of the Irish connection, another time to jump up, or something else – Missie O'Garro, especially, shows us that the St. Patrick's Day reality can be more diverse and complex. In his examination of traditions as disparate as May Day holidays, Boy Scout songs, flags and national anthems, and public school *esprit de corps* practices, Hobsbawm (1992: 9) identifies three overlapping types of invented tradition: they either facilitate social cohesion, legitimate forms of authority, or socialise conventions of behaviour. As a historian, Hobsbawm's interest is in hunting down the origins and facts – the history – of contemporary understandings. I believe that Howard Fergus seeks the same historical ends. My attention here, however, is focused upon the contemporary understandings of St. Patrick's Day, upon present-day meanings and uses, not upon the historical specificity or roots of the event. These contemporary understandings are, of course, often legitimated and justified by what I would refer to as "historical impressions" – impressions of past lived experiences, and impressions of historical readings and teachings (the socialisation of history in society). For Fergus and Cheddy, their historical impressions are historical realities, a process which we can trace back to when St. Patrick's Day became a national holiday on Montserrat (1985), and back to the rediscovery of the St. Patrick's Day rebellion (1971).

Because many Montserratians and tourists are under the impression that St. Patrick's Day is just another local holiday which has been celebrated since time immemorial, Sir Fergus's main objective has been to extend *his* personal understanding of St. Patrick's Day – and his sense of history and national identity – to that of a *collective* inter-subjective constellation. To this end, Fergus (1994: 75, my emphasis; see also Watkins 1924) recounts in great detail another historian's description of the 1768 St. Patrick's Day rebellion in his history of Montserrat:

> a day conveniently chosen since the people of the island unusually assembled to commemorate it. The Irish Roman Catholics were discriminated against, but the Irish connection was celebrated. The slaves working within Government House were to seize the swords of the gentlemen while those outside were to fire into the house using whatever missiles were at their disposal. They evidently had some arms because the plan was revealed when a *white* seamstress, noted for her drunkenness, heard two of the leaders discussing the disposition of their arms.

The colour of the woman has as much present-day psychological significance as the slave insurrection itself. According to Fergus's historical reality, it was not a black woman who exposed the conspiracy, but a drunken white woman.

For the British colonisers on Montserrat, those involved in the uprising had to be punished for their rebellious actions, actions which are now commemorated in all former slave societies. By October 1768, Fergus (1994: 75) continues, the insurrection was totally suppressed: "[n]ine of the ring-leaders were brutally executed, and some 30 were imprisoned pending banishment at the earliest opportunity". Little more is contained in Fergus's account. Montserratians are encouraged to commemorate the execution of the nine, but as Cheddy once commented to me, Fergus does not tell us anything about them: their names, the Estates that they worked on, or where they were executed are all missing from his account. Cheddy further noted that Fergus knew where the executions were held in Plymouth town, but that these details were omitted from his account, perhaps because the possible lack of specificity surrounding the slave uprising strengthens its mythical status, furthering a nationalist agenda which concentrates upon the present rather than the past. Whatever the reason for this surprising exclusion, Fergus (1994: 75) is keen to retain control over his historical reality, the slaves which he, as a nationalist scholar, turned into "national freedom-fighters". And it is his writings in newspapers, history books and poetry volumes where Fergus (1994: 76, my emphasis; see also George Irish writing in 1978 and 1985)[16] persuades and cajoles the rest of Montserrat to follow him, as evinced in his *History of Montserrat*:

> [t]his author had an occasion recently to warn against incipient distortion in the significance and celebration of the holiday. It was, in his view, beginning to resemble the style in which the Irish diaspora in the United States celebrate St Patrick's Day. The holiday was intended to honour our slave ancestors who bravely essayed to overthrow their oppressive European overlords – and these were English, Scottish *and* Irish.

MICHAEL MULLIN THE HISTORIAN AND THE HISTORY OF MONTSERRAT'S 1768 SLAVE REBELLION

Michael Mullin's more detailed, if inflammatory, account of the 1768 rebellion blends anthropological technique with historical fragments to evoke and provide insight into the life of slave and master on Montserrat, before, during and after the St. Patrick's Day rebellion. His account features in *Africa in America* (1992) where he analyses the relationship between slave acculturation (on plantations in the American south) and the changing nature of slave resistance (on plantations in the British Caribbean) between 1736 and 1831. Mullin makes extensive use of newspapers, Government and missionary records, diaries and plantation records, census and judicial archives to represent the outlook of individual actors,[17] and to suggest to the reader why most slaves never rebelled. In particular, his work allows the reader to appreciate the position of the creole leaders of rebellions trying to gain support from fellow slaves. In this way, Mullin's argument differs from those of Sir Fergus and Mr. Chedmond Browne who persist with the theory that the relationship between *all* African slaves and masters was a relationship of tension, struggle and revolt – the St. Patrick's rebellion being just one such instance.

Mullin (1992: 215–281) articulates three phases of slave resistance in the Caribbean: sudden, violent resistance from the new negroes of the New World bartered and sold into slavery between 1730 and 1760; conservative and wary resistance from 1760 to the early 1800s on many plantations; and vigorous and organised resistance against the planters by "the assimilateds" (second generation creoles) from the 1760s to the second quarter of the 1800s. From Trinidad to Montserrat, rebellions were mounted during all three phases, but only the campaigns mounted by the Maroons of St. Vincent can considered successful. Despite the many failures, it is crucial – to reiterate Cheddy – to record the many instances of resistance, to show West Indians (and Afro-Americans) of today that the conditions of slavery yesterday were not entirely passively tolerated but were actively resisted and confronted. One of the failures Mullin uses as a case study of the first of the Creole conspiracies is the 1768 St. Patrick's Day rebellion on Montserrat. His use of the Montserrat example substantiates recent commemorations of the event, and contrasts with Messenger's work and other expatriate scholarship which is sceptical of the idea that there was such a conspiracy at all (see below).

In the 1760s, Mullin records a population on Montserrat of 9,000 slaves and 1,300 whites, many of whom were Irish; the total population of whites was to decline to 434 by 1788. Mullin (1992: 219) begins his case study by explaining the timing for the 1768 conspiracy:

> [t]he presence of three Dutch vessels anchored offshore had inspired blacks to organise a mass escape by seizing a ship and sailing, perhaps, to Puerto Rico. The conspirators chose as their password a popular song, 'Fire in the Mountains', which when played by the black fiddler at the whites' St. Patrick's dance was to signal the beginning of the revolt.

According to Mullin (1992: 220-221) the plan for the uprising, one of the first major slave conspiracies in the Caribbean, was as follows:

> [t]o attack first at the dance, the conspirators reasoned, was to catch the white elite when it was concentrated, distracted, and could be taken in a rush. At the same time, house servants would secure their owners' swords, and slaves who were positioned outside would shoot the whites as they fled. News of the rising would run from ballroom to town then to the ridges above, where slaves would then light real fire in the mountains.

However, Mullin's (1992: 221, my emphasis) historical description of the failure of the rebellion is in marked contrast with Fergus's description in terms of the colour of the seamstress:

> [t]he plan unravelled disastrously as the slaves prepared for their own celebration. This party apparently revolved around a new dance that had been introduced by Antiguan blacks and was at the moment 'the rage' in Montserrat. When a conspirator returned to a *colored* seamstress and was told his costume for the fête was unfinished, he reproached

her angrily, "the thing I was going to do tonight, now I cannot do." For
her turn, the seamstress went to the authorities, who matched her account
with others they had heard and soon uncovered the whole.

The issue of the seamstress's colour is very important when we
bear in mind the present-day significance given to this failed
rebellion. In Mullin's historical version of the St. Patrick's Day
conspiracy, a coloured seamstress causes its failure; the onus
of blame, in this example, falls upon a coloured (free) slave rather
than a white colonial, thus undermining Cheddy's and Fergus's
use of the St. Patrick's Day commemoration to further their ethnic
and nationalist causes.

The uprising was "deep laid", with stores of arms hidden in
the mountains of Montserrat. But, once uncovered, Mullin (1992:
221) refers to an "atmosphere of murderous hysteria" which
overtook the whites on the island, "[a]s the plot broke [and] the
whites went berserk. They hacked, quartered, hanged, and starved
in gibbets any suspects whose owners were foolish enough to
send them to town for 'trials'."

If it wasn't for the colour of the seamstress, Mullin's account
of the St. Patrick's Day conspiracy would have assisted Sir Fergus
and Chedmond Browne in their work towards an independent
Montserratian national identity. Rather than attempt to verify
the intentional or unintentional historical accuracies of Fergus's
and Mullin's accounts, for me, what is important here is not what
they declare to be the historical truth of the rebellion – such
as the skin colour of the seamstress – but the way in which the
rebellion and the seamstress's colour is understood, used and
becomes their historical reality.

JOHN MESSENGER THE ANTHROPOLOGIST AND HIS BLACK IRISH OF MONTSERRAT

Using an historical approach similar to that used by Cheddy and
Sir Fergus, American anthropologist John Messenger casts doubt
upon both Cheddy's and Sir Fergus's support for the St. Patrick's
Day commemoration. Messenger does this by appealing to a 300
page unpublished history of Montserrat written from court records
in 1930 by a colonial agricultural worker, and "belonger", Mr. T.
Savage English (1930: 229). English briefly refers to the St. Patrick's
Day conspiracy as follows:

[i]n 1768 there was a negro conspiracy, given away, as almost always
seems to have happened in such cases anywhere in the West Indies,
by too much talking on the part of the conspirators. The story goes,

> that "the plot was discovered by a woman who heard two of the leaders
> disputing about the disposition of their arms. The plan was to have been
> carried into execution on St. Patrick's Day, which the inhabitants usually
> assembled to commemorate. The slaves within Government House were
> to have secured the swords of the gentleman, and those without to have
> fired into the house.

Controversially, Messenger (1994) uses this account in his academic
article "St. Patrick's Day in 'The Other Emerald Isle'", published
in the journal *Eire – Ireland*, to cast doubt upon the St. Patrick's
Day conspiracy. This academic anthropological position meant
that he was very reluctant to let any Montserratians see his article
when he showed it to me during one of his annual vacations to
Montserrat. After citing English, Messenger (1994: 16, my emphasis)
makes derogatory remarks about the 1768 uprising:

> [t]his *may be a legend* collected by English or a predecessor, and implied
> in it is that on this day the Irish would be vulnerable because of the
> drink customarily imbibed. To some locals, basing a festival on an
> unsuccessful slave revolt, *possibly recorded only in untrustworthy legend*,
> is as questionable as the effort by Afrophiles to change the name of
> the island [...].

Messenger dislikes the ways in which his anthropological writings
have been hijacked for other people's political ends such as those
of Sir Fergus and Cheddy, not to mention their adoption by the
Montserrat Tourist Board and visiting travel writers such as Stewart
(see chapter preface above). His article contains an implicit
sympathy with the historical Irish settlers of Montserrat, as well
as his contemporary Irish readers in Ireland. Messenger (1994:
13, my emphasis; see also 1969) seeks to further arouse the readers'
interests with the following highly controversial comments
connecting Ireland with Montserrat:

> [t]he Irish heritage is manifested in the phenotype of most islanders;
> in the English and possibly in the Creole that they speak; in place-names
> and surnames which are still employed; and in certain customs
> characteristic of, but not limited to, *the Black Irish*. Irish "cultural
> imponderables" revealed in motor habits, musical styles, systems of values,
> and codes of etiquette – prevail among the Black Irish, but are difficult
> to describe and *can only be sensed (verstehen)* by researchers who have
> resided for long periods in both Ireland and Africa.

According to Messenger (1994: 13), when he visited Montserrat
there were approximately one thousand of these in-bred "Black
Irish" living in the north of the island, "descendants of marriages
between Irish and slaves [....] to maintain the Caucasoid phenotype

and, for a few, the Irish tradition." This unsubstantiated claim, in particular, suggests that many of the Irish surnames used by Montserratians are the historical result of inter-ethnic marriage rather than former slaves acquiring their surnames from the Irish-named estates they worked on following their emancipation. Messenger (1973: 54) goes on to identify these hybridised blacks – the "Montserrat Irish" – in a 1946 census: they are the 6 percent "Mixed" or "Coloured" as opposed to the 93 percent "Negro" on the island. However, I must confess to having been completely unable to verify or find any *sense* in his pronouncements when I was on Montserrat, though I naturally lack Messenger's exclusive comparative ethnographic experience, and his obvious ethnological and statistical guile. The only Black Irish voices I came across came from the reverberations of Messenger's writings.

In 1993 Messenger, himself, was privy to the St. Patrick's Day events: the programme was very similar to the 1995 programme though, significantly, a "National Heroes Day" was included and, even in 1993, there was the suggestion that this day be moved to 1st August and that the Afrocentric interpretation of St. Patrick's Day be abandoned. Messenger (1994: 22–23) refers to the occasion as a poorly organised nativist revitalization movement, adding to the diversity of St. Patrick's Day impressions with the detail that one local claimed that "the slave rebellion of 1768 was successful and led to the immediate emancipation of slaves". This "St. Patrick's Day in 'The Other Emerald Isle'" article follows on from two important but similar articles by Messenger (1965; 1973) about Irish and African "retentions" on Montserrat. In the second of these articles, Messenger (1973: 55–56) declared that:

> "most of Montserratian culture today is a composite of African and Irish retentions, regional borrowings and internal innovations."

Messenger then went on to adopt Irish historian Father Aubrey Gwynn's (1929[a]: 393; see also Gwynn 1929[b]; 1930; 1931; 1932) phrase characterising Montserrat: "the most distinctively Irish settlement in the New World" – a throwaway line at the end of an article about Oliver Cromwell's expulsion of Irish Tories to the West Indies. Messenger (1975) used this *characterisation of Montserrat* in his *caricaturisation of Montserratians*, using it as the title of an article which has thereafter been cited often by tourists, academics, travel writers and Montserratians as proof of the Montserrat–Ireland connection. It was in this article that

Messenger (1975: 290) pressed home his other controversial claims: first, that the Irish landowners "treated their slaves with more care and kindness than did their English and Scottish counterparts"; and second, that "the Irish and other Europeans left an indelible genetic and cultural imprint on their former slaves"; there are also other similarities between Montserrat and Ireland stated such as the ingredients of goatwater stew, wakes, and high rainfall levels! Messenger's (1975: 296) article also includes a statistical breakdown on the Irish names found on Montserrat which are repeated – uncited – in the St. Patrick's Day Programme and other Montserrat Tourist Board publications.

Understandably, Fergus (1992: 17) has questioned the extent of this historically reconstructed reality of a Montserrat *past of Irish beginnings* and *present of Black Irish retentions*, preferring to describe the intermingling as a "touch of Ireland" on Montserrat. Furthermore, rather than attempt to prove or disprove Messenger's assertion about the sympathetic relationship between Irish landowners and their slaves, Fergus (1994: 77) prefers to make a slightly different point about slavery on Montserrat:

> "[t]here was really no comparison between the horrors of black slavery and the discrimination against Irish Catholics in Montserrat, but both groups in their different ways hankered after freedom."

In other words, all slaves on Montserrat were mistreated, whether by English or Irish slave-masters, and it is not creditable to equate English mistreatment of Irish Catholics with black slavery though both Irish Catholics and black slaves desired some form of independence. Second-class citizens on Montserrat, the Irish settlers congregated in the southernmost villages on the island such as St. Patrick's, enjoying a greater freedom amongst themselves – ironically living as "a colony within a colony" (Fergus 1994: 22). Cheddy, as ever, is more forthright in his rebuttal of Messenger's work: in his article "Burying the Irish Myth", Cheddy asserts that there was little social movement between levels of the plantocratic social structure – between English landholders, Irish farmers and "Afrikan" slaves;[18] he adds that one slave owner was as inhumane as another, whether they were English or Irish. Cheddy continues by dispelling the basis of Messenger's "Black Irish" label – that is, voluntary inter-ethnic marriages between slaves or freed slaves and Irish indentured labourers, freemen and landholders – and by pointing out that any coloureds on the island (260 in the 1787 census) were "the offspring of Afrikan women taken against their will by the european slave master":[19]

> Montserratians are Afrikans. [...] At no point in time throughout the 360 years of european occupation in the island of Montserrat is there any indication that the two ethnic groups merged, amalgamated, and formed a creole Afrikan-Irish society. If there's any doubt in your mind, just look at the faces around you.[20]

The leftovers of the Irish settler's stew on Montserrat still remains to be scavenged and picked over by these contemporary writers with their polarised positions. What is emerging from this debate are a variety of positions falling between the extremes of *no Irish retentions felt* and *many Irish retentions sensed*; let me add to this, though, that Messenger's (1991) academic *verstehen* sensings have elsewhere also included his haunting by "Brendan", a *leprechaun*, following his fieldwork in Ireland!

The future of St. Patrick's Day and the "Black Irish"

At present, St. Patrick's Day remains an example of contestation, of colonial and tourist impressionistic histories versus independent and nationalistic impressionistic histories, with many Montserratians also happy to just enjoy the week-long extension of the weekend. Throughout this chapter I have sought to show that there is, at the very least, an agenda for each person involved with the "Irishness" debate on Montserrat: the academics such as Fergus and Cheddy with their nationalist commemoration; Messenger (1994: 15) with his critique of a local "revitalization movement"; and the Irish-American visitors intent upon their celebrations. Working through the materials, it is apparent that there are but positions and impressions – just as Thesiger and Waugh saw and experienced different impressionistic realities of Haile Selassie's coronation. Each position articulated above is used, suppressed, manipulated, interpreted and reinterpreted. For my anthropologist self, they are the impressionistic positions of the "past and the present in the present" (Bloch 1977). Moreover, I have tried to show that in some cases it is possible for Cheddy and Sir Fergus to unite and share a reality, to create an inter-subjective constellation (see Chapter 3); and that Messenger's anthropological fault, here, is to privilege his historical reality at the expense of other respective positions and native realities.

Certainly, the St. Patrick's Day celebrations do attract excursionists and tourists to Montserrat, but the figures are too inconsistent across the years to be able to work out a trend for tourist activity on the island. I would like to conclude this chapter, then, by commenting further upon struggle to save or alter the St. Patrick's Day week as it is known and understood by people on Montserrat. It is my supposition that the tension described above – amongst and between Montserratians (Missie O'Garro, Doc, Pippa), Afrophiles (Fergus, Cheddy), anthropologists (Messenger, Mullin, Skinner), and those directly involved in the tourist industry (the Montserrat Tourist Board, tourists, British and Montserratian Governments) – will remain. Each different interest group (casual, political, academic, economic) has a different historical reality and understanding (personal, national, anthropological, financial) of St. Patrick's Day such that the groups are likely to continue with their trend to polarise between the activists (commemorators) and the tourism supporters (celebrators).

It is possible that Messenger's spiteful comments directed at the unnamed "Afrophiles" – the West Indian elite on Montserrat such as, presumably, Sir Fergus and Cheddy – also refer to one of the pre-eminent cultural activists of the 1970s, Dr. George Irish (University of the West Indies resident tutor on Montserrat prior to Fergus). Like Fergus, Irish has an history of activism, using articles and pamphlets to explain why Montserratians should celebrate 17th March. It was Irish (1974) who wrote that "Montserratian Negroes were among the front-line freedom-fighters of the New World", and that those involved in the St. Patrick's Day conspiracy were "noble warriors, lovers of freedom and self-determination" (Irish 1993: 12). He has also commented that "[t]he Irish imprint is more titular than real; the landmarks are more topographical than cultural or spiritual" (Irish 1993: 11). Irish's (1993: 9–16) work represents another Montserratian consciousness-raising enterprise, one running alongside Fergus's and Cheddy's endeavours. It is an attempt to change the way Montserratians think about themselves, others, their history and the history of others. Irish's (1993: 15) goal, however, is more extreme than Fergus's: he seeks "total liberation", perhaps sharing Cheddy's radical inter-subjectivity.

In an attempt to encourage tourism to Montserrat and to assist the Montserrat Tourist Board with their manufacture and control of the "the tourist gaze" (Urry 1994), the Government Information Unit printed a different account of the Irish influence on Montserrat in their leaflet on the history of St. Patrick's Day. In their leaflet they make the point that the white race of Irish settlers were in the majority on Montserrat and so "[i]t is natural therefore, that they would bring with them their customs, feast days, religion and culture, and these things would become an integral part of the society of those times" (Government Information Unit undated: 1). The Tourist Board's "natural" qualities, Messenger's "imponderables", Fergus's "legacy" and Irish's "imprint" all lie on the St. Patrick's Day continuum. Rather than reiterate Messenger's "Black Irish" message in a recent tourist guidebook, one designed to unveil the "special Montserrat package", Fergus (1992: vii, 14–17) opted to refer to Irish and/or African retentions on Montserrat as an amalgam – "a 'New World' interpretation", a cultural stew of Old World and New World. His book is aimed at encouraging tourists to Montserrat, but it also contains a warning that Montserrat does not become "transformed into an object for Euro-American consumption" (Fergus 1992: 64). This danger is also picked up by Laffey (1995: 30), an American student anthropologist who notes that the marketing behind this exotic island – where the Caribbean remains the way it used to be – "encourages the potential visitor to identify with the elite status of colonial rulers and with the power and deference they enjoyed, without the problematic and potentially guilt-provoking need for overt oppression." With the addition of Montserrat's Black Irish attraction, there is the distinct possibility that the friendly tourist consumption of Montserrat will eventually turn Montserratians into a spectacle to be consumed rather like the exotic Other in a cultural freak-show – "[Black Irish] ethnic tourism as the mirror image of racism" (MacCannell 1992: 170). Wary of this potential future, Fergus reminds us in *The Montserrat News* that Montserrat is more than just a tourist escape, that she is a home for Montserratians who should retain their sense of identity above that which the tourist pays them:

> "Montserrat's culture still rings with the melody of Europe and the rhythm of Africa [....] The Emerald Isle is more than a name, it is a beauty of culture and history."[21]

By writing these invitations to tourists, these histories to academics, these poems to expatriates, and these newspaper pieces to

Montserratians, Fergus is the only person out of the three "Afrophiles" (Cheddy, Fergus, Irish) to skilfully maintain his position on the island. Fergus is the consummate diplomat, the articulate barbarian Caliban on Montserrat.

This chapter has been a case study of several personal and institutional historical realities; a range of representations aimed at convincing undiscerning Montserratians, belongers and visitors. To date, the Montserrat Tourist Board would appear to be the predominant force in the St. Patrick's Day proceedings. Its influence is far-reaching, from the off-island tourism campaigns run throughout the year to the on-island publicity promotions such as its Tourism Awareness Program (ranging from history seminars for taxi drivers to tourism essay contests for schoolchildren and inter-hotel cooking competitions),[22] Tourism Week in November and its "Tourism is Everybody's Business" slogan and calypso-like song for the radio.[23] As part of Director of Tourism Leona Midgette's aim to "sensitise the public on the importance of tourism",[24] for the 1995 St. Patrick's Day tourist celebrations, the MTB sponsored the publication in *The Montserrat News* of John Bruton's (Taoiseach of Ireland) diplomatic letter of greeting to Montserrat. There, Bruton wrote about the significance of St. Patrick's Day for the "Irish":

> "[o]n St. Patrick's Day, people of Irish birth and descent throughout the world join in a celebration of our collective sense of Irishness. We recall with pride the accomplishments of our ancestors and the richness of Ireland's cultural heritage."[25]

It is this loose "collective sense of Irishness" which will continue to bring tourists to Montserrat. This shared Irish Diaspora-like reality is reinforced with the use of Irish emblems throughout Montserrat: the Montserrat Tourist Board's palm tree with a shamrock background; the ceremonial flag of Montserrat, "the Lady and the Cross"; "the badge of the colony", a blue flag with the flag of the Union in the top left quarter and a picture of Erin, wife of the first king of Ireland dressed in green, holding a brown cross and a golden harp, in the centre of the right half of the flag. These emblems, symbols of a national identity in Ireland, are – so Bruton declares – the "distinctively Irish dimension" in Montserrat's culture. [26]

The debate surrounding the celebration or commemoration of St. Patrick's Day on Montserrat lies at the heart of the various representations of Montserrat's emerald Caribbean identity –

whether Government promotion of tourism, Fergus's call for Montserratian nationalism, Irish's push for liberation, Cheddy's cry for self-determination, or the fickle fancies of the vacationer and travel writer ("[t]he Union jack should fly at half mast every St. Patrick's Day", in Fallon's mind [see below]).[27] Clearly any move of the St. Patrick's Day commemorations to 1st August would be a move towards the celebration end of the celebration–commemoration continuum. It would assist with the establishment of a celebratory tourist reality and encourage the increased "sensationalising" of the day and the islanders. The change would impose further the desires and views of short-term visitors upon Montserrat, and would undermine Fergus's and Cheddy's promotion of a Montserratian national solidarity.

In his article about an Irish American Unity Foundation tour to Montserrat, Jim Fallon notes that the conference group delegates all agreed that Montserratians, Irish-Americans and American blacks are all bonded together; the delegates also hoped that they could influence the Montserratian islanders with their particular version of Irish, African, West Indian and American history and heritage. Reminiscent of Messenger's use of English to undermine the Afrofile commemoration of a St. Patrick's Day rebellion, Fallon made the following qualified comment in his article:

> "*[A] man named Fergus*, a local historian and a University of West Indies professor, *said he thinks* St. Patrick's Day is celebrated not only to commemorate the island's Irish history, but also to remember the March 1768 slave rebellion."[28]

It is no small wonder, then, that the local Montserratian academics show such resilience in the face of their implicated dependence upon the tourist and the British. Only by continually persuading others of their alternative impressions of Montserrat's contested history are they able to impress their own historical realities upon other more powerful interest groups.

NOTES

1. Anon., 1993, no other references available.
2. Anon. [d], no other references available.
3. Anon. [c]: 4, no other references available.
4. Anon., 1994: 2, no other references available.
5. See Fergus's poem "March of Death" (Fergus, *Montserrat Times*, 19 March 1982: 5) and his newspaper articles: "A window on our history" (*Montserrat Mirror*, 28 January 1972: 8); "St. Patrick's Day, March 17" (*Montserrat*

Mirror, 14 March 1975: 7–8); "Why Celebrate St. Patrick's Day?" (*Montserrat Reporter*, 28 February 1986: 5); Fergus, H., "St. Patrick's Day in Focus" (*Montserrat Reporter*, 27 March 1992, no other references available).

6. Transcript of an interview between Chedmond Browne and Jonathan Skinner (10 July 1995: 1–2).

7. Transcript from ZJB Radio broadcasts (13 February 1995, no other references available).

8. Goods manufactured on Montserrat can already enter the EU at a lower rate of duty.

9. Anon., 1995: 5, no other references available.

10. Transcript from ZJB Radio broadcasts (13 February 1995, no other references available).

11. Anon., *Montserrat News*, 16 March 1995: 7, no other references available.

12. H.R.H. Elizabeth II, *Montserrat News*, 16 March 1995: 16.

13. "When Justice Came To Church" (Fergus, *The Montserrat Reporter*, 17 March 1995: 8).

14. Anon., *Montserrat Reporter*, 17 March 1995: 4, no other references available.

15. Meade, 17 March 1995: no other references available.

16. See Irish, *Montserrat Mirror*, 17 February 1978: 5; Irish, *The Montserrat Reporter*, 15 March 1985: 6–7).

17. See also Anon. [a]: no other references available.

18. Browne, *Pan-Afrikan Liberator*, June 1993: 4.

19. Browne, *Pan-Afrikan Liberator*, June 1993: 3.

20. Browne, *Pan-Afrikan Liberator*, June 1993: 4.

21. Fergus, *Montserrat News*, 18 November 1994: 17, 16.

22. Anon., *Montserrat News*, 14 October 1994: 19, no other references available.

23. See Anon., *Montserrat News*, 23 June 1995: 20.

24. Anon., *Montserrat Reporter*, 28 October 1994: 1, no other references available.

25. Bruton, *Montserrat News*, 24 March 1995: 12.

26. Bruton, *Montserrat News*, 24 March 1995: 12.

27. Fallon, *Irish Echo*, 28 July–3 August 1993: 18.

28. Fallon, *Irish Echo*, 28 July–3 August 1993: 18, my emphasis.

Dust settles but future is bleak

Polly Patullo reports from Montserrat on the grey, ash-ridden aftermath of a deadly eruption that has left those remaining on the island even more fearful and confused.

A Pɪᴄᴋ-Uᴘ truck packed with silent young men lurched up the hill away from the stricken flatlands of eastern Montserrat. "You don't see them?" someone called from the road. The men shook their heads, their eyes brimming with tears.

They had gone to search for relatives in Farm's village, which was devastated by Wednesday's eruption of the Soufriere Hills volcano. Ash poured over the crater rim down one of the ravines and into the river valleys, submerging villages as it did so.

Further down the road at a police checkpoint, groups of people stared down the coast towards the now empty airport. "He took everything. A whole village wiped out," said a taxi driver in disbelief. He was looking at a flat, grey steaming ash deposit where, 24 hours earlier, the community of Trants had stood.

Six people were killed and fifteen are missing after the worst day for this tiny seven by eleeven-mile British Dependent Territory, whose population has fallen from 11,000 to under 7,000 since the volcano started its current activity in April 1995.

The dead and missing – 40 were rescued by helicopter – were caught in one of the two "no-access" zones that stretch from coast to coast across the southern half of the island, taking in the capital, Plymouth.

Most residents were long ago evacuated to the north. But some insisted on staying, despite many warnings and what Governor Frank Savage called "strenuous" efforts to persuade them to leave. Others returned to the no-go areas to work their fields or tend their animals. For these once-green slopes were the agricultural heartland of Montserrat, home to many of the staunchly independent small farmers who till the volcanic soil.

"It will take courage to continue," Robert Allen said outside the hospital, itself relocated to a school in the safe north. Mr. Allen, a part-time farmer who produced a bouquet of fresh herbs from his car, was trying to visit his stepfather, who was burnt in the ash flow. "We're scared now," he admitted.

Down the west coast the classic greenery of a Caribbean landscape now gives way to uniform greyness. People wear dust masks to protect themselves from the swirling ash as they struggle to school or work.

In recent months a new capital has emerged around the small town of Salem to replace the boarded up, ghost-grey Plymouth. In Salem, businesses have re-opened. The internationally renowned calypso star Arrow has his Arrow Manshop in a neat row of wooden buildings, while government offices and banks have colonised smart villas owned by absentee expatriates.

But the uncertainty is becoming more acute, with the possibility of more evacuations in the face of further volcanic activity. The island remains cut off, the airport and port closed.

As the HMS Liverpool sails towards Montserrat to offer support, Montserratians can only hope that some day the volcano will go back to sleep.

• The Royal Fleet Auxiliary tanker Black Rover has been diverted from duties in the Caribbean to help HMS Liverpool on Montserrat. The vessel, with a crew of 53, is due to arrive on Sunday afternoon.

(Patullo, *The Guardian*, 28 June 1997: 17)

SOCIAL ANTHROPOLOGY AND SOCIAL COMMENTARY:
FROM COLONIAL CONTESTS TO MEANINGFUL
CLOSURE ON MONTSERRAT

In this conclusion I draw the book to a provisional close. I do this by commenting upon the literary and academic points I have been making whilst ending my presentation of social commentaries and impressions of Montserrat by genre groups of poets, calypsonians, tourists, and travel writers – as well as individuals such as Howard Fergus and Chedmond Browne. Both the indeterminate processes of writing and reading this text may be at a close, but life on and around Montserrat continues apace, and what Maurice Bloch (1977) terms the "long conversation" with the anthropologist's fieldsite continues apace in both the writer's and reader's imagination. All that has been suspended is the writer's collection and presentation of diverse realities and impressions of Montserrat, the writing process of representing some perspectives and connections, and the reader's reading of these representations and impressions. Howard Fergus is still writing poetry – about the volcano; Chedmond Browne is still contesting British colonialism from a more northerly cantonment; and I am still collecting and collating new representations and impressions of Montserrat – though from Britain.

Throughout this book I deliberately broke with the tradition of writing a text which presents a consistent presence, written with one, single, authorial voice. I wanted to construct a text which immersed the reader in the ethnographic present of fieldwork on Montserrat – be it through the anthropologist's eyes, or by interview with calypsonians or Cheddy, or by following tourists around the island – but also, in places, pulled the reader away from the island and the anthropologist's "long conversation" with the locals. To do this, to deconstruct and fragment the reader's presence, I inserted a temporal leap – a detached report of Montserrat's developing volcanic crisis – at the start of each chapter, reports which are a record apart from the ethnographic chapters. These reports I collected from "post-fieldwork", from when I was writing each chapter after I had already left Montserrat. This is one of my – postmodern – ways of recognising the partial nature of the text and the reading and writing interpretative and impressionistic processes; here I should reiterate that I reject the possibility of a complete loss of semantic or semiotic meaning: like a coil, signifier and signified are sometimes close and sometimes loose, all depending upon the eyes and ears of the beholder and beholden, hence my impressionistic turn towards an art of grammatology, a return from postliminy. I did this to break from the supposedly rigid boundaries of academic research and writing, from the persuasive illusions of space and time masquerading as ethnography.

Throughout this book I have maintained that writing is more than just the construction of an illusion because it is also an indeterminate activity or process which affects the writer's and reader's realities. A part of this argument stems from Dick Hobbs's (1993: 48) notion of "writing as field-work": for him, the writing process forces a new re-engagement with the fieldwork, recognising "that our experiential and interpretative faculties continue to function long after the gate to the field has been closed". For me, the field alters and affects the anthropologist's reality such that we never really leave the field. In this way, I am extending Anthony Cohen's (1992) work on "post-fieldwork fieldwork", blurring and querying the liminal distinctions between the pre- and the post- in fieldwork on metaphysical and phenomenological grounds.

From the start of the Academic Preface to the start of this Conclusion, the volcano situation has developed, shattering the closure of this text, tinkering with the reader's reality with e-mails from the Internet, pages from the World Wide Web and international reports from the Associated Press. These chapter prefaces in this book form their own developing narrative within the book narrative. They opened with the alerts in late July when I was evacuated from the island (see Chapter 1). Reuters covered the situation and their reports were posted on the CaribTalk 'beach bar' web site (see Chapter 2). The British papers such as *The Times*,

The Daily Telegraph, The Sun and even the Scottish paper *The Courier and Advertiser* picked up the news as soon as they found human-interest stories concerning their "locals" (see Chapter 3 and Chapter 4). On Montserrat, the newspapers wrote optimistic pieces; one even predicted a future for Montserrat in volcano tourism (see Chapter 5). The discussion in Chapter 6 about St. Patrick's Day was foregrounded by a useful travel writing article about the volcano and the Irish heritage on Montserrat. The volcano chapter preface to the Conclusion reporting deadly volcanic activities was written by Polly Patullo. Finally, true to life, the Postscript report at the end of this Conclusion leaves the island to its uncertain future – with super-heated gas, rock and ash flows tearing through the streets of the Plymouth where an anthropologist once trod, where Cheddy once flogged his newsletters, where Teknikal and the firefighters once sang together in Doc's house, and where Pippa once entertained. These messages are an artificial frame around this book, a book which has been filled in by chapters about Montserrat and the reading, writing and doing of anthropology. It is about these chapters – a sustained example of postmodern anthropology – that I shall now direct my more general comments in terms of anthropology and the anthropologist, and the various social commentaries and conversations on Montserrat. I then conclude this Conclusion by discussing Montserrat as an arena of theoretical and "empirical" contest and conquest.

I) BLURRED IMPRESSIONS – ANTHROPOLOGY AND THE ANTHROPOLOGIST

Let me recap on this book so far. My first impressions of Montserrat, in Chapter 1, are the impressions of an anthropologist. Prior to these impressions, I presented a theoretical Academic Preface to the book. In that Academic Preface I set out my anthropology which is uncomfortable and uncertain, postmodern and impressionistic; it was there that I set out the postmodern agenda which I was attempting to sustain in an ethnography of Montserrat. There, I argue that anthropologists gain but partial and relative impressions, the primary reason for holding an *a priori* stance towards realities. Furthermore, I – in my ethnographic studies of other people – envision a pragmatic but relative approach to diversity. I use an IF ... THEN approach to curtail relativism's slippery slope; universals, essences and truths are local truths, incommensurable realities which can only be juxtaposed and reconciled by the anthropologist once they are situated within their respective variables. It is, then, the anthropologist's task to fathom culture's criteria by peering into the various world-views – the "multiple subjective worlds" – in the field. Thus Tyler's (1986: 127) "perspectival relativity", anthropology, like history, is viewed as a heterogeneous and contested and contesting discipline without any universal trajectory. It becomes an uncertain subject, lacking a universal position and certain epistemological approach. Essentially, the rest of the book is an exemplification of this approach, one which results in a diverse range of different ethnographic impressions of Montserrat, various realities which I cautiously present in an experimental manner: notable individuals (Fergus, Cheddy), influential groups (calypsonians, development workers) and "historical" events (St. Patrick's Day).

Each chapter is an illustration of my postmodern impressionistic anthropology set out in the Academic Preface and the second chapter. By order, to force a catholic reading of this book, Chapter 1 immerses the reader without warning. Chapter 1 initiates the reader's relationship with the island. Here, I force away the virginity of the reader's Montserrat reality. In this chapter, Montserrat is built up through the author's presences. This, for me, is what life and fieldwork was like on Montserrat. I have tried not to remove myself or my fieldwork activities, mistakes and all, from this representation of my impressions. No doubt each reader, with each sensitive and indeterminate reading, will establish their own impressions from the text, and will, according to "the 'gestalt' of the text" (Iser 1988: 216), fill in the absences in the text wherever they are. I accept and acknowledge these characteristics of writing and reading, characteristics which differ from my lived experiences and which I try to communicate to others. With this in mind, I allow the reader more leeway in their reading – there are no pictures or maps outside this text for any pictures or maps would freeze, forever, an aspect of the reader's reality which relates to Montserrat. As I mentioned in the Academic Preface, reality is a blur, boundaries are unrealistic attempts at order, and distinctions are only local universals and should be recognised for what they are by the anthropologists who specialise in the natives' points of view. Indeed, even the impressions which feature in this book are partial impressions, arbitrary in selection, based upon my brief dip into the fieldwork mire. This book narrative comes, then, to a provisional close scarcely mentioning the traditional ethnographic categories of the kinship, geography, economics, politics of the island, and a comparison with other neighbouring islands.

From this loosely written opening, characters are drawn and personalities are described from my perspective. My approach thus reveals the muddle of fieldwork, the loose understandings built up by the anthropologist: in my case, I absorbed dialect by osmosis – there were no fixed or collective understandings for many words, or even activities. What was a passable and acceptable expression, opinion or action in one quarter of the island was not acceptable and not understood in another. Montserrat was "pock-marked" – for want of a better word – by various interest groups sharing realities. These "constellations" contested and competed with other groups, and sometimes they converged – from the individual level to small interest groups, to wider groups; for example, Doc, the firemen, Montserratians. Yet even for Doc, there are Goffmanesque roles which he is playing and presenting in everyday life; and if I continue with my own impressions of Doc, there is change and contest within himself – his "seemings" as Rorty (1996: 29) would describe them.

From a sample day on Montserrat, the impressions and representations of Montserrat slip and slide into a deconstruction of ethnography – what passes in this book as the second chapter. Leaving my ethnography of an anthropologist on Montserrat fresh in the reader's memory, I dip into social anthropological theory with Strathern's ethnography as partial connections and Rapport's description of social life as a "muddling-through" between different individuals' diverse world-views, both anthropologists practising Shweder's version of a romantic and rebellious anthropology. These anthropologists, like myself, like Geertz, Leach and Fernandez, are dealing with people and their messy lives. Writing about people, writing about unbounded individuals, anthropologists have to engage with the non-rational ideas and practices of people's lives. We have to interpret social behaviour, listen to locals, follow local events, research local knowledge and what is described as local culture. This local lore, local behaviour, local knowledge, is labelled local culture – culture is a cult of social consensus between people, the old "cliché of contestation" (Barnard & Spencer [1996: 141])

– but, as I have tried to show by alluding to the contests and competitions between individuals and social groups at work on the island, culture is also inchoate.

Culture and identity are persuasive tropes, powerful labels to unite or divide people. In the case of those on Montserrat, the individuals and groups demonstrate the diverse, contested and fragmentary nature of reality, culture and identity, whether it be Montserratian with Montserratian, Montserratian with expatriate, expatriate with expatriate or expatriate with Montserratian. Fergus shares little with Governor Savage or Union leader Cheddy, and less even with another poet, Doc – Doc's dialect, which I spoke around him and his friends, was incomprehensible to many other Montserratians on the island such as Pippa who lived just down the street. Though Fergus often occupies the Governor's residence when the Governor is off island, he does so for reasons very different from those of the Governor. Expatriates living on Montserrat do not socialise with Doc. Cheddy's historical reality is unfathomable to the Governor or most expatriates. Doc is sympathetic to Cheddy, but Pippa is sceptical of his colonised world-view. And so on.

As an anthropologist, as an "Arab Jew" on Montserrat, as a British colonial, as a poet, as a white tourist, I moved through Montserrat – a researcher, a chameleon on various walls, switching and jumping realities and situations from tourist's beach to poets' Maroon, from calypso session to firefighter get together. I would not, however, describe myself as a Machiavellian parasite latching onto informants, becoming a doppelgänger for the sake of research. My status as a researcher on the island was a special privilege. I had the good fortune to be able to share aspects of myself with diverse individuals and groups, partly as a result of sharing my personal interests, partly due to my personality, and partly because of my research position on Montserrat. In sum, I personified the ambiguous nature of reality – neither Montserratian nor tourist, British but not expatriate.

II) Social commentaries – poetry and calypso

As I mentioned at the end of the first chapter, I regularly attended the Writers' Maroon on Montserrat. I got to know the poets on the island by joining their meetings, socialising with them and eventually interviewing them. Howard Fergus, the most well-known poet on the island, preserves an aloof aura about him, so my contact with him was formal and occurred during the poetry meetings which he ran, his West Indian History classes, and my interview with him in his UWI office. It is in Chapter 2 that I concentrate upon the poets of Montserrat, Sir Fergus especially because of his interesting position and poetry on Montserrat. There, I partially explicate and contextualise his poetic reality. Poetry is the way in which Fergus expresses himself; it is his main expressive medium. Fergus "makes literary" his everyday impressions of his life and the people on Montserrat, using the public domain for what many would consider to be his private thoughts. In this book I concentrate upon Sir Fergus because his various positions on Montserrat make his impressions of Montserrat particularly interesting, and because his poetry can be related to the work of other "Barbarian & Commonwealth" poets. It is social commentary rather than abstract poetry. As such, his work is an example of indirect communication by word-wrapping (see Hendry and Watson 1997). Fergus's work also can be contrasted with that of Chedmond Browne, another intellectual who occupies a different historical reality on Montserrat and uses different modes of expression.

Just as different poets and historians represent Montserrat differently, giving us their diverse individual impressions of the island, so too the calypsonians discussed later in Chapter 4 give us different impressions of Montserrat. Each of the calypsonians writes songs and sings about the island – what Montserrat is, what Montserrat used to be, and what they want Montserrat to be. Calypso, I would argue, is like poetry, both private and public for some of the performers and creators. Both poetry and calypso are social commentaries, opportunities for the author to express their particular impressions of Montserrat. The difference between poetry and calypso is that poetry is *sometimes* performed to an audience whereas calypso is *usually* performed to an audience. But neither poetry nor calypso are products just for public consumption. To make this point, I include a presentation of calypso at a private local gathering in my examination of calypsos – and a few songs – about the island. This, then, is an example of calypso's creative nature, how calypso is written, played and toyed with, all to retain its topical position as social commentary.

There is the initial conversation with Top Secret about calypso as social and political commentary. There are three private scenes which I shared with Teknikal and some firefighters, all written in a play format to best convey an evening of musical treats with the firefighters' lyrical exchanges. There is the serious and poignant interview with Lord Alfredo. And finally, at the end of the chapter, I mention how calypso is internalised by many listeners, a point not lost on the Montserrat Tourist Board which created their own tourism jingle to advertise the benefits of tourism to Montserratians (see Chapter 6). Unlike the Maroon poets, calypsonians such as Teknikal, Top Secret, Lord Alfredo and others have their songs played on the radio, sold on the streets, repeated on people's lips and, if they can snappily reflect life's situations, the lyrics become popular catchphrases ("come better dan dat" was the retort putting down Ant when his eyes and mouth were hungrily chasing a school girl, as I mentioned in Chapter 1). It would appear, then, that though both poetry and calypso are social commentary, the former is uttered with *gravitas* whilst the latter is sung as bawdy *vox populi*.

III) Opposing conversations on Montserrat

Teknikal's social commentary is little known by the Technical Co-operation Officers (TCOs) from Britain who feature in Chapter 3. As I argue in Chapter 3, though the TCOs share the same title, they share little else with Teknikal, the calypsonian, or with other Montserratians. The TCOs do, however, share a certain degree of inter-subjectivity which I observe at one of their dinner parties, a "constellation" which contrasts with a Montserratian constellation witnessed at another dinner party. A constellation is a vaguely shared inter-subjectivity, similarity in a partial impression of reality, a loosely wrought interpretative community, an indeterminate Shwederian extension of Stanley Fish's "interpretative [reading] communities" and Nigel Rapport's loops of thought (world-views). The TCOs are international development workers from Britain who work and socialise together on Montserrat; they have shared interests, outlooks and attitudes. In Chapter 3 I contrast *TCO* development conversations at a New Year's dinner party with *Montserratian* development conversations on the same topic at one of Pippa's soirées. In the first presentation, the reader is less close to the scene of events: rather than experience the occasion through the anthropologist's eyes, here, the reader is a fly on the wall following the anthropologist at a distance. In the second presentation, the anthropologist is more sympathetic to and comfortable with the guests: here, the events unfold about Jonathan.

The purpose of Chapter 3 is not only to note the importance of the indigenous reactions and responses to the construction of Government Headquarters or to provide exacting transcripts of the evenings, it is to show through impressions that diverse realities can converge as well as diverge. On the subject of development there appear to exist two separate groups. This, then, is an example of expatriate individuals' realities converging, and Montserratian locals' realities converging to form two opposing constellations, an example of both inter-subjectivity (within the two groups) and incommensurability (between the two groups). In this case, inter-subjectivity is a conversational instance which reveals shared feelings and attitudes which I was able to verify by conducting further observation and interaction with the participants. Needless-to-say, even the spoken examples contained in Chapter 3 are as partial as the indeterminate nature of words' meanings when read and the assumptions and imaginations of the reader. Indeed, many conversations are examples of people talking past each other. Furthermore, the groups differ in substance and in kind. The expatriates are foreigners on Montserrat, judging and rating the island and the islanders according to previous postings; "artificial cesspit" is how Euan expresses his working and living frustrations. Their impressions of Montserrat are important because they live, work and interact with Montserratians on the island such as those at Pippa's party. Though their impressions of Montserrat vary, as a social group on the island they fall together in-between the Montserratians and the tourists – between those at Pippa's dinner party, calypsonians such as Belonger and the Montserratian firefighters and poets, and the fleeting visitors such as the tourists and travel-writers.

To investigate further the relationship between the individual and the group, I go on to consider the life and works of Chedmond Browne in the next-but-one chapter. In Chapter 5, I again investigate impressions of Montserrat through conversation, this time conversations with Cheddy. Cheddy is a well-known personality on the island, one who contrasts with Sir Fergus, especially with respect to his strong personal historical reality. Cheddy is a Garvey-like figure who courts trouble whereas Fergus is a Du Bois-like figure who courts publishers and diplomats. Cheddy has a bitter relationship with the Chief Technical Co-operation Officer, His Excellency Governor Savage. Chapter 5 approaches Cheddy just as I heard of him and just as I met him. Once again, the reading of the chapter begins by situating the writer and his relationship to his subject. I do this because it is important to show how the relationship with a subject is built up and how a world-view is accessed. Cheddy, like Fergus, was difficult to get to know, but for different reasons: as a rule, Cheddy does not talk with white people.

It could be argued that I am just engaged in Geertz's (1993[a]: 448) interpretative anthropology, that Cheddy is giving me a Montserratian reading of a Montserratian experience, suggesting a version of Geertz's (1993[a]: 3–30) Indian tale of the world on a platform on the back of an elephant on the back of a turtle on the back of an infinitude of turtles. Yet, I maintain that we have here something more than local interpretations, we have here the manifestation of local realities. I extend Geertz; and I criticise Geertz (1993[a]: 29) for giving us a tale which illustrates his point that "[c]ultural analysis is intrinsically incomplete" whilst at the same time failing to take on board the full ramifications of his own words with his presentation of a composite Balinese cockfight. My understanding of such interpretations which Geertz calls for is that there is an interpretative understanding of Balinese cockfights, one which lies with the Balinese themselves, one which the anthropologist can only report upon and translate into the anthropologist's own culture once the anthropologist has uncovered the symbolic keys to the socio-cultural activities. But this is an interpretative anthropology which places limitations upon interpretation. This is an interpretative anthropology which does not rest upon the back of turtle after turtle after turtle. Geertz's Indian tale does not match up with his Balinese example. For Geertz there is both no end to interpretations and an end to interpretations. According to Watson (1992: 138), Geertz's understanding of Balinese understandings stereotypes the Balinese. For me, it is more akin to the tale of the anthropologist standing on the back of a Balinese elephant which is standing upon a turtle which is standing still on a bedrock reality. My postmodern impressionistic anthropology shies away from such comfortable certainties. What I mean is that, unlike an ultimate interpretation – one with layers of interpretations and understandings, one layer under another but all with a base floor interpretation, that grounded turtle – all we have are shifting, depthless impressions of ourselves and others. Culture, history, ethnography and representation are all Baudrillard's simulacrum ("the collective hallucination that there is something solid outside the system" [Levin 1996: 280] such as natural values). My realities are therefore endless.

The chapter about Cheddy situates his role on Montserrat and represents his revolutionary work as leader of the Seamen's Union involved in an employment dispute with the British and Montserratian Governments. Like Fergus, Cheddy writes and articulates his reality in the public domain and, despite radio and classroom bans, he manages to promote his historical reality of emancipation right across Montserrat: his history which accounts for Montserrat's present colonial position, and the distribution of wealth across the island as well as internationally; his history which chronicles the continued oppression of black people. Though both are historians of Montserrat and the lives of Montserratians, Fergus has been the more successful at teaching and writing his history of Montserrat. Fergus has been lauded publicly whilst Cheddy has been condemned in the streets and the courtrooms. Both writers nevertheless hold past realities in the present to alter the future's anticipated reality. For me, these are two of many histories, fixed records bound up in a nation-building and consciousness-raising enterprise.

To return to the Academic Preface, we have already heard from Gilles Deleuze (via Young) of the insurmountable difficulty with defining and circumscribing an event, a coronation for example, or even a volcanic eruption. To this we can add the historian E.H. Carr's (1974: 8, 12) points that history is a reflection of the present and is not independent of the historian's interpretation. So we can build a case arguing that Fergus's history of Montserrat reflects his own position in time, as well as his position in Montserratian society; it reflects his-story. Both Carr and Young give us useful critiques of the belief in an objective and universal history, of a singular historical reality. Elaborating upon this historiography of history, extending a view of history beyond conceptions of history in which the past is a fiction of (and a charter for) the present, I suggest that the past is a record of our endless presents. In other words, the present is all that we have, and it is only in the present that the past has any meaning: history's meaning comes from the present. Yet, I do recognise that this is my (anti-)historical reality which many others – Fergus and Cheddy included – do not share.

A great deal has been written about the convergences and divergences between history and anthropology (anthropology as a history of the present [Evans-Pritchard 1962]), and the relationship between history and ethnography (how ethnography deals with "[t]he problem of writing the history of a present without a past" [Levi-Strauss 1977: 12, 3], and the problem of writing constructions of the past [Thomas 1996: 275]). My focus in this book has been upon the meaning and the understanding of history, the native's historical reality, and how these historical realities are used: how they are spread and are disseminated by Sir Fergus in books and newspapers, and by Cheddy in *The Pan-Afrikan Liberator*; how they are influenced and contested by the Government and expatriates, and how the histories are received by other people on Montserrat. All the interest groups featured in this book seek the pre-eminence of their history, and all parties contest and challenge each others' histories. Historical constellations are fleeting, formed and forged often by chance: for example, both Cheddy and Fergus's celebration of Montserrat's first Chief Minister, W.H. Bramble – as former President of the Montserrat Trade and Labour Union for Cheddy, as intellectual and political mentor for Fergus, common father of Montserrat's working class for both (see Fergus 1994: 151).

IV) ARENAS OF CONTEST: ST. PATRICK'S DAY AND THE "EMPIRICAL" GAZE

Though the two historians, Fergus and Cheddy, would not publicly align themselves, the poet and the port leader were once again thrown together during the week of 17 March 1995. In Chapter 6, I write about the Irish legacy on Montserrat and I give my ethnography of the Montserratian celebrations of St. Patrick's Day. During the week-long festival it was publicly announced that, in future, the unknown martyrs of the St. Patrick's Day 1768 rebellion could be commemorated at the August Emancipation

Commemoration which would be rechristened as Montserrat Achievers Day. This would be done so that the St. Patrick's Day celebrations would be more appealing to tourists without any local undercurrents of racial tension and slavery histories possibly tainting their experiences of Montserrat. Following this announcement during the 1995 celebrations, the public national figures Cheddy Browne and Howard Fergus were interviewed for public radio, each responding that the 17 March should always be connected with the attempted slave rebellion, Fergus going so far as to mention that the day should be named National Heroes Day. Here, Fergus and Cheddy's historical realities converged momentarily.

Fergus has always campaigned for the commemoration of St. Patrick's Day. It was Fergus who researched the failed rebellion and publicised certain aspects of the event in his poetry and histories of Montserrat. He established and made meaningful the island-wide St. Patrick's Day celebrations. To change the date of the activity would, for Fergus as well as Cheddy, break the connection between the historical reality of the date and its commemoration, turning a day of martyrdom – with tourists watching alongside – into a tourist celebration for the tourists. In this sense, the St. Patrick's Day celebrations are beginning to resemble Davydd Greenwood's (1977) example of the Alarde, a Basque festival in Fuenterrabia where the Spanish town inhabitants commemorate their defeat of a French siege in 1638. Both celebrations are local occasions imbued with authentic meaning for the participants, Montserratian or Basque. The re-enactment of Fuentarrabia's town solidarity against the French occurred as a local celebration, one which in 1969 the town council sought to capitalise upon by "re-enacting" the Alarde re-enactment twice in one day to make it available to an increasing number of tourists. This overt commodification of culture – "selling culture by the pound" as Greenwood (1977: 179) describes it – redefined, for the participants, the Alarde private ritual. It became a public show to be performed for outsiders. Though the double-bill re-enactment never came to pass, the town council's actions resulted in the town population's loss of interest in their performance of the Alarde. The town councillors had inadvertently violated the meaning of the ritual enactment: they had destroyed the "authenticity" of the ritual for the performers, resulting in a local reaction of indifference to any future performance of the ritual. Greenwood (1977: 178) explains this local Alarde *anomie* as a collapse of cultural meanings. Though unaware of the Alarde festival, both Cheddy and Sir Fergus seek to avoid any loss of the commemorative meaning they instil in the St. Patrick's Day week on Montserrat.

In Chapter 6, however, I do more than script an ethnography of St. Patrick's Day 1995 as an invented and increasingly commodified tradition. In the same chapter I pay special attention to some ethnic identity disputes raging between Sir Fergus and the anthropologist John Messenger concerning St. Patrick's Day and Irishness on contemporary Montserrat. Fergus uses St. Patrick's Day as a vehicle to develop Montserrat's creole national and cultural identity, and expressly refuses to accept that there is any significance in the vestiges of Irishness on Montserrat. Messenger ridicules the St. Patrick's Day events, preferring to use his own St. Patrick's Day ethnography to further his claim that there is a Black Irish ethnic category existing on Montserrat – an island where there are many "Irish retentions". Alongside these two interpretations of St. Patrick's Day I place the vivid "historical reconstructions" of the event given by the historian Michael Mullin. The future of St. Patrick's Day and the issue of "the Black Irish" is likely to continue to be just as hotly contested by diverse campaigners and causes; a fated – fêted – event and ethnicity for locals, tourists and governments. This identity politics on Montserrat is, in my mind, more reverberation than retention or reconstruction as identities old, new and mixed ripple through the island.

I was almost tempted down strictly historical pathways myself in my attempt to unravel all the competing agendas at work surrounding the Irish connection with Montserrat and the commemoration or celebration of St. Patrick's Day on Montserrat – with each self-interested party fielding a historical reality of and for Montserrat. Reading Fergus, Cheddy and Mullin, I was impelled towards answering some questions in my mind, and to providing an analysis which would unearth the truth and falsity about the Irish on Montserrat. Was the Irish influence lasting or transitory? Just exactly how did the St. Patrick's Day rebellion failed? What was the colour of the seamstress? I was tempted to resort to a historical approach to make sense of my ethnography of Montserrat, especially my impressions of St. Patrick's Day celebrations and John Messenger's "Black Irish". I wanted to present a historical excavation of the past which I could then use to frame, contextualise and interpret the present. However, history is diverse and heterogeneous; and an archaeology of an invented tradition does little to fathom contemporary meaning, nor does a historical approach take into account the ability of the present to frame and reconstruct the past; Trevor-Roper's (1992) disputed historical discovery that the kilt was invented by an Englishman, for example, serves little purpose in the present. I am not in the business of trying to establish historical benchmarks. Historical realism cannot assist with an understanding of the present, the time and place in which the history is written and read. For me, history remains another country.

Instead of confirming and co-founding – or rejecting and denying – the authenticity of the Black Irish or St. Patrick's Day, I have concentrated upon their contemporary significance. If Fergus and Cheddy establish their historical realities and try to assist with the establishment of other Montserratians' realities then the issue for the anthropologist becomes one of situating rather than eradicating the position from which the Black Irish label is being used, or the St. Patrick's Day commemoration supported. Here, I extend Richard Wood (1993: 58) and Handler & Linnekin's (1984: 286) analysis where they argue that "tradition" and "authenticity" are but assigned meanings defined in the present. For me, these terms belong to native realities. Moreover, I must remark that fieldwork results are blurred impressions and can never be categorised as authentic themselves. I agree with Hanson (1989: 888) when he asserts that the analytical task of the anthropologist is "not to strip away the invented portions of culture as inauthentic, but to understand the process by which they acquire authenticity". With respect to Montserrat, the factuality of Fergus's St. Patrick's Day (doubted by expatriates) and Messenger's "Black Irish" (questioned by Fergus) become a non-issue for the anthropologist: for the anthropologist, uncovering the names of the St. Patrick's Day "martyrs" is as unnecessary as pathologising the names of those buried in the Tomb of the Unknown Soldier (see also Ingersoll & Nickell 1987). Thus the historical and cultural substantiation, or repudiation, of links between the "white" Irish of the Emerald Isle and the Black Irish of the Other Emerald Isle becomes an inappropriate line of investigation, and one which will always be inconclusive. My anthropological investigation is into how the native realities (including Messenger's) are held, not to confirm or refute them.

Montserrat is "the locus of struggle" (Bourdieu 1984: 11). It is the place where writers, poets and singers all attempt to grasp the meaning of the social structures and practices before them, and to render the meaning understandable to the reader and listener. They have their agendas and intentions, but I would like to suggest after Dell Hymes (1973: 201, 196) that that "difference is in our understanding, not in kind". For me, this means that we each have personal, creative, indeterminate and impressionistic readings and that it depends on how we treat and take these texts rather than follow the course of the text. One of the results of this treatment is that the text is derailed from its interpretative tramlines. This is why I have made use of my own loose and indeterminate "constellations" in this book, rather than rely upon Fish's (1988: 325) "interpretative communities". In doing so, I wish to preserve the creative, "idiosyncratic subjectivity" which Howell (1994: 326) seeks to eradicate and Fish does not cater for. Whereas Howell (1994: 335) seeks to close down the different meaning constructions recorded from the ethnographic situation by citing our reading and writing conventions and cultures – and her impression that "subjectivity is an illusion and need not concern us" – I side with Rapport (1997[b]: 114) who has argued that the interpretative community can be "exegetically plural", that "textual interpretation will more likely be multiple and inconsistent than singular and shared, even at one and the same event".

In the Chapter 6 chapter preface, Lucretia Stewart (1996) writes about the Irish heritage of Montserrat. Her travel writing piece in The Independent (with Travel Notes) combines news about the island with news about the rumbling volcano. Tourist visitors have read about Montserrat and some of the islanders in the marketing of Montserrat but, as the local papers pick up international stories or articles about Montserrat, the islanders also read about themselves and other islanders on Montserrat. Montserratians are thus aware of the tourist attractions Montserrat offers, and they are also aware of the expatriate/tourist lifestyle on Montserrat. Because these different constellations – opposing world-views are familiar with each other – I believe that it is acceptable to set them together, expatriate with local (development worker with Montserratian) or tourist perspective with local history (the demands of the visitor with the needs of the local historian). In this book I emphasise the contrasting positions and contested representations of impressions. My aim is to show how people's beliefs, convictions and impressions all elide each other. I do not seek to crash together the development workers at the TCOs party with the Montserratians at Pippa's soirée; or to show up Messenger with a promotion of Cheddy's version of Montserrat's history; or to expose the Montserrat Tourist Board's declaration of Montserrat's Irish connection with Fergus's Macmillan Caribbean Guide to Montserrat; or to pit Montserrat's Heroes Day against Montserrat Achievers Day. The resulting read, then, is hopefully an edifying collage of dynamically represented impressions; a narrative as edifying as Fernandez's (1986: 172–187) account of narratives of jurisprudence among the Kpelle where success is measured upon a criterion of resourcefulness more than any polarity of truth or falsity, "edification by puzzlement". The end product should be a book with a narrative more edifying, peripheral and elliptical than systematic, divisionary, and universally commensurable (see Rorty 1996: 369–370).

Both travel writing (such as by Stewart) and anthropology (such as by Messenger and Skinner) are connected in that they try to cater to restricted audiences – the magazine or journal reader and the academic community. The two genres further correspond with respect to their topics and analysis: the ethnographic monograph evolved from the travel report as far as Justin Stagl and Christopher Pinney (1996: 122) are concerned. Away from home, many travel writers and anthropologists perform a spatial schizophrenia in their travel narratives of Pratt's (1992: 6) "contact zone", "the space of colonial encounters"; their "imperial eye" essentialising and textualising all before it in a vain scientific quest for the exact description of everything, for a narrative which bears upon the quest rather than a scientific narrative which is relevant to systems of knowledge outside the text (Pratt 1992: 153, 34, 77). This fixing of fluid realities by writing is what Simmel (1964: 353) refers to as the "objectification of the subjective". The newspaper articles here, in this book, differ slightly from Fergus's articles in the papers, the anti-colonial editorials, the Maroon poetry, the calypso commentaries and the local understandings

of Messenger's Black Irish. Unlike the other impressions of
Montserrat, these chapter prefaces are not examples of
"autoethnographic expression" ("instances in which colonised
subjects undertake to represent themselves in ways that engage
with the coloniser's own terms"), or "transculturation" ("how
subordinated or marginal groups select and invent from materials
transmitted to them by a dominant or metropolitan culture"),
to try and loosely apply Pratt (1992: 7, 6) to the rest of this book
and to the Tourist Board's marketing of Montserrat.

Bruner (1991: 241) uses Said and Foucault to explore the power
relationship between tourist and native. He suggests that though
the tourist experience is advertised as a profound transformation
of the self, it is, in fact, the native self which undergoes change
due to contact with the tourist, and that because it is the tourist
and tourist industry which has the power and money in the
relationship, they are able "to decide what stories will be told
– by whom, in what discursive space – so that others in the system,
such as the Africans [or West Indians], have to base their actions
on what is essentially someone else's story." I would like to suggest
that this occurs on Montserrat as Messenger's Black Irish trope
becomes a tourism tag. Furthermore, with internal as well as
external newspaper tourist marketing, the Montserrat Tourist Board's
controversial marketing epithet "Montserrat – The Way The
Caribbean Used To Be" has had both an off-island and on-island
influence upon the behaviour, attitude and impressions of tourists
and Montserratians. One of the consequences of the marketing
of Montserrat is that Montserrat becomes enshrined as colonial
British with a twist of Irish mystery, sometimes tagged as "The
Emerald Isle of the Caribbean" or "The Other Emerald Isle". With
its "breath of Eire in the Caribbean", those involved in the travel
industry maximise Montserrat's Irish connection: the Irish place
names, surnames and alleged Irish brogue; the Irish stews, jigs
and stories; the shamrock on Government House and Erin, the
mermaid on the national flag. Finally, authority is lent to these
New World Ireland citations by invoking John Messenger's
academic expertise on ethnicity and the Black Irish; here, indeed,
is an anthropological loop to follow, an academic self-fulfilling
prophecy.

The travel writers' reports which I have presented during the
course of this book are at odds with the impressions of Montserrat

represented by Cheddy, Fergus, some of the calypsonians, Maroon members, and other Montserratians. This difference is well-expressed in Susan Laffey's (1995: 34) work where she refers to the travel writer's humorous coupling of black ethnicity with the Irish to produce the Black Irish "ethnic spectacle" for the tourist; Stewart's examination of Miss Sweeney is a good example of this. Laffey and I both disagree with the static and homogenising portrayal of Montserratians by the travel writers when they write about them as comic and exotic creatures, especially the surprise and shared joke with the reader at the incongruity of an Irish ethnicity with a black skin colour. These reactions are the result of a challenge to Euro-American cultural understandings as to the presumed incommensurability of Irish culture with black skin colour. Lampooning the local is also a way in which both Messenger and Stewart can reassure themselves amongst their readers. These reactions are of interest because they give valuable insight – "unmentionable glimpses" (Leach 1984) – into the nature of the author. It is the tourist, though, who is left with the power to frame the tourist-native encounter, and the possibility of re-ordering their Euro-American inter-subjective constellations.

Montserrat is an island of contest and contradiction, of English and Irish place names (Wapping and Plymouth, St. Patrick's and Galway's), where the Queen's Birthday is celebrated alongside St. Patrick's Day festivities. Montserrat is where Pratt's (1992: 6) "transculturation" takes place. Montserrat is the contact zone where calypsonians, poets, development workers and union leaders all seek to influence each other, representing, framing, and marketing the island. With so many parties involved in Montserrat the construction, there is no sole controlling force dictating Montserrat's tourist image, and so it is not possible to say categorically that Montserratians are the exploited, dominated hosts in any "host-guest" tourism relationship (see Smith 1977); there is too much local play and cashing in on the traditional notions of Ireland on Montserrat – the signs and seductions of rural friendliness, quaint charm and Gaelic myth, Celto-centrism.

Ireland with a black creole; better than "the real thing", no pale imitation or copy (quite literally?): my final chapter preface impressions of Montserrat and Montserratians are represented by travel writers, those who make their home in homelessness (Chambers 1994: 246). These writers are able to occupy what

David Spurr (1993: 16) describes as "the position of visual authority" with their panoptic control in their writing over all that they survey. Spurr (1993: 16) distinguishes between travel writing and anthropological monographs, but notes that a form of writing with a "commanding view" is found in both writing genres – not because anthropology's ethnographies are necessarily born out of colonial conditions, but because the anthropologist author attempts to describe, write, and represent the social reality of their gaze. Spurr (1993: 187), like Tyler, seeks strategies of textual representation which do not hold such "a totalizing authority over the objects of representation." Spurr toys with James Clifford's desire to overthrow not only the monologic authority of the ethnographer, but also the dialogic and polyphonic experiments in ethnography which, for Clifford (1988: 54), are all present in the ethnographers' discordant and incoherent participant observation but are glossed over in the ethnographers' vain attempts at writing a coherent and ordered narrative. Clifford is left behind, though, when Spurr engages in the Derridean deconstruction of journalism and ethnography: for Spurr (1993: 188), Clifford fails to overcome the "virtuoso orchestration" of author(s) engaged in polyphonic or heteroglossic ethnographic writing – even authorial control shared between members of different cultures does not entirely loosen the voice of authority of the scriptor(s). In other words, Derridean declarations (free-floating signifiers, fluid meanings, an unstable language without correspondence between words and things and thoughts) allow Spurr (1993: 195) to resist colonial discourse by "maintaining a perpetual openness to the unexpected". It would appear to be the case that meaning plays on a coil with Gellner at one end and Derrida claiming to be somewhere at the other end; I write "somewhere" towards the Derridean end of this coil because I believe that there is coherence and order to Derrida's work such that his "differential" and "deferred" work about the restlessness of meaning does not equate with the clarity of his extreme philosophical thesis.

Spurr uses his examination of the nature of authorial power and authority in travel writing and ethnographic forms of writing to help him to break free from the authority of the writer. Unfortunately, it is impossible to achieve this goal, complete freedom from the author. This is because the author gains authority from laying down their avenues of meaning, and from producing the text – particularly so when the text purports to represent social reality. There may be many avenues of meaning, according to Barthes and reader response theory – some which are not anticipated by the author – but the text has some of the author's authority imprinted into it, even if it is just as a rough guide. With this in mind, I have sought to continually locate myself in my writing, as well as show how my writing occurs; I want readers of my text to be loosely guided, and to be able to fathom the tenuous connection between ethnography the social process and ethnography the written product. Rather than end with Derrida in my Conclusion, I stay close to Clifford: both Clifford and I partake in the examination and production of texts, all of which have a degree of authority and voice to them. Neither of us believe that it is possible for a text to lose its authority completely, no matter the number of authors or experimental nature of the writing. In *Orientalism – Western Conceptions of the Orient*, Said (1991: 325, author's emphasis) answers this epistemological problem – and his own question, "[h]ow does one *represent* other cultures?" – not by rejecting Western scholarship or the ability of written ethnography to authoritatively represent reality (see Asad 1980), but by arguing that texts about the Orient should be shaped by the experience of the Orient and should at least attempt to contain, or speak with, the voices of the Orient; in other words, that there should not be an accumulation of texts with each text on the Orient simply relying upon other texts on the Orient (Said 1991: 328, 20), an argument relevant to the field of anthropology. For me, Said is simply forcefully reiterating anthropology's fieldwork ambitions. This reminds me of Miller's ethnographic critique of cultural studies which I mentioned in the Academic Preface.

Despite resisting the hackneyed "postmodern" label (personal communication), and though his *Orientalism* has been criticised for doing to Western scholarship what Western scholarship has done to the Orient (Porter 1993), I applaud Said's maintenance of meaning in his cultural analysis. In my work – in the ethnography which I have presented, and in the theory with which I have packaged the ethnography – I too have sustained an interrogation of meaning, and I have paid some consideration to the literary understandings of the reader and not just those of the writer. In so doing, I have queried our ability to give an accurate and authentic representation of reality – one of modernism's central tenets (Walsh 1992: 7). The results of my approach are not nihilistic or schizophrenic; I do not aim to de(con)struct the semiotic chain, rather, I suggest that there is some metaphoric looseness in the semiotic system, a factor which must be taken into account by the ethnographer typically writing an integrated ethnography with "narrative closure and semiotic framing" (Harkin 1995: 665) and working with the assumption that native life is as coherent as it is in the ethnographic narrative. Meaning, I am arguing, is not lost; meaning, as I mention in Chapter 2, is ductile: meaning – which is composed out of the relationship between signifier and signified – works like a coil, sometimes tight, sometimes loose; hence, meaning is never precise, but is always impressionistic.

I began this book by addressing the impulse to write and connect with others. Let me end my Conclusion in similar vein, by drawing upon Nietzsche (1990: 33) where he opens his collection of thoughts, *Beyond Good and Evil*, by describing what philosophers hold as the "will to truth" which is essentially an appetite for fundamental desires, eternal truths and exact meaning. This "will to truth", Nietzsche (1990: 33) – the perspectivist – criticises as an assumption which philosophers hold so dear to their hearts. Nietzsche calls it a prejudice. I suggest that this imperative, this "will to truth", this modernist prejudice, lies at the heart of both the human and inhuman sciences. Moreover, this "impulse to truth" (what Nietzsche [1911: 80] derides as a "mobile army of metaphors, metonymies and anthropomorphism") – to understand, to order, to make sense and meaning – also lies outside the academic world. In this book I have attempted to show that not only does the anthropologist attempt to represent his or her own social realities (Chapter 1), but so do other interest groups and expressive individuals: Sir Fergus and the Maroon poets (Chapter 2); the development workers and Montserratians living and working on Montserrat (Chapter 3); the calypsonians (Chapter 4); Cheddy and the Pan-Afrikanists and port workers on the island (Chapter 5); the historians, the tourists, travel writers, local Government and Montserrat Tourist Board (Chapter 6).

In all of the chapters in this book, I have represented impressions of Montserrat to the reader. These representations I have shown to be fleeting, partial and impressionistic. I mentioned in the Academic Preface that these impressions are a sensory phenomenalism with the anthropological goals of Malinowski and Leach, the semiotics of de Saussure and Geertz, the semantics of Parkin, and the inchoate spaces created by Fernandez. Successive chapters represented some of the various collective (inter-subjective constellations) and individual impressions of Montserrat, exemplifying the calypso contests, poetic parodies, union struggles, and St. Patrick's Day protests. The reading of these ethnographic chapters as representations of impressions from contrasting and contesting groups and individuals should be a feature of not just my ethnography but of other ethnographies and attempted representations of social realities. In "writing about writing and reading impressions" I hope not to deride other writings but to open them out for impressionistic readings and revisionist interpretations just like Geertz's (1989) literary re-use of well-known anthropologists' work in *Works and Lives – The Anthropologist as Author*. Here, perhaps, my constrained relativism, my sustained postmodernism, my constellations of shifting realities, my uncomfortable and uncertain anthropology may be of some use.

Unfortunately, underpinning even my own fieldwork activities there was an intense "will to truth" – a determination to "get to the bottom of things", an ethnographic ambition "to cover events". These insecurities led me to tape-record interviews with my informants and friends at the end of the year despite all of our previous untapped conversations. I also felt the need to collect as many "concrete" examples of newspaper, poetry and travel article representations of Montserrat. It was only when I entered the writing phase that I realised that reality at large cannot be precisely represented and pinned down; this does not mean do not seek the end of ethnography as anthropological praxis, I seek rather just to problematise modernist assumptions, what Mitchell (1992: 312), in Saidian terms, refers to as "the citationary nature of Orientalism". Even inviolable reality itself is open to various interpretations (see Trigg 1980: 200) and re-examinations (Rorty 1996: 17–69). This book, then, is an articulation and exemplification of my suppositionless anthropology.

To conclude my Conclusion, this chapter has both summarised the previous chapters in this book and drawn them together to show that the academic world thirsts after meaningful truths.

This craving runs so strong, and so deep, that the academic world would rather create well-worked illusions feigning to be truth – a singular historical reality, one meta-narrative, accurate and authentic representations of reality – than countenance an edifying plurality of realities, shifting positions, partial connections and impressionistic realities. This book has taken an ethnographic location, Montserrat, and shown that a place is an arena of contest. It has shown that people represent their realities in expressive, creative and – in this case study – individual ways. Perhaps this also suggests that this ordering desire, which we all carry, is manifested for some in writing, in singing, in reading and in speaking.

When Rorty (1996: 387, author's emphasis) writes that "[a]nything can be discoursed of abnormally, just as anything can become edifying and anything can be systematized", I take this to mean that examples, ethnographic for instance – or "naturalistic" as in the context of this philosopher's quote – can be brought in to flesh out any argument; that our examples illustrate our opinions. I can use my ethnography of Montserrat to build a theory of the Caribbean or further afield; I can use my ethnography of Montserrat to reify Montserrat from other islands and people in the world; or I can use my ethnography of Montserrat as a way of entering into a "long [- challenging, contesting, probing, edifying -] conversation" with myself, Montserratians, anthropologists, and others. From this trio of possible directions, my postmodern choice approach to Montserrat and anthropology has represented both as travellers' tales, as edifying impressions, rickety constituents of our meaningful edifice of signification.

Eruption Reaches Montserrat capital

A VOLCANIC eruption on the island of Montserrat sent super-heated gas, rock and ash tearing through the deserted capital Plymouth, apparently setting alight homes and buildings abandoned two years ago. Plumes of smoke and flame could be seen from Salem, a town about 5 miles to the north in an area considered safe from the Soufriere Hills volcano.

It is the first time the fiery debris has reached Plymouth, evacuated along with the rest of the southern half of the island when the volcano sprang into life in July 1995. The deputy chief scientist at Montserrat Volcano Observatory, Jill Norton, said eruptions in the past few days had filled a ravine on the volcano's south-western flank and left Plymouth exposed.

Eruptions in the past two years have prompted nearly half of the British colony's 11,000 residents to flee. −AP, SALEM.

(Associated Press, *The Guardian*, 5 August 1997: 9)

REFERENCES

In this work a diverse array of sources have been utilised – letters, journals, manuscripts, tapes, files, newspapers, photocopies, guidebooks, advertisements, anthologies. To facilitate future research on Montserrat, references are as full as possible and have been arranged in numerical fashion.

1. General references
    1.1. General references
    1.2. General poetry volume references
    1.3 General music references

2. Montserrat references
    2.1. Montserrat references
    2.2. Montserrat music references
    2.3. References to Howard Fergus's work
        2.3.1. Fergus – Anthologies
        2.3.2. Fergus – Histories
        2.3.3. Fergus – Histories cited from newspapers
        2.3.4. Fergus – Poems cited from newspapers
    2.4. Montserrat travel writing references
    2.5. References to Montserrat news pieces
        2.5.1. Chapter prefaces and postscript
        2.5.2. *Pan-Afrikan Liberator* pieces
        2.5.3. Montserrat newspaper pieces

1. General References

1.1. General References

Achebe, C., "The African Writer and the English Language" in, Williams, P. & L. Chrisman (eds.), *Colonial Discourse and Post-Colonial Theory – A Reader*, Hemel Hempstead: Harvester Wheatsheaf, 1993, pp. 428–434.

Amit, V. (ed.), *Constructing the Field: Ethnographic Fieldwork in the Contemporary World*, London: Routledge, 2000.

Angrosino, M., "Dub Poetry and West Indian Identity" in, Benson, P. (ed.), *Anthropology and Literature*, Chicago: University of Chicago Press, 1993, pp. 73–88.

Appignanesi, R. & C. Garratt & Z. Sardar & P. Curry (eds.), *Postmodernism for Beginners*, Cambridge: Icon Books, 1995.

Asad, T., "Introduction" in, Asad, T. (ed.), *Anthropology and the Colonial Encounter*, London: Ithaca Press, 1973, pp. 9–20.

Asad, T., "Orientalism", *English Historical Review*, 95(376), 1980, pp. 648–649.

Ashcroft, B. & G. Griffiths & H. Tiffin (eds.), *The Empire Writes Back – Theory and Practice in Post-Colonial Literatures*, London: Routledge, 1989.

Atkinson, P., *The Ethnographic Imagination – Textual Constructions of Reality*, London: Routledge, 1990.

Atkinson, P., *Medical Talk and Medical Work – The Liturgy of the Clinic*, London: Sage Publications, 1995.

Barnard, A. & J. Spencer, "Culture" entry in, Barnard, A. & J. Spencer (eds.), *Encyclopaedia of Anthropology*, London: Routledge, 1996, pp. 136–143.

Barthes, R. [a], "The Death of the Author" in, Lodge, D. (ed.), *Modern Criticism and Theory – A Reader*, London: Longman, 1988, pp. 167–172.

Barthes, R. [b], "Textual Analysis: Poe's 'Valdemar'" in, Lodge, D. (ed.), *Modern Criticism and Theory – A Reader*, London: Longman, 1988, pp. 172–195.

Bauman, R., *Verbal Art as Performance*, Prospect Heights, Illinois: Waveland Press, Inc., 1984.

Berger, P. & T. Luckmann, *The Social Construction of Reality – A Treatise on the Sociology of Knowledge*, London: Penguin, 1971[1966].

Bhabha, H., "Foreword" in, Fanon, F., *Black Skin, White Masks*, London: Pluto Press, 1991, pp. vii–xxvi.

Bhabha, H., *The Location of Culture*, London: Routledge, 1994.

Birth, K., "Bakrnal: Coup, Carnival, and Calypso in Trinidad", *Ethnology*, 33(2), 1994, pp. 165–177.

Bloch, M., "The Past and the Present in the Present", *MAN*, 12(2), 1977, pp. 278–292.

Bloch, B., "Foreword" in, Mannoni, O., *Prospero and Caliban: the Psychology of Colonization*, Ann Arbor: University of Michigan Press, 1990, pp. v–xx.

Boissevain, J., *Friends of Friends: Networks, Manipulators and Coalitions*, Oxford: Basil Blackwell, 1974.

Bourdieu, P., *Homo Academicus*, Stanford: Stanford University Press, 1984.

Brathwaite, E., Autobiographical article, *Timehri – Savacou*, 2, 1970, pp. 35–44, no other references available.

Brokensha, D. & D. Warren & O. Werner, "Introduction" in, Brokensha D. & D. Warren & O. Werner (eds.), *Indigenous Knowledge Systems and*

Development, Washington, University Press of America Incorporated, 1980, pp. 1–8.

Brotherston, G. (ed.), *José Enrique Rodó: ARIEL*, Cambridge: Cambridge University Press, 1967.

Bruner, E., "Transformation of Self in Tourism", *Annals of Tourism Research*, 18(2), 1991, pp. 238–250.

Bruner, E., "Introduction: The Ethnographic Self and the Personal Self" in, Benson, P. (ed.), *Anthropology and Literature*, Chicago: University of Illinois Press, 1993, pp. 1–26.

Burgess, R., *In the Field – An Introduction to Field Research*, London: Routledge, 1993.

Calvino, I., *If on a Winter's Night a Traveller*, London: Minerva, 1992.

Campbell, S., "Carnival, Calypso, and Class Struggle in Nineteenth Century Trinidad", *History Workshop Journal*, 26, 1988, pp. 1–28.

Carr, E., *What is History?*, Harmondsworth: Penguin, 1974.

Chambers, I., "Leaky Habitats and Broken Grammar" in, Robertson, G. & M. Mash & L. Tickner & J. Bird & B. Curtis & T. Putnam (eds.), *Travellers' Tales – Narratives of Home and Displacement*, London: Routledge, 1994, pp. 245–249.

Clifford, J., *The Predicament of Culture: Twentieth-Century Ethnography, Literature and Art*, Cambridge: Harvard University Press, 1988.

Cohen, A., *Whalsay – Symbol, Segment and Boundary in a Shetland Island Community*, Manchester: Manchester University Press, 1987.

Cohen, A., "Post-Fieldwork Fieldwork", *Journal of Anthropological Research*, 48(4), 1992, pp. 339–354.

Cohen, A., *Self Consciousness – An Alternative Anthropology of Identity*, London: Routledge, 1995.

Cohen, A. & N. Rapport, "Introduction – Consciousness in Anthropology" in, Cohen, A. & N. Rapport (eds.), *Questions of Consciousness*, London: Routledge, 1995, pp. 1–20.

Crapanzano, V., *Tuhami: Portrait of a Moroccan*, Chicago: University of Chicago Press, 1980.

Crapanzano, V., *Hermes' Dilemma & Hamlet's Desire – On the Epistemology of Interpretation*, London: Harvard University Press, 1992.

Crawford, R., *Devolving English Literature*, Oxford: Oxford University Press, 1992.

Crawford, R., Television interview about Scotland, BBC2, 1993.

Cronon, E., *Black Moses: The Story of Marcus Garvey and the Universal Negro Improvement Association*, London: University of Wisconsin Press, 1969.

Derrida, J., *Dissemination*, London: Athlone Press, 1993.

Dolman, A., "Paradise Lost? The Past Performance and Future Prospects of Small Island Developing Countries", in E. Dommen and P. Hein (eds.) *States, Microstates and Islands*, London: Croom Helm, 1985, pp. 40–69.

Donham, D., "Beyond the Domestic Mode of Production", *Man*, 16(4), 1981, pp. 515–541.

Dumont, L., *Homo Heirarchicus: The Caste System and its Implications*, London: Weidenfeld & Nicholson, 1970.

Dumont, L., *Essays on Individualism: Modern Ideology in Anthropological Perspective*, Chicago: University of Chicago Press, 1986.

Dwyer, K., *Moroccan Dialogues – Anthropology in Question*, Prospect Heights, Illinois: Waveland Press, Inc., 1982.

Eriksen, T., *Us and Them in Modern Soceities – Ethnicity and Nationalism in Trindad, Mauritius and Beyond*, Oslo: Scandinavian University Press (Universitetsforlaget), 1992.

Escobar, E., "Anthropology and the Development Encounter: the Making and Marketing of Development Anthropology", *American Ethnologist*, 18(4), 1991, pp. 658–682.

Evans-Pritchard, E., *Essays in Social Anthroplogy*, London: Faber & Faber, 1962.

Fallon, J., "The Black Irish", findings of the Florida Unity Conference Group about Montserrat's Irish-African connection, *Irish Echo*, 27 July–3 August 1993, p. 18.

Fanon, F., *Black Skin, White Masks*, London: Pluto Press, 1991.

Fernandez, J., "Symbolic Consensus in a Fang Reformative Cult", *American Anthropologist*, 67, 1965, pp. 902–927, no other references available.

Fernandez, J., "Afterword: At the Center of the Human Condition", *Semiotica*, 46(2), 1983, pp. 323–330.

Fernandez, J., *Persuasions and Performances – The Play of Tropes in Culture*, Bloomington: Indiana University Press, 1986.

Fetterman, D., "The Ethnographic Evaluator" in, Eddy, E. & W. Partridge (eds.), *Applied Anthropology in America*, New York: Columbia University Press, 1987, pp. 340–366.

Firth, R., "Engagement and Detachment: Reflections on Applying Social Anthropology to Social Affairs", *Human Organization*, 40(3), Fall 1981, pp. 193–201.

Fish, S., "Interpreting the Valorium" in, Lodge, D. (ed.), *Modern Criticism and Theory – A Reader*, London: Longman, 1988, pp. 311–329.

Gates, H., "Critical Fanonism", *Critical Inquiry*, 17, 1991, pp. 457–470.

Geertz, C., *Islam Observed – Religious Development in Morocco and Indonesia*, London: University of Chicago Press, 1968.

Geertz, C., *Works and Lives – The Anthropologist as Author*, Cambridge: Polity Press, 1989.

Geertz, C. [a], *The Interpretation of Cultures*, London: Fontana Press, 1993.

Geertz, C. [b], *Local Knowledge – Further Essays in Interpretative Anthropology*, London: Fontana Press, 1993.

Geertz, C., *After the Fact*, Cambridge, Massacheusetts: Harvard University Press, 1995.

Gellner, E., *Postmodernism, Reason and Religion,* London: Routledge, 1993.

Good., B., *Medicine, Rationality, and Experience – An Anthropological Perspective*, Cambridge: Cambridge University Press, 1994.

Goodman, N., *Ways of Worldmaking*, Indianapolis: Hackett Publishing, 1978.

Greenwood, D., "Culture by the Pound: An Anthropological Perspective on Tourism as Cultural Commoditization" in, Smith, V. (ed.), *Hosts and Guests – The Anthropology of Tourism*, Philadelphia: University of Pennsylvania, 1977, pp. 37–52.

Gupta, A. & J. Ferguson (eds.), *Anthropological Locations: Boundaries and Grounds of a Field Science*, California: University of California Press, 1997.

Hammersley, M., *Reading Ethnographic Research: A Critical Guide*, London: Longman, 1993.

Handler, R. & J. Linnekin, "Tradition, Genuine or Spurious", *Journal of Folklore Studies*, 97(385), 1984, pp. 273–290.

Hanley, C., "Island Studio Attracts Rock Stars", *Sunday Cape Cod Times*, 5 August 1984, p. 48.

200 Before the Volcano

Hanson, A., "Does God Have a Body? Truth, Reality and Cultural Relativism", *Man*, 14(3), 1979, pp. 515–529.

Hanson, A., "The Making of the Maori: Cultural Invention and its Logic", *American Anthropologist*, 91(4), 1989, pp. 890–902.

Harkin, M., "Modernist Anthropology and Tourism of the Authentic", *Annals of Tourism Research*, 22(3), 1995, pp. 650–670.

Hart, K., "Swimming into the Human Current", *Cambridge Anthropology*, 14(3), 1990, pp. 3–10.

Hastrup. K., *A Passage to Anthropology – Between Experience and Theory*, London: Routledge, 1995.

Hebdige, H., *Cut "n" mix: Culture, Identity and Caribbean Music*, London: Comedia Routledge, 1987.

Hendry, J., & C. Watson, "Introduction" in, Hendry, J. and C. Watson (eds.), *Indirection, Intention and Diplomacy*, London: Routledge, 2001, pp. 1–15.

Hirabayashi, E. & D. Warren & W. Owen, "That Focus on the 'Other 40%': A Myth of Development" in, Brokensha D. & D. Warren & O. Werner (eds.), *Indigenous Knowledge Systems and Development*, Washington, University Press of America, 1980, pp. 353–362.

Hirst, P., "Is it Rational to Reject Relativism?" in, Overing, J. (ed.), *Reason and Morality*, London: Tavistock Publications, 1985, pp. 85–103.

Hobart, M., "Introduction: the Growth of Ignorance" in, Hobart, M. (ed.), *An Anthropological Critique of Development – The Growth of Ignorance*, London: Routledge, 1993, pp. 1–30.

Hobbs, D., "Peers, Careers, and Academic Fears: Writing as Field-Work" in, Hobbs, D. & T. May (eds.), *Interpreting the Field – Accounts of Ethnography*, Oxford: Clarendon Press, 1993, pp. 45–66.

Hobsbawm, E., "Introduction: Inventing Traditions" in, Hobsbawm, E. & T. Ranger (eds.), *The Invention of Tradition*, Cambridge: Cambridge University Press, 1992, pp. 1–14.

Holy, L. & M. Stuchlik, *Actions, Norms and Representations – Foundations of Anthropological Inquiry*, Cambridge: Cambridge University Press, 1983.

Holy, L., "Introduction – Description, Generalization and Comparison: Two Paradigms" in, Holy, L. (ed.), *Comparative Anthropology*, Oxford: Basil Blackwell, 1987, pp. 1–21.

Howell, S., "'Reading Culture': Or How Anthropological Texts Create Fieldwork Expectations and Shape Future Texts" in, Archetti, E. (ed.), *Exploring the Written – Anthropology and the Multiplicity of Writing*, Oslo: Scandinavian University Press, 1994, pp. 317–336.

Hymes, D., "An Ethnographic Perspective", *New Literary History*, "What is Literature?" special edition, 5(1), 1973, pp. 187–201.

Ingersoll, D. & J. Nickell, "The Most Important Monument: The Tomb of the Unknown Soldier" in, Ingersoll, D. & G. Bronitsky (eds.), *Mirror and Metaphor – Material and Social Constructions of Reality*, London: University Press of America, 1987, pp. 199–228.

Iser, W., "The Reading Process: a Phenomenological Approach" in, Lodge, D. (ed.), *Modern Criticism and Theory – A Reader*, London: Longman, 1988, pp. 212–228.

Jackson, M. *Minima Ethnographica: Intersubjectivity and the Anthropological Project*, Chicago: University of Chicago Press, 1998.

James, A. & J. Hockey & A. Dawson (eds.), *After Writing Culture – Epistemology and Praxis in Contemporary Anthropology*, London: Routledge, 1997.

Jameson, F., "Postmodernism, Or, The Logic of Late Capitalism", *New Left Review*, 146, 1984, pp. 53–93.

Jameson, F., *POSTMODERNISM, or, the Cultural Logic of Late Capitalism*, London: Verso, 1991.

Kuhn, T., *The Structure of Scientific Revolutions*, Chicago: University of Chicago Press, 1970.

Kuper, A., *Anthropology and Anthropologists – The Modern British School*, London: Routledge, 1991.

Lash, S., "Genealogy and the Body: Foucault/Deleuze/Nietzsche" in, Featherstone, M. & M. Hepworth & B. Turner (eds.), *The Body: Social Process and Cultural Theory*, London: Sage, 1995, pp. 256–280.

Lazarus–Black, M., *Legitimate Acts and Illegal Encounters: Law and Society in Antigua and Barbuda*, Smithsonian Series in Ethnographic Inquiry, London: Smithsonian Institution Press, 1994.

Leach, E., *Rethinking Anthropology*, London: Athlone Press, 1982 [1961].

Leach, E., "Glimpses of the Unmentionable in the History of British Social Anthropology", *Annual Review of Anthropology*, 13, 1984, pp. 1–23.

Leach, E., *Social Anthropology*, Glasgow: Fontana Press, 1986.

Leach, E., "Tribal Ethnography: Past, Present, Future" in, Chapman, M. & E. Tonkin & M. McDonald (eds.), *History and Ethnicity*, London: Routledge, 1989, pp. 34–47.

Leenhardt, M., *Do Kamo: Person and Myth in Melanesian World*, translated by Basia Gulati, Chicago: University of Chicago Press, 1979 [1947].

Levin, C., *Jean Baudrillard – a Study in Cultural Metaphysics*, Hemel Hempstead: Simon & Schuster, 1996.

Levi-Strauss, C., *Structural Anthropology 1*, London: Penguin, 1977.

Lewin, O., "Calypso" in, Sadie, S. (ed.), *The Newgrove Dictionary of Music and Musicians*, London: Macmillan, 1980, p. 634.

Lewis, I., *Social Anthropology in Perspective – The Relevance of Social Anthropology*, Cambridge: Cambridge University Press, 1988.

Lindquist, G., "Travelling by the Other's Cognitive Maps or Going Native and Coming Back", *Ethnos*, 60(1–2), 1995, pp. 5–40.

Lyotard, J., *The Postmodern Condition: A Report on Knowledge*, Manchester: Manchester University Press, 1992.

MacCannell, D., *The Tourist – A New Theory of the Leisure Class*, New York: Schocken Books, 1989.

MacCannell, D., *Empty Meeting Grounds: The Tourist Papers*, New York: Routledge, 1992.

Madan, G., *Livre sans nom: Twelve Reflections*, 12, privately printed, 1934, no other references available.

Mair, L., *Studies in Applied Anthropology*, London: Athlone Press, 1957.

Malinowski, B., *Argonauts of the Western Pacific – An Account of Native Enterprise and Adventure in the Archipelagoes of Melanesian New Guinea*, London: Routledge & Kegan Paul, 1978 [1922].

Malinowski, B., *The Sexual Life of Savages in North-Western Melanesia – An Ethnographic Account of Courtship, Marriage, and Family Life Among the Natives of the Trobriand Islands, British New Guinea*, London: Routledge & Kegan Paul, 1982 [1929].

Mannoni, O., *Prospero and Caliban: the Psychology of Colonization*, Ann Arbor: University of Michigan Press, 1990.

Marcus, G. & J. Clifford (eds.), *Writing Culture – The Poetics and Politics of Ethnography*, London: University of California Press, 1986.

Marcus, G. & M. Fischer, *Anthropology as Cultural Critique – An Experimental Moment in the Human Sciences*, Chicago: University of Chicago Press, 1986.

McGinn, B., "How Irish is Montserrat?", *Irish Roots*, 1, 1994, pp. 20–23.

Messenger, J., *Inis Beag: Isle of Ireland*, New York: Holt, Rinehart and Winston, 1969.

Messenger, J., "Brendan Revisited", *Anthropology and Humanism Quarterly*, 16(2), 1991, pp. 63–68.

Miller, D., *MODERNITY – An Ethnographic Approach: Dualism and Mass Consumption in Trinidad*, Oxford: Berg, 1994.

Miner, H., "Body Ritual Among the Nacirema", *American Anthropologist*, 58(3), 1956, pp. 503–507.

Mitchell, T., "Orientalism and the Exhibitionary Order" in, Dirks, N. (ed.), *Colonialism and Culture*, Ann Arbor: University of Michigan Press, 1992, pp. 289–317.

Myers, H., "Trinidad and Tobago" in, Sadie, S. (ed.), *The Newgrove Dictionary of Music and Musicians*, London: Macmillan, 1980, pp. 146–150.

Naipaul, V., *The Mimic Men*, London: Penguin, 1969.

Naipaul, V., *Miguel Street*, London: Penguin Books, 1971.

Nash, C. (ed.), *Narrative in Culture – The Uses of Storytelling in the Sciences, Philosophy, and Literature*, London: Routledge, 1994.

Nietzsche, F., *Early Greek Philosophy and Other Essays*, Edinburgh: Darien Press, 1911, pp. 171–192.

Nietzsche, F., *Beyond Good and Evil*, London: Penguin Books, 1990.

Olwig, K. & K. Hastrup (eds.), *Siting Culture: the Shifting Anthropological Object*, London: Routledge, 1997.

Ottenberg, S., "Thirty Years of Fieldnotes: Changing Relationships to the Text" in, Sanjek, R. (ed.), *Fieldnotes: The Makings of Anthropology*, London: Cornell University Press, 1990.

Overing, J., "Introduction" in, Overing, J. (ed.), *Reason and Morality*, London: Tavistock Publications, 1985, pp. 1–29.

Owens, J., *Dread – The Rastafarians of Jamaica*, London: Heinemann, 1984.

Parkin, D., "Introduction" in, Parkin, D. (ed.), *Semantic Anthropology*, London: Academic Press, 1982, pp. xi–li.

Patton, J., "Communication and Cultural Identity Through Calypso and Poetic Discourse", *Bulletin of Eastern Caribbean Affairs*, 19(3), September 1994, pp. 53–68.

Pêcheux, M., *Language, Semantics and Ideology: Stating the Obvious*, London: Macmillan, 1982.

Peck, J. & M. Coyle, *Literary Terms and Criticism*, London: Macmillan Education, 1989.

Pool, G., "Culture, Language and Revolution in Grenada", *Anthropologica*, 46(1), 1994, pp. 73–107.

Pool, R., "Postmodern Ethnography?", *Critique of Anthropology*, 11(4), 1991, pp. 309–331.

Porter, D., "*Orientalism and Its Problems*" in, Williams, P. & L. Chrisman (eds.), *Colonial Discourse and Post-Colonial Theory – A Reader*, Hemel Hempstead: Harvester Wheatsheaf, 1993, pp. 150–161.

Pratt, M., *Imperial Eyes: Travel Writing and Transculturation*, London: Routledge, 1992.

Rabinow, P., *Reflections on Fieldwork in Morocco*, Berkeley: University of California Press, 1977.

Radcliffe-Brown, A., *The Andaman Islanders*, Cambridge, 1922, no other references available.

Radcliffe-Brown, A., *Structure and Function in Primitive Society*, London: Routledge & Kegan Paul, 1979.

Rapport, N., *Talking Violence – An Anthropological Interpretation of Conversation in the City*, St. John's, Newfoundland: Memorial University of Newfoundland, Institute of Social and Economic Research Publications [ISER], 34, 1987.

Rapport, N., *Diverse World-Views in an English Village*, Edinburgh: Edinburgh University Press, 1993.

Rapport, N., *The Prose and the Passion – Anthropology, Literature and the Writing of E.M. Forster*, Manchester: Manchester University Press, 1994.

Rapport, N. [a], *Transcendent Individual – Towards a Literary and Liberal Anthropology*, London: Routledge, 1997.

Rapport, N. [b], review of Archetti, E. (ed.), *Exploring the Written – Anthropology and the Multiplicity of Writing* (Oslo, Norway: Scandinavian University Press (Universitetsforlaget AS), 1994), *Social Anthropology*, 5(1), 1997, pp. 112–114.

Retamar, R., *Caliban and Other Essays*, Minnesota: University of Minnesota Press, 1989.

Riches, D., "Power as a Representational Model" in, Fardon, R. (ed), *Power and Knowledge: Anthropological and Sociological Approaches*, Edinburgh: Edinburgh Academic Press, 1985, pp. 83–102.

Ritzer, G., *Sociological Theory*, London: McGraw-Hill, 1996.

Rohlehr, G., "Sparrow and the Language of Calypso", *Savacou*, 2, 1970, pp. 88–99.

Rorty, R., *Philosophy and the Mirror of Nature*, Oxford: Blackwell, 1996.

Rorty, R., Guest lecture, St. Andrews University, 30 April 1997.

Said, E., *Orientalism*, London: Penguin, 1991[1978].

Sarup, M., *An Introductory Guide to Post-Structuralism and Postmodernism*, Hemel Hempstead: Harverster Wheatsheaf, 1993.

Saussure, F., "The object of study" in, Lodge, D. (ed.), *Modern Criticism and Theory – A Reader*, London: Longman, 1988, pp. 2–10.

Schneider, D., "Kinship and Biology" in, Schneider, D. & A. Coale & M. Levy & S. Tomkins (eds.), *Aspects of Analysis of Family Structure*, Princeton: Princeton University Press, 1965, pp. 83–101.

Schneider, D., "Notes Toward a Theory of Culture" in, Basso, K. & H. Selby (eds.), *Meaning in Anthropology*, Albuquerque: University of New Mexico Press, 1976, pp. 197–220.

Schneider, D., *Schneider on Schneider – The Conversion of the Jews and Other Anthropological Stories*, David M. Schneider as told to Richard Handler, edited and transcribed by Handler, R., London: Duke University Press, 1995.

Scholte, B., "The Literary Turn in Contemporary Anthropology – Review Article on Writing Culture", *Critique of Anthropology*, 7(1), 1987, pp. 33–47.

Searle, C., *Words Unchained – Language and Revolution in Grenada*, London: Zed Books, 1984.

Shakespeare, W., *The Tempest*, Harlow: Longman, 1984 [1610].

Shklovsky, V., "Art as Technique" in, Lodge, D. (ed.), *Modern Criticism and Theory – A Reader*, London: Longman, 1988, pp. 16–30.

Simmel, G., *The Sociology of Georg Simmel*, translated and edited by Kurt Wolff, New York: Free Press, 1964.

Shweder, R., "Anthropology's Romantic Rebellion Against the Enlightenment, or There's More to Thinking Than Reason and Evidence" in, Shweder, R. & R. LeVine (eds.), *Culture Theory*, Cambridge: Cambidge University Press, 1984, p. 27–66.

Shweder, R., *Thinking Through Cultures*, London: Harvard University Press, 1991.

Skinner, J., "The Post-Colonial Sideshow", *Cascando*, 4, 1994, pp. 73–76.

Smith, D., "Them and Uz: Douglas Dunn's Technique" in, Crawford, C. & D. Kinloch (eds.), *Reading Douglas Dunn*, Edinburgh: Edinburgh University Press, 1992, pp. 80–93.

Smith, V. (ed.), *Hosts and Guests – The Anthropology of Tourism*, Philadelphia: University of Pennsylvania, 1977.

Spivak, G., *The Post-Colonial Critic: Interviews, Strategies, Dialogues*, edited by Harasym, S., London: Routledge, 1990.

Spurr, D., *The Rhetoric of Empire – Colonial Discourse in Journalism, Travel Writing and Imperial Administration*, London: Duke University Press, 1993.

Stagl, J., & C. Pinney, "Introduction: from Travel Writing to Ethnography" in, Stagl, J. & C. Pinney (eds.), *History and Anthropology*, (Special Edition: "From Travel Writing to Ethnography"), 9(2 & 3), 1996, pp. 121–124.

Strathern, M., "Out of Context – The Persuasive Fictions of Anthropology", *Current Anthropology*, 28(3), 1987, pp. 251–270.

Strathern, M., *Partial Connections*, Savage, Maryland: Rowman and Littlefield, 1991.

Synnott, A., *The Body Social – Symbolism, Self and Society*, London: Routledge, 1993.

Thesiger, W., *The Life of My Choice*, London: Collins, 1987.

Thiong'o, N., "The Language of African Literature" in, Williams, P. & L. Chrisman (eds.), *Colonial Discourse and Post-Colonial Theory – A Reader*, Hemel Hempstead: Harvester Wheatsheaf, 1993, pp. 435–456.

Thomas, N., "History and Anthropology" entry in, Barnard, A. & J. Spencer (eds.), *Encyclopaedia of Anthropology*, London: Routledge, 1996, pp. 272–277.

Thompson, D. (ed.), *The Concise Oxford Dictionary*, 9th ed., London: Oxford University Press, 1995.

Thompson, V., *Africa and Unity: The Evolution of Pan-Africanism*, London: Longman, 1969.

Trevor-Roper, H., "The Invention of Tradition: The Highland Tradition of Scotland" in, Hobsbawm, E. & T. Ranger (eds.), *The Invention of Tradition*, Cambridge: Cambridge University Press, 1992, pp. 15–41.

Trigg, R., *Reality at Risk: A Defence of Realism in Philosophy and the Sciences*, Brighton: Harvester Press, 1980.

Tsing, A., *In the Realm of the Diamond Queen: Marginality in an Out-of-the-Way Place*, Princeton: Princeton University Press, 1993.

Turner, V., *Dramas, Fields, and Metaphors – Symbolic Action in Human Society*, New York: Cornell University Press, 1996.

Tyler, S., "Post-Modern Ethnography: From Document of the Occult to Occult Document" in, Marcus, G. & J. Clifford (eds.), *Writing Culture – The Poetics and Politics of Ethnography*, Berkeley: University of California Press, 1986, pp. 122–140.

Urry, J., *The Tourist Gaze – Leisure and Travel in Contemporary Societies*, London: Sage Publications, 1994.

van den Berghe, P., "Tourism" entry in, Spencer, J. & A. Barnard (eds.), *The Encyclopaedia of Social and Cultural Anthropology*, London: Routledge, 1996.

Van Maanen, J., *Tales of the Field: On Writing Ethnography*, Chicago: University of Chicago Press, 1988.

Wagner, R., *The Invention of Culture*. Chicago: Chicago University Press, 1981.

Walsh, K., *The Representation of the Past: Museums and Heritage in the Post-Modern World*, London: Routledge, 1992.

Warner, K., "Ethnicity and the contemporary calypso" in, Yelvington, K. (ed.), *Trinidad Ethnicity*, Knoxville: University of Tennessee Press, 1993, pp. 275–291.

Warren, D. & P. Meehan, "Applied Ethnoscience and a Dialogical Approach to Rural Development" in, Brokensha D. & D. Warren & O. Werner (eds.), *Indigenous Knowledge Systems and Development*, Washington: University Press of America, 1980, pp. 363–375.

Watson, B., "Autobiography, Anthropology and the Experience of Indonesia" in, Okely, J., & H. Callaway (eds.), *Anthropology and Autobiography*, London: Routledge, 1992, pp. 134–146.

Waugh, E., *When the Going Was Good*, London: Penguin, 1951.

Wood, R., "Tourism, Culture and the Sociology of Development" in, Hitchcock, M. & V. King & M. Parnwell (eds.), *Tourism in South-East Asia*, London: Routledge, 1993, pp. 48–70.

Young, R., *White Mythologies – Writing History and the West*, London: Routledge, 1992.

1.2. GENERAL POETRY VOLUME REFERENCES

Burnett, P. (ed.), *The Penguin Book of Caribbean Verse in English*, London: Penguin Books, 1986.

D'Aguiar, F., *British Subjects*, Newcastle upon Tyne: Bloodaxe Books, 1993

Dunn, D., *Barbarians*, London: Faber and Faber, 1979.

Dunn, D., *Selected Poems 1964–1983*, London: Faber and Faber, 1986.

Harrison, T., *Selected Poems*, Harmondsworth: Viking, Penguin Books, 1984.

McWatt, M. & H. Simmons-McDonald (eds.), *A World of Poetry for CXC*, Oxford: Heinemann Educational Publishers, 1994.

Morgan, E., *Selected Poems*, Manchester: Carcanet Press, 1985.

Walcott, D., *Omeros*, London: Faber & Faber, 1990.

Zephaniah, B., *City Psalms*, Newcastle upon Tyne: Bloodaxe Books, 1992.

1.3. GENERAL MUSIC REFERENCES

Mighty Sparrow [a], "Jean and Dinah", calypso, Slinger "Mighty Sparrow" Francisco, Trinidad, in, *Mighty Sparrow – Volume One*, Ice Records, 1992, no other references available.

Mighty Sparrow [b], "Wood in the Fire", calypso, Slinger "Mighty Sparrow" Francisco, Trinidad, in, *Mighty Sparrow – Volume Two*, Ice Records, 1992, no other references available.

Mighty Sparrow [b], "Sell de Pussy", calypso, Slinger "Mighty Sparrow" Francisco, Trindad, in, *Mighty Sparrow – Volume Two*, Ice Records, 1992, no other references available.

Nevis Culturama Committee, *Nevis's Culturama Anniversary Magazine 1974–1994*, booklet including calypso songs, Nevis: Nevis Printing Ltd., 1994, p. 55.

2. Montserrat References

2.1. *Montserrat References*

Akenson, D., *If the Irish Ran the World: Montserrat, 1630–1730*, London: McGill-Queen's University Press, 1997.

Anon. [a], *"A Natural, Civil, and Religious History of Monteserrat in the West-Indies, Including a Particular Account of the Struggles of the Free Coloured Inhabitants ... by a Wesleyan Missionary who Resided Five Years in the Island"*, undated missionary manuscript, "History of Montserrat" section (pp. 46–47), West Indies biographical box 588, Methodist Missionary Society Archives, School of Oriental and African Studies Library, University of London, no other references available.

Anon. [b], "Calypso Workshop – Criteria for Judging", undated calypso handout from the Division of Culture, no other references available.

Anon. [c], "The Place, Montserrat" in, *American University of the Caribbean (AUC) – School of Medicine – Bulletin*, undated, no other references available.

Anon. [d], *West Indies Real Estate and Advertisement Brochure*, brochure used throughout 1994–1995, undated, no other references available.

Anon., "Caribbean Basin Docile at a Glance" in, *Caribbean Basin Docile*, 1993, no other references available.

Anon., *The Montserrat Springs Hotel*, brochure with prices, 1994/5, Boca Raton, Florida: CPS Graphics, 1994, no other references available.

Anon., Vue Pointe Hotel advertisement in, James, G. (ed.), *The Official St. Patrick's Day Programme 1995*, 20-page pamphlet, Montserrat: George James Publishing, 1995, p. 5, no other references available.

Dewar, A., *Music in the Alliouagana (Montserrat) Cultural Tradition*, April 1977, unpublished thesis, Montserrat Public Library.

English, T., *Records of Montserrat*, reported name – T. Savage English, unpublished manuscript, Montserrat Public Library, 1930.

Flasher, "The History and Evolution of Calypso in Montserrat", undated, unpublished lecture script held by Ms Yvonne Weekes (Division of Culture), possibly by Desmond "Flasher" Daley, no other references available.

Government Information Unit, "St. Patrick's Day", 2-page information leaflet, no other references available.

Gwynn, A. [a], "Early Irish Emigration to the West Indies", *Studies*, September 1929, pp. 337–393.

Gwynn, A. [b], "Early Irish Emigration to the West Indies", *Studies*, December 1929, pp. 648–663.

Gwynn, A., "Cromwell's Policy of Transportation – Part I", *Studies*, December 1930, pp. 607–623.

Gwynn, A., "Cromwell's Policy of Transportation – Part II", *Studies*, June 1931, pp. 291–305.

Gwynn, A., "First Irish Priests in the New World", *Studies*, June 1932, pp. 213–228.

Irish, G., *Alliouagana Voices*, 1972, no other references available.

Irish, G., "Why Celebrate March 17", pamphlet, Plymouth, Montserrat, 1974.

Irish, G., *Alliouagana Folk*, Plymouth, Montserrat: Montserrat Printery Ltd., Montserrat Allied Workers' Union [MAWU] and JAGPI Production, 1985.

Irish, G., *Perspectives for Alliouagana – Reflections on Life in Montserrat*, New York: JAGPI Productions and Caribbean Research Center, 1990.

Irish, G., *Life in a Colonial Crucible – Labor & Social Change in Montserrat, 1946– Present*, Plymouth, Montserrat: JAGPI Productions, 1991.

Irish, G., *Further Perspectives for Alliouagana – Journalism and Change*, Plymouth, Montserrat & New York: JAGPI Productions and the Caribbean Research Center, 1993.

James, G. (ed.), *The Official St. Patrick's Day Programme 1995*, 20-page pamphlet, Montserrat: George James Publishing, 1995.

Laffey, S., *Representing Paradise: Euro-American Desires and Cultural Understandings in Touristic Images of Montserrat, West Indies*, unpublished MA Anthropology Thesis, Texas University, Austin, 1995.

Meade, R., "Message for St. Patrick's Day from the Honourable Chief Minister" in, James, G. (ed.), *The Official St. Patrick's Day Programme 1995*, 20-page pamphlet, Montserrat: George James Publishing, 1995, p. 6.

Meade, R., "Message for St. Patrick's Day 1995 by The Honourable Chief Minister Reuben T. Meade", Government Press Release, 17 March 1995, no other references available.

Messenger, J., "Excerpts from John Messenger's essay on 'The Irish of Montserrat' 1965", unpublished copy, 1965, no other references available.

Messenger, J., "African Retentions in Montserrat", *African Arts*, 6(4), 1973, pp. 54–57.

Messenger, J., "Montserrat: The Most Distinctively Irish Settlement in the New World", *Ethnicity*, 2, 1975, pp. 281–303.

Messenger, J., "St. Patrick's Day in 'The Other Emerald Isle'", *Eire – Ireland*, Earrach – Spring 1994, pp. 12–23.

Montserrat Dept. of Tourism, *Holiday Montserrat – The Way The Caribbean Used To Be: An Official Tourist Guide of the Montserrat Dept. of Tourism 1993/ 94*, St. John's, Antigua: West Indies Publishing Ltd., 1993.

Mullin, M., *Africa in America: Slave Acculturation and Resistance in the American South and the British Caribbean, 1736–1831*, Chicago: University of Illinois Press, 1992.

Overseas Development Agency, *British Overseas Aid Annual Review 1994*, London: Totem Group, 1994.

Savage, F., "Message from H.E. The Governor F.J. Savage – St. Patrick's Day 1995" in, James, G. (ed.), *The Official St. Patrick's Day Programme 1995*, 20-page pamphlet, Montserrat: George James Publishing, 1995, p. 4.

Skinner, J., "Licence Revoked: When Calypso Goes Too Far" in, Hendry, J. & C. Watson (eds.), *Indirection, Intention and Diplomacy*, London: Routledge, 2001, pp. 181–200.

Skinner, J., "British Constructions with Constitutions: The Formal and Informal Nature of 'Island' Relations on Montserrat and Gibraltar" in, Skinner, J. (ed.), Special Edition: Managing Island Life, *Social Identities: Journal for the Study of Race, Nation and Culture*, 8(2), 2002, pp. 301–320.

Watkins, F., *Handbook of the Leeward Islands*, London: West India Committee, 1924.

2.2. MONTSERRAT MUSIC REFERENCES

Accident, "Iraq's Invasion", calypso, Earl "Accident" Blake, Montserrat, 1990.

Arrow, "Dis is Awe Culture", calypso, Alphonsus "Arrow" Cassell, Montserrat, calypso cited in, Arrow, *Hold on To Your Property*, calypso, Alphonsus "Arrow" Cassell, Montserrat, calypso in, *Arrow on Target* album, 1971, no other references available.

Arrow, "Ole Time Calypso Medley", calypso, Alphonsus "Arrow" Cassell, Montserrat, from, *Arrow – Classics*, Plymouth: Montserrat, 1994; also containing "Montserrat Culture" with "Montserrat English" variations [1974].

Belonger, "Bring Dem Back", calypso, Pat "Belonger" Ryan, Montserrat, 1988.

Cepeke, "White Man's World", calypso, Cecil "Cepeke" Lake, Montserrat, 1992.

Collis, "Determination", calypso, Rachael Collis, Montserrat, 1992.

Cutter, "Lift This Nation", calypso, Ishmael "Cutter" Skerrit, Montserrat, 1994.

Duberry, E. (arranger), *Emeral City Festival Volume 1*, compilation of Montserrat Festival hit songs, Rome, Italy and St. Michael, Barbados: Mango Media Organization, no other references available.

Edgecombe, D., "Montserrat – My Country", national song, (Denzil Edgecombe, not to be confused with David Edgecombe, editor of *The Montserrat Reporter*), *Montserrat Reporter*, 30 June 1995: p. 1, no other references available.

Hero, "Body-to-Body", calypso, Justin "Hero" Cassell, Montserrat, 1986.

Lord Alfredo, "Push to the Rear", calypso, Archibald "Lord Alfredo" Mills, Montserrat, 1980.

Lord Alfredo, "Socialism Jam", calypso, Archibald "Lord Alfredo" Mills, Montserrat, 1980.

Q-Pid, "What's Inside The Box", calypso, Herman "Q-Pid" Francis (also known as "Cupid"), Montserrat, calypso, *Montserrat Reporter*, 18 December 1987, p. 4, no other references available.

Rockamaya, "Montserrat is for Montserratians", calypso, Charles "Rockamaya" Weekes, Montserrat, 1993.

Spoiler, "Wet Me Down", Road March song, Glanville "Spoiler" Roach, Montserrat, 1994.

Teknikal, "A News Dem A Look", calypso, Sean "Teknikal" Martin, Montserrat, 1994.

The Patriot, "Save This Country", calypso, Lenroy "The Patriot" Tuitt, Montserrat, 1982.

Top Secret, "Tropical Gal", calypso, Neville "Top Secret" Greenaway, Montserrat, 1994; see also "Top Secret's", Top Secret's 1994 calypsos, *Montserrat News*, 4(35), 16 December 1994, p. 9.

Top Secret, "Don't Rock The Boat Dada", calypso, Neville "Top Secret" Greenaway, Montserrat, 1994; see also "Top Secret's", Top Secret's 1994 calypsos, *The Montserrat News*, 5(35), 16 December 1994, p. 9.

2.3. REFERENCES TO HOWARD FERGUS'S WORK

2.3.1. Fergus – Anthologies

Fergus, H., *Cotton Rhymes*, Woodstock, Ontario: Woodstock Print & Litho., 1976.

Fergus, H. [a], *Green Innocence*, St. Augustine, Trinidad: Multimedia Production Centre, 1978.

Fergus, H., *Stop the Carnival*, Plymouth, Montserrat: University of the West Indies Extra-Mural Department, 1980.

Fergus, H. (ed.), *Flowers Blooming Late*, Plymouth, Montserrat: Montserrat Times, 1984.

Fergus, H., *Politics as Sport*, Plymouth, Montserrat: Summit Communications, Montserrat Times, 1987.

Fergus, H. (ed.), *Horrors of a Hurricane – Poems*, Plymouth, Montserrat: Montserrat Times, 1990.

Fergus, H. [a], *Calabash of Gold – Selected Poems*, London: Linda Lee Books, 1993.

Fergus, H. [a], *Eruption – Ten Volcano Poems*, Plymouth, Montserrat: Montserrat Printery, 1995.

Fergus, H. [a], *Lara Rains and Colonial Rites*, Leeds: Peepal Tree Press – Poetry, 1998.

Fergus, H. (ed.) [b], *HOPE – Fiftieth Anniversary Anthology of Poems: Celebrating the University of the West Indies and Montserratian Hope during a Volcanic Crisis*, University of the West Indies School of Continuing Studies: Montserrat, 1998.

Fergus, H. & A. Markham (eds.), *Hugo Versus Montserrat*, Londonderry, Northern Ireland: Linda Lee Books, distributed by New Beacon Books, 1989.

Fergus, H. & L. Rowden (eds.), *Dark Against the Sky – An Anthology of Poems and Short Stories from Montserrat*, Kingston, Jamaica: U.W.I. Publishers' Association, 1990.

2.3.2. Fergus – Histories

Fergus, H., *History of Alliouagana: A Short History of Montserrat*, Plymouth, Montserrat: Montserrat Printery, 1975.

Fergus, H. [b], *Montserrat: The LAST ENGLISH COLONY? Prospects for Independence – Two Essays on Montserrat*, Plymouth, Montserrat: Montserrat Printery, 1978.

Fergus, H., *WILLIAM HENRY BRAMBLE: HIS LIFE AND TIMES*, Groves, Montserrat: Montserrat Times, 1983.

Fergus, H., *Montserrat – Emerald Isle of the Caribbean*, London: Macmillan Caribbean Guides, 1992 [1983].

Fergus, H., *RULE BRITANNIA – Politics in British Montserrat*, Plymouth, Montserrat: University Centre, 1985.

Fergus, H. [b], "Where History and Culture Make Beauty" in, Montserrat Dept. of Tourism, *Holiday Montserrat – The Way The Caribbean Used To Be: An Official Tourist Guide of the Montserrat Dept. of Tourism 1993/94*, St. John's, Antigua: West Indies Publishing, 1993, p. 2.

Fergus, H., *Montserrat: History of a Caribbean Colony*, London: Macmillan Caribbean, 1994.

Fergus, H. [b], "Celebration of Achievement by Dr Howard Fergus" in James, G. (ed.), *The Official St. Patrick's Day Programme 1995*, 20-page pamphlet, Montserrat: George James Publishing, 1995, p. 7.

Fergus, H., *Gallery of Montserrat: Prominent People in Our History*, Kingston, Jamaica: Canoe Press, University of West Indies, 1996.

2.3.3. Fergus – Histories Cited From Newspapers

Fergus, H., "A Window on Our History – St. Patrick's Day 1768", *Montserrat Mirror*, 28 January 1972, p. 8, no other references available.

Fergus, H., "St. Patrick's Day, March 17", *Montserrat Mirror*, 14 March 1975, pp. 7–8, no other references available.

Fergus., H., "Why Celebrate St. Patrick's Day?", *Montserrat Reporter*, 28 February 1986, p. 5, no other references available.

Fergus, H., "St. Patrick's Day in Focus", *Montserrat Reporter*, 27 March 1992, no other references available.

Fergus, H., "This Emerald Isle – Where History and Culture Make Beauty", *Montserrat News*, 4(32), 18 November 1994, p. 17, continued on p. 16.

Fergus, H., "Lady & the Harp for Bramble", *Montserrat Reporter*, 11(26), 30 June 1995, p. 1 and back cover.

2.3.4. Fergus – Poems Cited From Newspapers

Fergus, H., "This Land Is Mine", poem, *Montserrat Mirror*, 2 July 1976, p. 4, no other references available.

Fergus, H., "March of Death", poem, *Montserrat Times*, 19 March 1982, p. 5, no other references available.

Fergus, H., "When Justice Came To Church", poem, *Montserrat Reporter*, 11(11), 17 March 1995, p. 8.

Fergus, H., "Easter", poem, *Montserrat News*, 5(13), 13 April 1995, p. 1.

Fergus, H., "A Question of Emblems", poem, *Montserrat News*, 5(26), 7 July 1995, p. 13.

2.4. REFERENCES TO MONTSERRAT NEWS PIECES

2.4.1. Chapter Prefaces and Postscript

Anon., "Volcano Island Call", *Courier and Advertiser*, 26 August 1995, p. 13, no other references available.

Anon., "Student Recalls Volcano Island Ordeal", *Courier and Advertiser*, 6 September 1995, p. 4, no other references available.

Anon., "Business as Usual for the Tourism Industry", *Montserrat Reporter*, 22 September 1995, p. 2, no other references available.

Associated Press, "Eruption Reaches Montserrat capital", *Guardian*, 5 August 1997, p. 9.

Ferguson, J., "Volcano Update for 7/26/95", CaribTalk Web page, 28 July 1995.

Global Volcanism Network, "Soufriere Hills, Montserrat", e-mail, 19 July 1995.

Patullo, P., "Dust Settles But Future is Bleak", *Guardian*, 28 June 1997, p. 17.

Stewart, L., "Emerald Isle Taken by Storm", *Independent on Sunday*, 4 February 1996, pp. 51–52.

2.4.2. *Pan-Afrikan Liberator* Pieces

Anon., "An Act for the Abolition of Slavery in Montserrat", a report on the 1834 Act, *The Pan-Afrikan Liberator*, 1(1), August 1992, p. 1, continued on p. 3, no other references available.

Anon., "KNOW YOUR HISTORY", slogan, *Pan-Afrikan Liberator*, 1(1), August 1992, p. 2, no other references available.

Anon., "KNOWLEDGE IS POWER", slogan, *Pan-Afrikan Liberator*, 1(1), August 1992, p. 4, no other references available.

Anon., "*Stop Press* Free Speech Banned – Executive Council Exercises Might Cancels 'Conscious Connection'", *Pan-Afrikan Liberator*, 2(3), October 1993, p. 5, no other references available.

Anon., "Kwame Ture Tells The People To Seek Independence", *Pan-Afrikan Liberator*, 2(12), April/May 1995, p. 8, no other references available.

Browne, C., "Message From the Publisher", *Pan-Afrikan Liberator*, 1(1), August 1992, p. 2.

Browne, C., "Burying the Irish Myth", reported name – Mwongozi Shujaa C. Browne, *Pan-Afrikan Liberator*, 1(11), June 1993, p. 1–4.

Browne, C., "Book Review: Montserrat – History of a Caribbean Colony", *Pan-Afrikan Liberator*, 2(8), October 1994, pp. 7–8.

Browne, C., "Seamen Union Smashed With A Whimper – Continuing Saga of Britain's Agenda for Montserrat Played Out", *Pan-Afrikan Liberator*, 2(11), January/February 1995, pp. 1–5.

Cassell, J., "Country Policy Plan or Grant-in-Aid?", second part of a two-part serial of an interview with Governor Frank Savage, reported in *Pan-Afrikan Liberator*, 2(3), October 1993, pp. 1–4.

Garvey, M., "The Rule of Intelligence – Marcus Garvey Glorifies the Mind of Man – Speaking to the People of Montserrat", historical speech made by Marcus Garvey on Montserrat, *Pan-Afrikan Liberator*, 2(1), August 1993, pp. 1–4, entire edition.

Lake, P., "'Them' And 'Us'", poem (25th May 1992), *Pan-Afrikan Liberator*, 1(3), October 1992, p. 3.

Ras Atiba, "The Mental Emancipator", *Pan-Afrikan Liberator*, 1(1), August 1992, p. 4.

White, P., "Breaking The Dependency Cycle", *Pan-Afrikan Liberator*, 1(10), May 1993, pp. 1–3.

2.4.3. Montserrat Newspaper Pieces

Anon., "'In Bad Taste' Says Hero", Feedback Letter to the Editor, *Montserrat Reporter*, 23 January 1987, p. 4, no other references available.

Anon., "In Support of Chedmond Browne", editorial, *Montserrat Reporter*, 29 October 1993, p. 4, no other references available.

Anon., "Tourism Week 1994: October 20 – November 5 – Program of Activities – Preliminary Draft", *Montserrat News*, 4(27), 14 October 1994, p. 19, no other references available.

Anon., "Independence", *Montserrat News*, 4(33), 2nd December 1994, p. 15, no other references available.

Anon., "Millie", *Montserrat News*, 5(3), 20 January 1995, p. 24, back cover, no other references available.

Anon., "High Court Opens With a March and Prayers", *Montserrat Reporter*, 11(10), 10 March 1995, p. 1, no other references available.

Anon., "Montserrat: 3 in 1", *Montserrat News*, 5(10), 16 March 1995, p. 7, no other references available.

Anon., "Good Manners", editorial, *Montserrat Reporter*, 11(11), 17 March 1995, p. 4, no other references available.

Anon., untitled report about the dismissal of four Port employees, *Montserrat News*, Port Extra edition, 5(16), 2 May 1995, p. 9, no other references available.

Anon., "Port Rocks the Boat – Workers Go Back To Work On Monday", *Montserrat Reporter*, 11(17), 5 May 1995, p. 1, headline article, no other references available.

Anon., "Fergus for Assignments in Botswana and Washington", *Montserrat Reporter*, 11(17), 5 May 1995, p. 10, no other references available.

Anon., "Tourism is Everybody's Business", *Montserrat News*, 5(24), 23 June 1995, p. 20, no other references available.

Browne, C., "The Montserrat Seamen and Waterfront Workers Union Speaks Out", Port Offer to the Management, *Montserrat News*, 5(2), 13 January 1995, pp. 12–13.

Browne, C., "The Montserrat Seamen and Waterfront Workers Union Speaks Out", Port offer to the management, *Montserrat Reporter*, 11(2), 13 January 1995, p. 7.

Bruton, J., "St. Patrick's Day", letters for the occasion, *Montserrat News*, 5(11), 24 March 1995, p. 12.

Edgecombe, D., "Night of the Invisible Artistes", *Montserrat Mirror*, 10 January 1975, p. 2, no other references available.

Edgecombe, D., "Hero Reigns Again", *Montserrat Reporter*, 16 January 1987, no other references available.

Edgecombe, D., "No Skin-Tight Outfit for Hero", *Montserrat Reporter*, 30 January 1987, no other references available.

Edgecombe, D., "The Case of the Suspicious Ballots", *Montserrat Reporter*, 23 October 1987, p. 4, no other references available.

Edgecombe, D., "ZJB Is Not Playing Q-Pid's Song", *Montserrat Reporter*, 18 December 1987, p. 1, headline article, no other references available.

Edgecombe, D., "Let Q-Pid's Song Be Played", editorial, *Montserrat Reporter*, 18 December 1987, p. 4, no other references available.

Edgecombe, D. & A. Burns, "Hustler is the new Calypso Monarch" in, Edgecombe D. & Burns, A., "Festival '88 Highlights", *Montserrat Reporter*, 13 January 1989, pp. 6–7, no other references available.

Elizabeth II, H.R.H., "Commonwealth Day Message 1995", *Montserrat News*, 5(10), 16 March 1995, p. 16.

Fenton, D., "The Conscious Connection Programme Cancelled – Let Browne Talk", *Montserrat Reporter*, 22 October 1993, p. 14 and back page, no other references available.

Galloway, W., "'Our Culture is Dying'", *Montserrat Reporter*, 13 January 1989, p. 5.

G.S.C., "Letter to the Editor", *Montserrat Mirror*, 29 April 1967, p. 1, continued on p. 4, no other references available.

Irish, G., "Reflections on March 17", *Montserrat Mirror*, 17 February 1978, p. 5, no other references available.

Irish, G., "Reflections on St. Patrick's", *Montserrat Reporter*, 15 March 1985, pp. 6–7, no other references available.

Lewis, R., "1994 Calypsonians", *Montserrat Reporter*, 10(45), 2 December 1994, back cover.

Samuel, H., "Letter to the Editor", *Montserrat Reporter*, 5 November 1993, p. 6, no other references available.

Staff Reporter, "Francis Looks Inside 'De Box'", *Montserrat Times* – Christmas Issue, 23 December 1987, no other references available.

Index

Abdul (Weekes), 11, 90, 127

academic preface, xii-xiv, xxxi, xxxiii, xxxv, 31-32, 53, 55, 78, 172-174, 181, 191, 193; and academic preface (xii-xxxvii)

Amerindian, 34, 40, 42, 44, 46, 112; and Alliouagana 34, 40, 44, 46, 48, 112, 149

Amy, 7-8, 10, 23-26

anthropology, xii-xxxvii, 28, 29, 30, 33, 171, 173-5, 180-2, 187, 190-1, 193-4; and academic preface (xii-xxxvii); see evocative; see impressions; see uncertainty; see uncomfortable

anthropological, xiii-xviii, xxi-xvi, xxxi, xxxiii, xxxv, xxxviii, 19, 29, 42, 53, 133, 145, 157, 160, 163, 164, 175, 186, 188, 190, 193

anthropologist, the, xiii-xviii, 33, 40, 53-56, 75-78, 86, 153, 159, 164-165,171-5, 180, 184, 187, 190, 192-3, 194; as Jonathan/Jono 1-21, 97-106; and Skinner on Montserrat xxxi-xxxiii, 11, 21, 28, 29, 31, 32, 33, 35, 56-67, 72, 80, 163, 171, 173, 175, 176, 179; see academic preface (xii-xxxvii)

Arrow – Alphonsus Cassell, 87-8, 91, 107, 107n.9, 107n.11, 107n.12, 136, 169

authenticity, 11, 112, 142-3, 183, 185, 192, 194

Barbarian poetry, 23, 35, 83, 165, 177; and barbarian features 36-39; and 'barbarian' Fergus 42-50; see Fergus

Barthes, Roland, xxviii, xxxv, 32, 34, 191

Baudrillard, Jean, 181

belonger, 49, 54, 84, 88, 94, 124, 159, 166

Belonger – Pat Ryan, 85-6, 88, 93-4, 107n.8, 149, 154, 179

Bhabha, Homi, xxxiii, 38, 49

Black identity/ethnicity, xxx, 2, 9, 16, 18, 24, 28, 33, 37, 39, 65-7, 71-2, 89, 93, 111, 113, 148, 152-3, 156, 158, 162, 167, 189; and chapter 5 (110-135), 154, 181; and consciousness xiii, 6, 9, 47, 75, 114

Black Irish, xxxvi, 28, 34, 46, ch.5 141, 153, 159, 163, 165, 184-5, 188-9; and Messenger section (159-163), 165, 188; and Montserrat Irish 2, 161; see Messenger; see St. Patrick's Day

Bramble, William, 27-8, 45, 47-8, 51n.26, 132, 147, 182

Brathwaite, Kamau, 37

British Dependent Territory (BDT), xxxv, 8-9, 34-5, 40, 53, 71,